E 植物図鑑

NCYCLOPEDIA OF FLOWERS

Makoto AZUMA

Shunsuke SHIINOKI

ENCYCLOPEDIA OF FLOWERS III

First Edition	5 December, 2016
Artworks	Makoto Azuma
Photographs	Shunsuke Shiinoki
Supervise	AMKK (Azuma Makoto Kaju Kenkyusho)
Design	Kenya Hara + Kaoru Matsuno + Megumi Ohno
	Hara Design Institute (Nippon Design Center, Inc.)
Publisher	Hideaki Yasuda
Published	Seigensha Art Publishing, Inc.
	Higashi-iru, Karasuma-Sanjo Nakagyo-ku,
	Kyoto, 604-8136 Japan
	Tel +81 75 252 6766
	Fax +81 75 252 6770
	http://www.seigensha.com
Cooperation	Kyoko Wada
Editor	Mizue Nakamura	HeHe
	Eriko Kamada	Seigensha Art Publishing, Inc
Printed and Bound	SunM color, co., Ltd
Printing Director	Masuo Taniguchi	SunM color, co.,Ltd

ISBN 978-4-86152-571-1 C0072

E 植物図鑑
NCYCLOPEDIA OF FLOWERS III

Makoto AZUMA
Shunsuke SHIINOKI

東 信
椎木俊介

SEIGENSHA ART PUBLISHING

E III

植物図鑑

NCYCLOPEDIA OF FLOWERS

Makoto AZUMA

Shunsuke SHIINOKI

東 信

椎木俊介

COEXISTENCE ———— p. 17

［koʊɪgzɪstəns］共生, 共在, 両立, 併存

地上のすべての種は、連続し、等価であり、必然である。
互いにかかわり合い、交じり合い、共生する。

［kō-ig-ˈzistən(t)s］symbiosis, compatibility

All varieties on earth are connected, equivalent,
and are necessary. They affect one another, commingle,
and exist together in a symbiotic relationship.

HYBRID ———————— p. 75

［háɪbrɪd］雑種, 混成, 交配, 超境

ある種は自然交配によって、ある種はさらなる美を求め
人工交配されることによって、あるいは環境の変化によって
更新されつつある自然の姿。

［ˈhī-brəd］cross, mix, crossbreed

One variety is a result of natural crossbreeding,
another is a product of artificial crossbreeding
for the purpose of beauty. Yet another one is created through
changes in the environment that yield a new, natural form.

CHIAROSCURO ———— p. 121

［kɪˌɑːrəˈskʊərəʊ］光と闇, 対比法, カラバッジェスク

一度限りの儚い生が光に浮かび上がっては、闇へと浸潤していく。
生と死の鬩ぎ合い。容赦ない時の経過と肢体の変貌。明滅する命の臨海。

［ˈkjaːro-skyur-(ˌ)ō］light and shadow, comparison method,
caravaggesque

A fleeting, singular life rises up into the light, only to melt
into the darkness once again. A struggle of life and death,
a transformation of limbs within the merciless lapse of time.
A flickering sea of life.

WHOLE

———— p. 149

[hóʊl] すべて, 全体, 完全, 統合

季節感も固有の風土も特定の種も決まりきった定義もない。
あるのは、混沌。わたしたちが生きる世界のミクロコスモス。

['hōl] all, entire, complete, integral

Any sense of seasons, the particularity of a climate,
or the special quality of a breed no longer possesses a fixed
definition. Chaos. A microcosm of the world we live in.

TONDO

———— p. 237

[tɒndəʊ] 円形, 浮彫, 幾何学模様, 神話

古代ギリシアに起を発し、ルネサンス期に昇華された円形の宗教画。
崇拝のかたち。神秘の構造。遠心状に放たれた生命の大輪。

['tän-(ˌ)dō] circle, relief, geometric pattern, myth

Originating in ancient Greece, circular religious paintings were
particularly refined during the Renaissance era. Expressions of
adoration, structuring of mystery, and large flowers of life,
irradiated in a centrifugal fashion.

APPEARANCE

———— p. 261

[əpí(ə)rəns] 存在, 形相, 現れ, 姿勢

刻々と朽ちゆき、姿かたちを変えていく生命の移ろいを捉え、
静止した時間に封じ込められた植物の肖像。

[ə-'pir-ən(t)s] existence, look, posture

With time held in abeyance, a portrait that captures
the moment of a life's blossom in full glory,
gradually withering and changing.

AUTOGENESIS ——————— p. 317

[ɔːtəʊˈdʒɛnɪsɪs] 自生，繁殖，土着，進化

意思を持つ自然。自ら根を張り、枝葉を伸ばし絡み合い、
繰り返される淘汰と増殖。種を超えて結び合う、ひとつの生命体。

[ô'tō-jĕn'ĭ-sĭs] **spontaneous generation, proliferation, aboriginality, evolution**

Nature, with the will to take root and grow entanglements
of branches. Repeated selection, proliferation and cross-
fertilization, to generate one organism.

More roots to be exposed │ Makoto Azuma
まだ見ぬ原風景へ │ 東 信 ——————— p. 9

List of Flower Names　植物名リスト ——————— p. 368
Index of Flower Names　索引 ——————— p. 440
Profiles　　　　　　　略歴 ——————— p. 479

まだ見ぬ原風景へ
More roots to be exposed

東 信　フラワーアーティスト
Makoto Azuma　Flower Artist

　　　　2014年7月、私は砂漠のただ中にいた。『Encyclopedia of Flowers Ⅱ』を上梓した直後の夏のことだ。アメリカ、ネバタ州のブラックロック砂漠。延々と干上がった地面は、およそ生命の欠片さえも寄せ付ける気配すらない。そこからさらに不毛な宇宙に向けて、私は《式》と活けた花を打ち上げることを巧んでいた。《EXOBIOTANICA》と名付けたこのプロジェクトは、それぞれ地上30,000メートルの未知の領域へと植物を送り出す試みである。大地から絶たれ、重力からも解き放たれ、水も大気も逸した生命の源をすべからくもぎ取られた究極の環境下で、植物はいったいどんな姿をわれわれに見せてくれるというのだろうか。

　　　　私を常に突き動かしているのは、このような未だ見ぬ植物の姿である。花の究極の美とは何か？　その命を表現するとはどういうことな

　　　In July 2014, I stood in the middle of the desert. It was the summer right after the publication of *Encyclopedia of Flowers Ⅱ*, and the place was the Black Rock Desert in Nevada, USA. There wasn't the slightest sign of life whatsoever on the interminably parched earth. From there I was planning to launch my "Shiki" and my flower arrangements, toward the even more barren realms of outer space. The "EXOBIOTANICA" project is based on the idea to shoot plans up 30,000 meters into the vast unknown. Cut off from the soil, and free from the forces of gravity, I wondered how they would present themselves to us down here in such an extreme environment without water, air, or any other source of life.

　　　It is such never-before-seen appearances of flowers that keep stimulating me. What is the ultimate beauty of flowers? How can such kind of life be expressed? Will I be able to bring that out to the fullest

のか？ それをいかに最大限引き出すことができるか？ という尽きることのない問いである。切り花として流通し、市場で取引される商品としての命は、花屋に届けられるときには既に仮死状態にある。人間の手によってもぎ取られた命を引き受ける以上、自然界でありのままに生きていたよりもさらにその存在を強く表したい、そして美を際立たせることが使命ではないかと自問自答を繰り返している。私がしきりに「殺して生かす」と言うのは、このためだ。花を凍結させる。烈火を注ぐ。海中に沈める。真空状態にする。花々が徐々に朽ちて死にゆくまで放置する。私が取り組むプロジェクトは植物を極限状態に強いるため、得てして暴力的にさえ映るかもしれない。ただ、死と拮抗する状態でしか見せることができない極限の美はある。私は取り憑かれるように、次の、またそ

extent? All these are inexhaustible questions. Flowers distributed and traded as a product in the form of cut flowers are already in a state of apparent death when they arrive at the florist's. Taking over the life that has been torn off by human hand, I have been convincing myself that my mission should be to express its existence and highlight its beauty even stronger than it used to be in its original natural environment. This is what I refer to when I talk about "killing to let live." I freeze flowers. I fire them. Drown them. Vacuum-pack them. I leave the flowers alone as they gradually decay and finally die. As my projects involve forcing flowers into extreme states, they may appear somewhat violent. But there exists a kind of beauty that only reveals itself in the face of death. As if possessed, I am driven by my projects, one after another, like in a chain of trials.

の先の次への試練にも近いプロジェクトに駆り立てられていく。

　こうした非日常的なプロジェクトと比べてみれば、並行して制作している『Encyclopedia of Flowers』は対極にあるかもしれない。日課のごとく都内のアトリエで花を活けては、撮影を淡々と進める。外界から完全に閉ざされた空間で、細部にわたって完璧に手をくだし、徹底的にコントロールする。そこには一切のノイズは介さず、一寸の隙さえ許容しない。ただただ神経を研ぎ澄まし、黙して花に対峙する。そして2年の月日をかけてつくり貯めた作品を最終的には1冊の本に封じ込め、定着させることで完成する。今年でこのプロジェクトを開始して6年の月日が経ち、今回は3冊目の刊行となる。黙して、愚直に、辛抱強く、積み上げては定着し、それを絶え間なく繰り返し、持続していくこと。

Compared to such extraordinary projects, this *Encyclopedia of Flowers* that I have been putting together in parallel marks the other end of the spectrum. As part of my daily routine, I arrange flowers in my Tokyo atelier, and photograph them in a pragmatic manner. In a space completely shut from the outside world, I dedicate my attention to every painstaking detail, striving for complete control and perfection. I don't permit any noise, not even the tiniest gap. All I do is silently confront the flowers with my senses sharpened. The works created this way over a period of two years are eventually confined into one book, and everything is fixed and finished. Six years since the launch of this project, this year the third volume sees the light of day. Silently, honestly and patiently, I continue to stack them one by one, again and again. It goes on and on, there is no end. That's the very core of this project.

終わりはない。それがこのプロジェクトの核心だ。

　こうして続けてきた『Encyclopedia of Flowers』は、人間の欲望のありようを記録する定点観測だ。人間のあくなき美への欲望に駆られる花卉市場には、常に同じ種の花が並ぶわけではない。時代の流行り廃りによって種が絶たれる花、新たに交配されることで誕生する種と2年という短期間にも更新を要するほど様変わりする。その一方で、われわれの足跡を刻むアクティブな現状報告でもある。よって、当然のことながら『Encyclopedia of Flowers』には、さまざまなプロジェクトが根深く入り組んでいる。本書には、新シリーズ3作を含むこれまでで最多の7シリーズを収録した。それもひとえに、われわれが多岐にわたって植物の表現を追求していた結果の現れだ。

The *Encyclopedia of Flowers* project is an ongoing fixed-point observation of human desires. On the flower market that is propelled by humans' inexhaustible thirst for beauty, there aren't always flowers of the same kind on offer. Fashions change, and as some kinds become extinct and new ones are created through crossbreeding, there is a demand for changes in the product line in intervals as short as two years. On the other hand, it's also an active status report in which we leave our footprints. So quite naturally there are a variety of projects flowing into the *Encyclopedia of Flowers*. This book contains a total of seven series, including three new ones. All these present the results of our efforts aimed to create a rich diversity of floral depictions.

　The new series "CHIAROSCURO" developed out of "APPE-ARANCE" (contained in vol. 1), which expresses the transition and

新シリーズ「CHIAROSCURO」は、生命の移ろいとその存在感を表した「APPEARANCE」（第1巻収録）の発展系である。それは、およそ 6,000 本の花を重ね、120センチメートル立方のボックス型という巨大な花の塊として活けたプロジェクト《Box Flowers》（2015 年）と無関係ではない。花の塊は日ごとに腐臭を帯びた液体を流しながら萎れ、腐り、乾き、黴びていった。 1ヶ月間、その変化を定点観測したのがこのプロジェクトの全貌だ。「CHIAROSCURO」は、このような時間の経過を一瞬に凝縮したシリーズである。生と死の対比をイタリア語で Chiaro＝光とScuro＝闇との対比の構図で際立たせた。

　「TONDO」もまた、イタリア語に由来する。ルネサンス期に描かれた円形の宗教画の様式である。このシリーズは、自然界では存在し

presence of life, and is not unrelated to the "Box Flowers" (2015), a huge box-shaped arrangement of about 6,000 flowers in a 120×120cm cube. The lump of flowers withered, decayed, dried and became moldy as it exuded more and more putrid smell and fluid each day. This project showcases the results of a month-long stationary observation. "CHIAROSCURO" is a series in which that period of time is condensed into a brief moment. The layout, described using the Italian terms "chiaro" (light) and "scuro" (dark), was chosen with the aim to highlight the contrast between life and death.

　"TONDO" is another word derived from Italian, referring to a Renaissance style of round-shaped religious paintings. This series is rooted in my experience arranging flowers in situations that would never come about in nature as part of the "In Bloom" project (2015).

得ないようなシチュエーションで花を活ける《In Bloom》（2015年）の体験が根っこにある。フィリピン・ネグロス島の海上に約1万本もの真っ赤なヘリコニアを高さ5メートルにも活け込んだ塊は、まさに植物が見せる奇跡の光景だった。「TONDO」の衒いのない真俯瞰の構図には、ここで一輪一輪をあらためて直視してもらいたいとの思いがある。その色彩、組成、フォルム。目の前に存在しているという神秘。一輪の花でさえ、奇跡としか言いようがない聖なる花への祈りだ。

　2005年から盆栽を四角く組んだ金属のフレームに吊る《式》というインスタレーションを展開しているが、これは最もミニマルに自然と人間の関係を問う作品である。近年は、いまや廃墟となった火力発電所や共産党本部の大ホールでのインスタレーションを行っている。こうした人工

The 5-meter-high arrangement of a total of about 10,000 bright red Heliconia in the sea at Negros in the Philippines was a truly miraculous sight. The unpretentious overhead view shots in "TONDO" reflect my desire to have the reader look straight down at every single flower – its color, its composition, its form. It is a mystery that stands right there. Every single flower is a prayer to the sacred flower that can only be described as a marvel.

　　Since 2005 I have been working on my "Shiki" installations of bonsai trees hung up in cubic metal frames. These are works that explore the relationship between man and nature in the most minimalist way. In recent years I did installations at a now closed thermal power plant, and in a hall at the Communist Party headquarters. Such artificial structures all disintegrate and rot away, before plants eventually take

の構造物はいずれ滅び、朽ち果て、やがて植物が根を張り生い茂って、まるで何事もなかったように原っぱへと戻っていくだろう。人間が築き上げた文明の脆さと自然の生命力との軋轢。計りしれない自然の生命力への畏敬が「AUTOGENESIS」シリーズへと繋がっている。

　当初の『Encyclopedia of Flowers』は、ミクロコスモスとしての東京から発信するという意味合いが濃かったように思う。しかし、その後われわれの活動は五大陸に及び、生態系すら飛び出し成層圏まで至った。『Encyclopedia of Flowers』は、もはや閉ざされたアトリエで制作された箱庭ではなく、世界のランドスケープ、強いていえば地球ものとも借景に取り込んだプロジェクトに昇華しつつある。さらにこの先も、われわれは植物が見せる新たなランドスケープを目にすることになるだろう。

root and grow, back in the field, as if nothing had ever happened. It is a clash between the fragility of civilization built by mankind, and the vitality of nature. A sense of reverence for the immeasurable vital force of nature is what eventually inspired the "AUTOGENESIS" series.

I think the idea of transmitting from the microcosm Tokyo was reflected quite prominently in the original *Encyclopedia of Flowers*. But after that, our endeavors expanded across the five continents, beyond ecosystems, and into the stratosphere. The *Encyclopedia of Flowers* is no longer a miniature garden made in the closed space of an atelier, but has evolved into a project that incorporates landscapes around the world, or even the entire globe, into its borrowed landscapes. From here, we will continue to witness more new landscapes as presented to us by flowers.

COEXISTENCE

COEXISTENCE   08

COEXISTENCE 09

COEXISTENCE 11

COEXISTENCE 13

COEXISTENCE 15

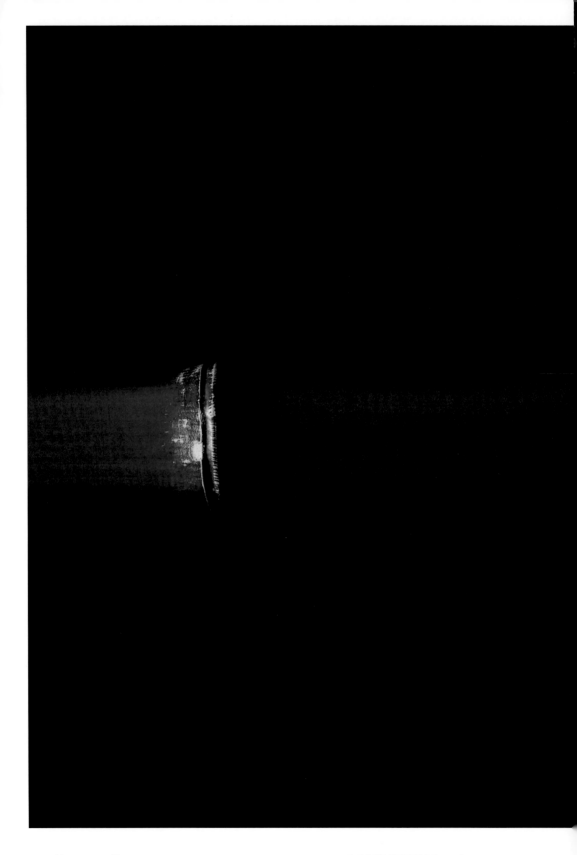

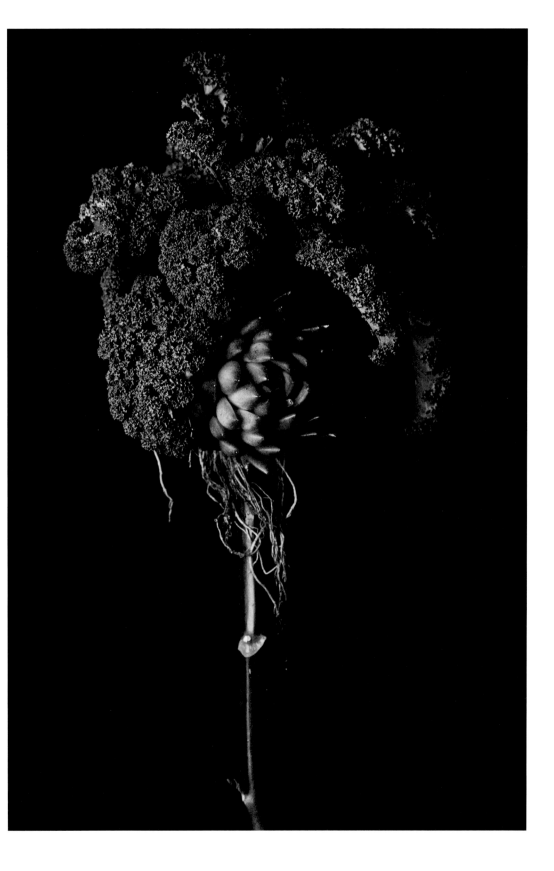

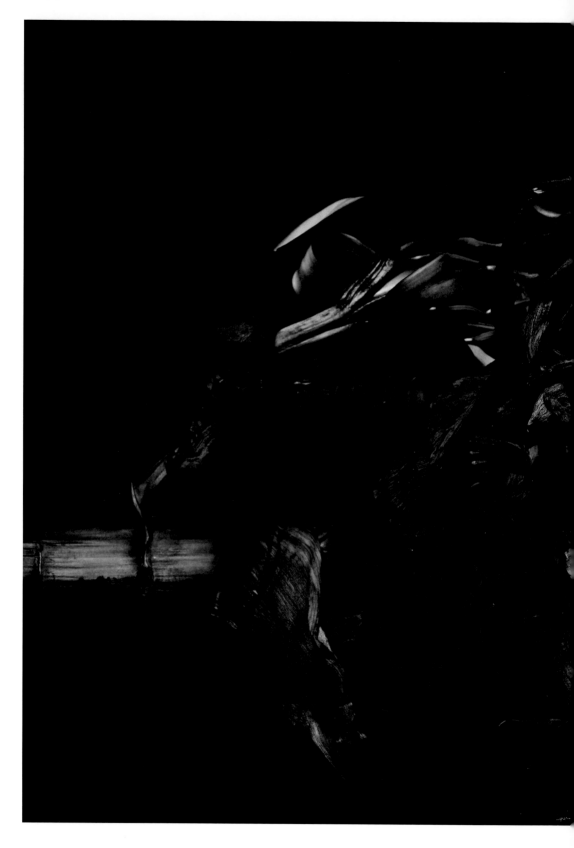

COEXISTENCE 22

COEXISTENCE   28

HYBRID

HYBRID 01

HYBRID 02

HYBRID 04

HYBRID 06

HYBRID 08

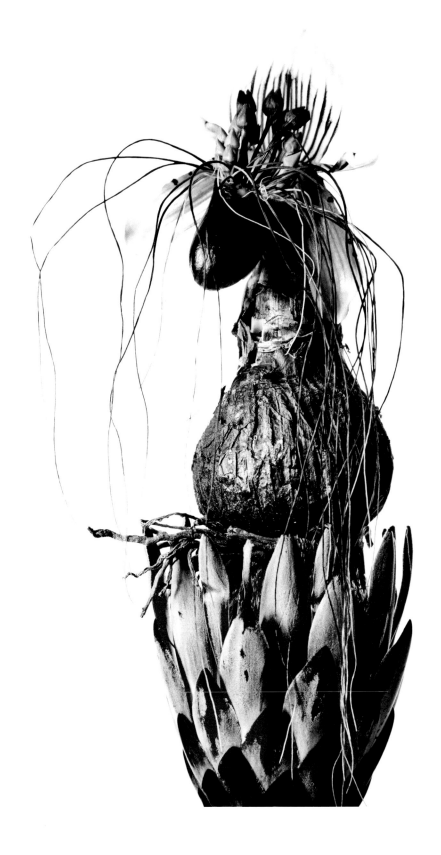

HYBRID 11

HYBRID 14

HYBRID 15

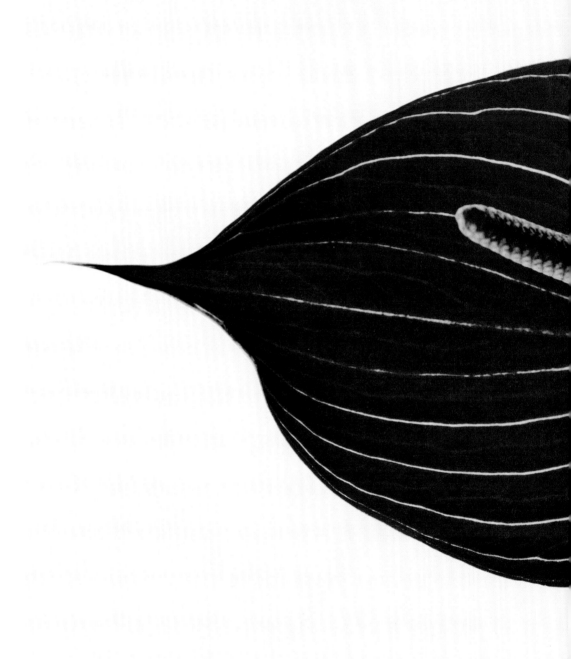

HYBRID 16

HYBRID 18

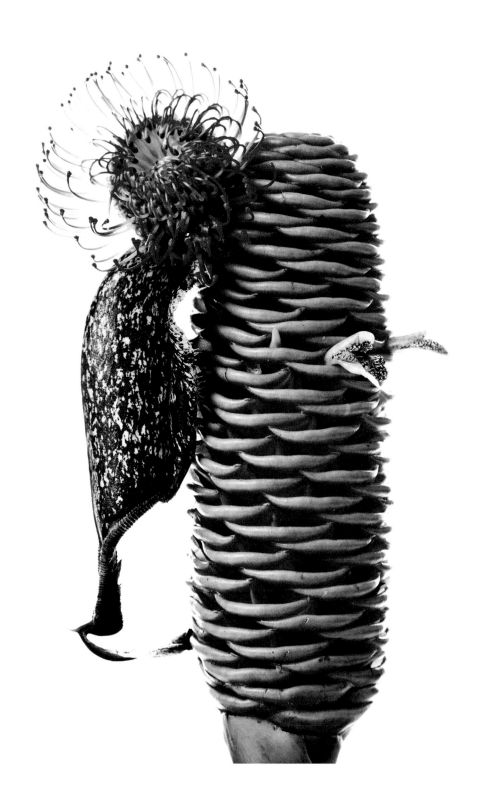

HYBRID 20

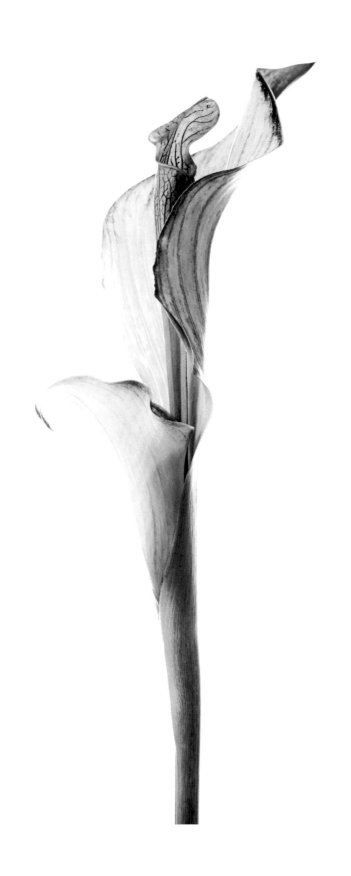

CHIAROSCURO

CHIAROSCURO   01

CHIAROSCURO   02

CHIAROSCURO 03

CHIAROSCURO   05

CHIAROSCURO   06

CHIAROSCURO 08

CHIAROSCURO   09

CHIAROSCURO 11

CHIAROSCURO   12

CHIAROSCURO   13

WHOLE

WHOLE 01

WHOLE 02

WHOLE 03

WHOLE   04

WHOLE 05

WHOLE 06

WHOLE   07

WHOLE   08

WHOLE 09

WHOLE 10

WHOLE 11

WHOLE 12

WHOLE 13

WHOLE 14

WHOLE 15

WHOLE 16

WHOLE 17

WHOLE 18

WHOLE   19

WHOLE 20

WHOLE 21

WHOLE 22

WHOLE 23

WHOLE 24

WHOLE 25

WHOLE   27

WHOLE 28

WHOLE 30

WHOLE 31

WHOLE 32

WHOLE 33

WHOLE 34

WHOLE 35

WHOLE 37

WHOLE 38

WHOLE   39

WHOLE 40

WHOLE 41

WHOLE   42

WHOLE 43

TONDO

TONDO 01 | 02

TONDO 21

APPEARANCE

APPEARANCE   01

APPEARANCE 02

APPEARANCE 06

APPEARANCE 07

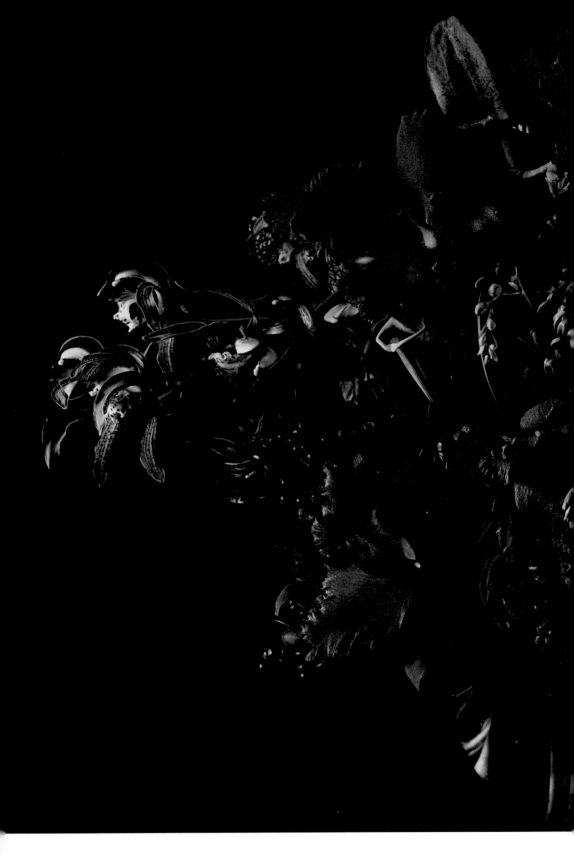

APPEARANCE   08

APPEARANCE 10

APPEARANCE   11

APPEARANCE 12

APPEARANCE   13

APPEARANCE   14

APPEARANCE 15

APPEARANCE   16

APPEARANCE   17

APPEARANCE   18

APPEARANCE   19

APPEARANCE 20

APPEARANCE   21

APPEARANCE 22

APPEARANCE   23

APPEARANCE 26

APPEARANCE   27

AUTOGENESIS

AUTOGENESIS   10

AUTOGENESIS 11

AUTOGENESIS 12

AUTOGENESIS 13

AUTOGENESIS 14

346———347

AUTOGENESIS 15

AUTOGENESIS 18

AUTOGENESIS 19

AUTOGENESIS 20

AUTOGENESIS 21

AUTOGENESIS 22

AUTOGENESIS 23

List of Flower Names　植物名リスト

Index of Flower Names　索引

植物名は世界共通で使われているラテン語表記による正式名「学名」と一般名「和名」を併記した。学名と園芸品種名の採用については『国際植物命名規約』および『国際栽培植物命名規約』に基づき検討し下記の通り植物名を表記した。

学名表記について:

1) 原則、二名法に則り、〈属名＋種小名〉で表記した。命名者名の記載がある場合は、命名者名を種小名に続けて記した。なお、本書では命名年号は省略している。

2) 園芸品種名は、上記〈属名＋種小名〉に続けて ″で括り表記した。園芸品種名が入る場合は、命名者名を省略している。園芸品種名が特定できない場合は、〈属名＋（種小名）＋命名者名〉で表記した。

3) 種小名が特定できない場合は、〈属名＋園芸品種名〉で表記した。

表記例:
アロエ＝ Aloe、エケベリア＝ Echeveria、グズマニア＝ Guzmania、
グレビレア＝ Grevillea、トケイソウ＝ Passiflora、
ブバルディア＝ Bouvardia、プロテア＝ Protea、
ベロニカ＝ Veronica、カーネーション＝ Dianthus、
グラプトベリア＝ Graptoveria、センペルビウム＝ Sempervivum、
ネオレゲリア＝ Neoregelia、ヒューケラ＝ Heuchere、
ユリ＝ Lilium

4) 亜種、変種の場合は、〈属名＋種小名〉に続けて「subsp.」（＝亜種）、「var.」（＝変種）の略号で表記した。

5) ランの学名においては、人工的に作られた交配種の種小名のみ大文字で表記している。

6) 以下については特記の通り採用・表記した。

ゼンマイ＝シダ科の植物に見られる渦巻き状のことを指し、シダ科の何の植物のゼンマイかによって学名が異なる。
ブローディア＝トリテレイアへ変更している。
クロユリ／バイモユリ＝ユリ科ではなく、学名のフリチラリアに統一した。
ドリテノプシス＝ファレノプシスに統一した。
グラプトベリア＝エケベリアの新種。品種名があるものはすべて品種名に統一した。
ムスカリ／ベレバリア＝近縁種である旧名ムスカリの名称だったが近年ベレバリアの品種に変更された。
ジンジャー＝実際にジンジャーではない品種もその名称で流通しているため、ジンジャーの表記で統一している。

和名表記について:

和名については読者の便宜を図ることを目的として下記の通り表記した。

1) 原則、学名表記に準拠し、〈属名・種小名〉で表記した。

表記例:
チューリップ・トルケスタニカ

ただし、特に園芸品種で、属名が流通上で一般的に使われておらず浸透していない、あるいは流通名と属名に混同が生じてしまう可能性がある属・種については、一般的に認知度の高い流通名（あるいは園芸品種名）を採用した。正式な学名については、ラテン語表記を参照して頂きたい。

2) 学名の品種名と異なる和名の品種名を使用している主な種類は以下の通りである。

オナガカンアオイ［緑鵬（りょくほう）］、
アエオニウム［黒法師（くろほうし）］、カラー［エチオピカブレナ］、
カライトソウ、カワラタケ、キバナホウチャクソウ、キブシ、
クリスマスローズ・フェチダス、
クリスマスローズ［ダブルラズベリーリップル］、
クロトン［曙（あけぼの）］、クロホオズキ、ゲットウ、コウゾリナ、
コショウ、コルチカム［アルバ］、サワギキョウ、サンタンカ、
シオデ［イタリアンベリー］、シネラリア［ティアブルー］、
スズラン、セイヨウスユキソウ、セッカダイズ、タイワンホトトギス、
ツバキ、ツルウメモドキ、トクサ、トケイソウ、トベラ、
ノラニンジン、ハナトラノオ、ビオラセア・フレグランス、
プッシュカン、フウラン［白雲閣（はくうんかく）］、ヤトロファ、
ルリタマアザミ［ベッチーズブルー］、ワスレナグサ

3) 園芸品種名が特定できる場合は、種小名の表記を省き、属名に続けて［］で括り表記した。※ランは例外とする

表記例:
ガーベラ［アナクレート］

4) サボテンについては、〈属名＋種小名〉の原則に拠らず、〈属名〉の代わりに〈科名〉である「サボテン」を記した。正式な学名については、ラテン語表記を参照して頂きたい。

表記例:
サボテン［赤城（あかぎ）］

5) 原則、和名はカタカナで表記し、園芸品種名で主に漢字表記で流通している種については、漢字表記を採用し、ふりがなを平仮名で併記した。

6) 学名のラテン語、および欧文のカナ表記については、現実的、慣用的側面を考慮し、あえて本書内では統一を行っていない。読者の利用および検索の便をはかるために和名として既に定着し、流通名として使用および掲載頻度が高いカナ表記を適宜採用した。よって、一部のカナ表記については併存している。

[Explanatory notes]

Flowers' names are described using global common Latin scientific names, along with their popular English names (popular Japanese names in the Japanese section). Scientific names and horticultural variety names have been reviewed based on the "International Code of Botanical Nomenclature" and "International Code of Nomenclature for Cultivated Plants", and are indicated as follows.

Notation of scientific names:

1) Generally indicated as [Generic name + specific name] according to the binomial nomenclature. Where names of nomenclators are included, they follow after the respective specific name. Years of nomenclature are not indicated.

2) Horticultural variety names are indicated in single quotation marks, following the [Generic name + specific name]. Where horticultural variety names are included, the name of the respective nomenclator is omitted. Where horticultural variety names are not identified, names are indicated as [Generic name + (specific name) + nomenclator's name].

3) Where specific names are not identified, names are indicated as [Generic name + Horticultural variety name].

Examples:
Aloe, Echeveria, Guzmania, Grevillea, Passiflora, Bouvardia, Protea, Veronica, Dianthus, Graptoveria, Sempervivum, Neoregelia, Heuchere, Lilium.

4) Subspecies or variant species are indicated as "subsp." and "var." respectively following after the [Generic name + specific name].

5) Regarding scientific names of orchids, only the specific names of artificial crossbreeds are indicated in capital letters.

6) Special rules for the indication of names are adopted as follows.

Examples:
Generally refers to ferns with helical patterns, whereas different scientific names are used to indicate Osmunda japonica from different families of ferns.
Brodiaea: Changed to "Triteleia".
Fritillaria camtschatcensis / Fritillaria verticillata: Generally indicated not as Liliaceae but under the scientific name "Fritillaria".
Doritaenopsis: Generally indicated as "Phalaenopsis".
Graptoveria: New breed of Echeveria. Items with variety

names are generally indicated with the respective names.
Muscari/Bellevalia: The former variety name "Muscari" was recently changed to "Bellevalia".
Ginger: As even species that are not actually ginger are distributed under this name, they are generally indicated as "Ginger".

Names of Flowers │ COEXISTENCE

December, 2014——August, 2016 in Tokyo

01   p. 19

1 *Fritillaria imperialis* 'Rubra Maxima'
　フリチラリア［ルブラマキシマ］
2 *Cryptanthus bivittatus* 'Pink Starlight'
　クリプタンサス［ピンクスターライト］

02   p. 21

1 *Fritillaria meleagris* L.
　フリチラリア・メレアグリス
2 *Arpophyllum giganteum* Hartw. ex Lindl.
　アーポフィラム・ギガンテウム

03   p. 23

1 *Convallaria majalis* L.
　スズラン
2 *Zantedeschia aethiopica* 'Green Goddess'
　カラー［グリーンゴッデス］

04   pp. 24–25

1 *Juniperus chinensis* var. *sargentii*
　イブキ［真柏（しんぱく）］
2 *Aloe* 'Flamingo'
　アロエ［フラミンゴ］

05 — p. 27

1 *Paphiopedilum* Norito Hasegawa 'Gold Rush'
パフィオペディラム・ノリトハセガワ［ゴールドラッシュ］
2 *Papaver nudicaule* L.
ポピー・アイスランドポピー
3 *Paphiopedilum venustum* 'Petit Light'
パフィオペディラム・ベナスタム［プチライト］

06 — p. 29

1 *Echeveria* 'Yamatobini'
エケベリア［大和美尼（やまとびに）］
2 *Dianthus caryophyllus* 'Dom Pedro'
カーネーション［ドンペドロ］

07 — p. 31

1 *Fritillaria persica* 'Ivory Bells'
フリチラリア［アイボリーベル］
2 *Bellevalia paradoxa* 'Green Pearl'
ベレバリア［グリーンパール］

08 — p. 33

1 *Hippeastrum correiense* (Bury) Worsley
アマリリス・コリエンシス
2 *Alpinia zerumbet* (Pers.) B. L. Burtt and R. M. Sm.
ゲットウ
3 *Cynara scolymus* L.
アーティチョーク

09   pp. 34–35

1   *Pitacairnia wendlandii* Baker
　ピトカイルニア・ウェンドランディ
2   *Vriesea carinata* 'Christiane'
　フリーセア [クリスティアーナ]
3   *Musa minor* Nakai
　バショウ [キングバナナ]
4   *Aechmea fendleri* 'Del Mar'
　エクメア [デルマー]

5   *Curcuma cordata*
　'Jewel of Thailand'
　クルクマ [ジュエルオブタイランド]
6   *Heliconia magnifica* W. J. Kress
　ヘリコニア・マグニフィカ
7   *Dionaea muscipula*
　'Cluster Traps'
　ハエトリグサ [クラスタートラップス]
8   *Sarracenia purpurea* L.
　サラセニア・プルプレア

10   p. 37

1   *Iris spuria* subsp. *ochroleuca* (L.) Dykes
　アヤメ・オクラレルカ
2   *Zantedeschia aethiopica* 'White Swan'
　カラー [エチオピカブレナ]

11   p. 39

1   *Dahlia* 'Micchan'
　ダリア [ミッチャン]
2   *Fritillaria uva-vulpis* Rix
　フリチラリア・ウバブルビス

12   p. 41

1   *Tillandsia* 'Cotton Candy'
　チランジア [コットンキャンディ]
2   *Protea cynaroides* 'Arctic Ice'
　プロテア・キングプロテア [アークティックアイス]

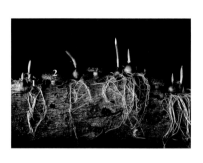

13   pp. 42–43
___

1 *Narcissus tazetta* 'Shirofusa Suisen'
   スイセン［白房スイセン（しろふさすいせん）］
2 *Lentinula edodes* (Berk.) Pegler
   シイタケ

14   p. 45
___

1 *Iris × hollandica* 'Blue Diamond'
   アヤメ・ダッチアイリス［ブルーダイヤモンド］
2 *Juniperus chinensis* var. sargentii
   イブキ［真柏（しんぱく）］

15   p. 47
___

1 *Gladiolus murielae* Kelway
   グラジオラス・ムリエラ
2 *Bambuseae* Kunth ex Dumort.
   タケ
3 *Phalaenopsis* Sogo Yukidian 'V3'
   ファレノプシス・ソゴユキディアン［V3（ぶいすりー）］
4 *Pinus parviflora* Sieb. & Zucc.
   マツ［五葉松（ごようまつ）］

16   pp. 48–49
___

1 *Bambuseae* Kunth ex Dumort.
   タケ
2 *Camellia sasanqua* Thunb.
   サザンカ
3 *Hyacinthus orientalis* 'Blue Jacket'
   ヒヤシンス［ブルージャケット］

17   p. 51

1 *Picris hieracioides* L.subsp. *japonica* (Thunb.) Krylov
コウゾリナ
2 *Stachyurus praecox* Siebold et Zucc.
キブシ
3 *Tulipa* 'Super Parrot'
チューリップ［スーパーパーロット］

18   p. 53

1 *Brassica oleracea* 'Purple Pop'
ハボタン［パープルポップ］
2 *Echeveria* 'Sofuren'
エケベリア［相府蓮（そうふれん）］

19   p. 55

1 *Chrysanthemum* × *morifolium* 'Green Shamrock'
キク［グリーンシャムロック］
2 *Nigella damascena* L.
ニゲラの実
3 *Anthurium andreanum* 'Fuchsia Green'
アンスリウム［フューシャグリーン］

20   p. 57

1 *Lilium maculatum* 'Apricot Fudge'
ユリ・スカシユリ［アプリコットファッジ］
2 *Ranunculus asiaticus* 'Morocco Mhamid'
ラナンキュラス［モロッコマーミド］

21   p. 59
——
1   *Cyathea spinulosa* Wall. ex Hook.
    ヘゴゼンマイ
2   *Nepenthes* 'Rebecca Soper'
    ネペンテス［レベッカソーパー］

22   pp. 60–61
——
1   *Rosa* 'Red Elegance'
    バラ［レッドエレガンス］
2   *Doryanthes excelsa* Correa
    ガイミアリリー

23   p. 63
——
1   *Lupinus luteus* 'Kibana Lupinus'
    ルピナス［黄花ルピナス（きばなるぴなす）］
2   *Leucospermum cordifolium* 'High Gold'
    ピンクッション［ハイゴールド］

24   p. 65
——
1   *Anthurium andreanum* 'Alula Pink'
    アンスリウム［アルーラピンク］
2   *Lilium orientalis* 'Sheila'
    ユリ［セーラ］

25 pp. 66–67
___

1 *Pinus parviflora* Sieb. & Zucc.
マツ［五葉松（ごようまつ）］
2 *Citrus medica* var. *sarcodactylis*
ブッシュカン

26 p. 69
___

1 *Tulipa* 'Flaming Spring Green'
チューリップ［フレミングスプリンググリーン］
2 *Fritillaria thunbergii* Miq.
フリチラリア・バイモユリ

27 p. 71
___

1 *Allium* 'Pinocchio'
アリウム［ピノキオ］
2 *Equisetum hyemale* L.
トクサ
3 *Fockea edulis* 'Kaseijin'
フォッケア［火星人（かせいじん）］

28 pp. 72–73
___

1 *Nelumbo nucifera* 'Ouren'
ハス［桜蓮（おうれん）］

Names of Flowers │ HYBRID

December, 2014——August, 2016 in Tokyo

01   p. 77

1 *Sarracenia leucophylla* Raf.
サラセニア・レウコフィラ
2 *Lilium ochroleucum* Wall. ex Baker
ユリ・ウコンユリ
3 *Obregonia denegrii* Frič
サボテン［帝冠（ていかん）］
4 *Protea barbigera* 'Niobe'
プロテア［ニオベ］

02   p. 79

1 *Paphiopedilum* 'St. Swithin'
パフィオペディラム［セントスイシン］
2 *Iris germanica* 'Dusky Challenger'
アヤメ・ジャーマンアイリス［ダスキーチャレンジャー］

03   p. 81

1 *Vriesea carinata* 'Christiane'
フリーセア［クリスティアーナ］
2 *Chrysanthemum* × *morifolium* 'Yo'
キク［陽（よう）］
3 *Protea grandiceps* Tratt.
プロテア・グランディケプス

04   pp. 82–83

1 *Nepenthes rafflesiana* 'Koshikawa'
ネペンテス・ラフレシアナ［コシカワ］
2 *Dendrochilum magnum* Rchb. f.
デンドロキラム・マグナム
3 *Stemona japonica* (Blume) Miq.
リキュウソウ

05   p. 85
—

1   *Paphiopedilum niveum* (Rchb. f.) Stein
    パフィオペディラム・ニベウム
2   *Protea cynaroides* 'Red Rex'
    プロテア・キングプロテア［レッドレックス］

06   p. 87
—

1   *Tulipa turkestanica* (Regel) Regel
    チューリップ・トルケスタニカ
2   *Clematis florida* 'Alba Plena'
    クレマチス［アルバプレナ］
3   *Papaver nudicaule* L.
    ポピー・アイスランドポピー

07   p. 89
—

1   *Heliconia xanthovillosa* 'Shogun'
    ヘリコニア［ショウグン］
2   *Paphiopedilum platyphyllum* T. Yukawa
    パフィオペディラム・プラティフィラム

08   pp. 90–91
—

1   *Anthurium andreanum* 'Tropical Red'
    アンスリウム［トロピカルレッド］
2   *Papaver nudicaule* L.
    ポピー・アイスランドポピー

09   p. 93
—

1 *Tacca chantrieri* André
  タッカ・シャントリエリ
2 *Paphiopedilum callosum* (Rchb. f.) Stein
  パフィオペディラム・カローサム
3 *Hippeastrum × hybridum* 'Red Lion'
  アマリリス［レッドライオン］
4 *Protea* 'Pink Ice'
  プロテア［ピンクアイス］

10   p. 95
—

1 *Passiflora caerulea* 'Clear Sky'
  トケイソウ［クリアスカイ］
2 *Iris germanica* 'Wench'
  アヤメ・ジャーマンアイリス［ウエンチ］

11   pp. 96–97
—

1 *Protea barbigera* 'Niobe'
  プロテア［ニオベ］
2 *Drimiopsis maculata* Lindl. & Paxton
  ドリミオプシス・マクラータ

12   p. 99
—

1 *Heliconia rostrata* Ruiz & Pavon
  ヘリコニア・ロストラータ
2 *Paphiopedilum* Maudiae 'The Queen'
  パフィオペディラム・モーディエ［クイーン］
3 *Nepenthes* 'Dyeriana'
  ネペンテス［ダイエリアナ］

13   p. 101
—

1 *Sarracenia flava* var. *rubricorpora* 'Red Burgundy'
　サラセニア・フラバ・ルブリコーポラ［レッドバーガンディ］
2 *Anthurium andreanum* 'Sierra Magic'
　アンスリウム［シエラマジック］

14   pp. 102–103
—

1 *Paphiopedilum* Maudiae 'The Queen'
　パフィオペディラム・モーディエ［クイーン］
2 *Passiflora* 'Incense'
　トケイソウ［インセンス］

15   p. 105
—

1 *Lilium hansonii* Leichtlin ex D. D. T. Moore
　ユリ・タケシマユリ
2 *Mammillaria albilanata* Backeb.
　サボテン［希望丸（きぼうまる）］

16   pp. 106–107
—

1 *Anthurium andreanum* 'Safari'
　アンスリウム［サファリ］
2 *Rosa* 'Red Pompon'
　バラ［レッドポンポン］

17   p. 109
—

1 *Arisaema urashima* Hara
ウラシマソウの実
2 *Papaver orientale* (L.)
ポピー・オリエンタルポピー

18   p. 111
—

1 *Leucospermum cordifolium* 'Succession'
ピンクッション［サクセション］
2 *Nepenthes rafflesiana* var. *gigantea*
ネペンテス・ラフレシアナ・ギガンテア
3 *Zingiber spectabile* 'Golden Shampoo'
ジンジャー［ゴールデンシャンプー］

19   p. 113
—

1 *Allium amethystinum* 'Red Mohican'
アリウム［レッドモヒカン］
2 *Zantedeschia aethiopica* 'Captain Promise'
カラー［キャプテンプロミス］
3 *Vanda* 'Deep Purple Spots'
バンダ［ディープパープルスポット］

20   pp. 114–115
—

1 *Haworthia fasciata* 'Juni no Maki'
ハオルチア［十二の巻（じゅうにのまき）］
2 *Cynara scolymus* L.
アーティチョーク

21   p. 117

1   *Sarracenia alata* var. *ornata*
    サラセニア・アラータ・オルナタ
2   *Zantedeschia aethiopica* 'Captain Durance'
    カラー［キャプテンデュランス］

22   p. 119

1   *Nelumbo nucifera* 'Daikouho'
    ハス［大紅袍（だいこうほう）］
2   *Caladium* 'Scarlet Beauty'
    カラジウム［スカーレットビューティー］
3   *Curcuma alismatifolia* 'Pink Pearl'
    クルクマ［ピンクパール］

List of Flower Names │ CHIAROSCURO

December, 2014——August, 2016 in Tokyo

01   pp. 122–123

1 *Dahlia* 'Junai no Kimi'
   ダリア［純愛の君（じゅんあいのきみ）］
2 *Rubus fruticosus* L.
   ルブス・ブラックベリー
3 *Cynara scolymus* L.
   アーティチョーク
4 *Clematis texensis* 'Scarlet'
   クレマチス［スカーレット］
5 *Helianthus annuus* 'Tohoku Yae'
   ヒマワリ［東北八重（とうほくやえ）］
6 *Dahlia* 'Garnet'
   ダリア［ガーネット］
7 *Agapanthus africanus*
   'June Bride'
   アガパンサス［ジューンブライド］

8 *Echinacea purpurea* 'Hot Papaya'
   エキナセア［ホットパパイヤ］
9 *Serruria* 'Pretty n Pink'
   セルリア［プリティピンク］
10 *Scabiosa atropurpurea*
   'Moco Purple'
   スカビオサ［モコパープル］
11 *Anigozanthos flavidus*
   'Orange Cross'
   カンガルーポー［オレンジクロス］
12 *Delphinium elatum*
   'Aurora Blue Imp'
   デルフィニウム［オーロラブルーインプ］

02   pp. 124–125

1 *Callistephus chinensis*
   'Shaggy Pink Flash'
   アスター［シャギーピンクフラッシュ］
2 *Pelargonium graveolens*
   'Snowflake'
   ペラルゴニウム［スノーフレーク］
3 *Dahlia* 'Sinbad'
   ダリア［シンドバッド］
4 *Rosa* 'All 4 Love'
   バラ［オール4ラブ（おーるふぉーらぶ）］
5 *Delphinium grandiflorum*
   'Super Sky Blue'
   デルフィニウム［スーパースカイブルー］

6 *Hydrangea arborescens*
   'Hayes Starburst'
   アジサイ［ヘイズスターバースト］
7 *Dahlia* 'Matador'
   ダリア［マタドール］
8 *Vanda* 'Robert's Delight Blue'
   バンダ［ロバートデライトブルー］
9 *Lilium orientalis* 'Carolina'
   ユリ［カロリーナ］
10 *Rosa* 'Avalanche'
   バラ［アバランチェ］

03　　　　pp. 126–127

1 *Dahlia* 'Murakingyo'
ダリア [群金魚（むらきんぎょ）]

2 *Dahlia* 'Kokucho'
ダリア [黒蝶（こくちょう）]

3 *Dianthus barbatus* 'Green Trick'
ナデシコ [グリーントリュフ]

4 *Gerbera* 'Miguel'
ガーベラ [ミゲル]

5 *Rosa* 'Freedom'
バラ [フリーダム]

6 *Moluccella laevis* L.
モルセラ・ラエヴィス

7 *Dianthus caryophyllus* 'Master'
カーネーション [マスター]

8 *Zinnia elegans* 'Queen Lime'
ジニア [クイーンライム]

9 *Protea barbigera* 'Niobe'
プロテア [ニオベ]

10 *Lilium longiflorum* 'Pure Horn'
ユリ・テッポウユリ [ピュアホルン]

11 *Chrysanthemum* × *morifolium*
'Saffina'
キク [サフィーナ]

12 *Anthurium andreanum*
'ARCS Purple'
アンスリウム [ARCSパープル
（えーあーるしーえすぱーぷる）]

13 *Vanda* 'Pat Delight'
バンダ [パットデライト]

14 *Chrysanthemum* × *morifolium*
'Saba'
キク [サバ]

04　　　　pp. 128–129

1 *Celosia argentea* var. *cristata*
'Sakata Pride'
ケイトウ [サカタプライド]

2 *Anthurium clarinervium* Matuda
アンスリウム・クラリネルヴィウム

3 *Dionaea muscipula*
'Dingleys Giant'
ハエトリグサ [ディングレイズジャイアント]

4 *Zantedeschia aethiopica* 'Aquila'
カラー [アキーラ]

5 *Zinnia haageana* 'Persian Carpet'
ジニア [ペルシャンカーペット]

6 *Equisetum hyemale* L.
トクサ

7 *Rosa* 'Tamango'
バラ [タマンゴ]

8 *Aechmea wittmackiana*
'Scarlet Berry'
エクメア [スカーレットベリー]

9 *Huperzia squarrosa*
(G.Forst.) Trev.
フペルジア・スクアローサ

10 *Gentiana triflora* var. *japonica*
'Pastel Bell'
リンドウ [パステルベル]

11 *Codiaeum variegatum* 'Akebono'
クロトン [曙（あけぼの）]

12 *Paeonia lactiflora* 'Bunker Hill'
シャクヤク [バンカーヒル]

05   pp. 130–131

1   *Hydrangea macrophylla*
    'Hawaiian Blue'
    アジサイ［ハワイアンブルー］

2   *Dahlia* 'Biedermannsdorf'
    ダリア［ビーデルマンズドルフ］

3   *Tagetes erecta* 'Sovereign'
    マリーゴールド［ソブリン］

4   *Gerbera* 'Tomahawk'
    ガーベラ［トマホーク］

5   *Clematis integrifolia*
    'Miss Sumire'
    クレマチス［ミススミレ］

6   *Vanda* 'Variety'
    バンダ［バラエティ］

7   *Centaurea macrocephala*
    Muss. Puschk. ex Willd.
    オウゴンヤグルマギク

8   *Clematis texensis* 'Scarlet'
    クレマチス［スカーレット］

06   pp. 132–133

1   *Nepenthes* 'Chelsonii'
    ネペンテス［チェルソニー］

2   *Sarracenia* 'Night Sky'
    サラセニア［ナイトスカイ］

3   *Colmanara* Wildcat
    'Golden Red Star'
    コルマナラ・ワイルドキャット
    ［ゴールデンレッドスター］

4   *Paeonia lactiflora* 'Bunker Hill'
    シャクヤク［バンカーヒル］

5   *Dahlia* 'Santa Claus'
    ダリア［サンタクロース］

6   *Gerbera* 'Stanza'
    ガーベラ［スタンザ］

7   *Anthurium andreanum* 'Trinidad'
    アンスリウム［トリニダ］

07   pp. 134–135

1 *Vanda* 'Pachara Delight'
   バンダ［パチャラデライト］

2 *Callistephus chinensis*
   'Shaggy Pink Flash'
   アスター［シャギーピンクフラッシュ］

3 *Amaranthus caudatus* 'Viridis'
   アマランサス［ハンギンググリーン］

4 *Trachelium caeruleum*
   'Devotion Purple'
   ユウギリソウ［ディボーションパープル］

5 *Gerbera* 'Black Pearl'
   ガーベラ　［ブラックパール］

6 *Oncidium* Moon Shadow 'Tiger Tail'
   オンシジューム・ムーンシャドウ
   ［タイガーテイル］

7 *Paphiopedilum* Hassallii
   'Saint Mary'
   パフィオペディラム・ハッサリー
   ［セイントマリー］

8 *Kniphofia uvaria* 'Bees' Lemon'
   トリトマ［ビーズレモン］

9 *Vriesea carinata* 'Christiane'
   フリーセア［クリスティアーナ］

10 *Stachys byzantina*
   'Primrose Heron'
   ラムズイヤー［プリムローズヘロン］

11 *Cyathea spinulosa* Wall. ex Hook.
   ヘゴゼンマイ

12 *Globba winitii* 'Green Dragon'
   グロッバ［グリーンドラゴン］

13 *Brassia verrucosa*
   Bateman ex Lindl.
   ブラッシア・ベルコーサ

14 *Dianthus caryophyllus* 'Duelo'
   カーネーション［デュエロ］

15 *Crocosmia* 'Lucifer'
   クロコスミア［ルシファー］

08   pp. 136–137

1 *Echinops ritro* 'Veitch's Blue'
   ルリタマアザミ［ベッチーズブルー］

2 *Dianthus barbatus* 'Green Trick'
   ナデシコ［グリーントリュフ］

3 *Dahlia* 'JyuJyu'
   ダリア［JyuJyu（じゅじゅ）］

4 *Gerbera* 'Last Dance'
   ガーベラ［ラストダンス］

5 *Sarracenia purpurea* L.
   サラセニア・プルプレア

6 *Helichrysum bracteatum*
   (Vent.) Andrews
   ヘリクリサム

7 *Dahlia* 'Antique Red × Peach Pie'
   ダリア［アンティークレッド × ピーチパイ］

8 *Epidendrum* Star Valley
   'Violet Queen'
   エピデンドラム・スターバレー
   ［バイオレットクイーン］

9 *Veronica spicata* 'Red Fox'
   ベロニカ［レッドフォックス］

10 *Phalaenopsis* 'Palermo'
   ファレノプシス［パレルモ］

09 pp. 138–139

1 *Gentiana triflora* var. *japonica*
'Ashiro no Banshu'
リンドウ［安代の晩秋（あしろのばんしゅう）］

2 *Heliconia latispatha* 'Red Inazuma'
ヘリコニア［レッドイナズマ］

3 *Zingiber spectabile* 'Golden Shampoo'
ジンジャー［ゴールデンシャンプー］

4 *Chrysanthemum × morifolium*
'Green Shamrock'
キク［グリーンシャムロック］

5 *Anthurium andreanum* 'Amigo'
アンスリウム［アミーゴ］

6 *Sedum spectabile* 'Autumn Joy'
セダム［オータムジョイ］

7 *Echeveria* 'Shichifukujin'
エケベリア［七福神（しちふくじん）］

8 *Curcuma alismatifolia*
'Eternal Pink'
クルクマ［エターナルピンク］

10 pp. 140–141

1 *Allium amethystinum*
'Red Mohican'
アリウム［レッドモヒカン］

2 *Passiflora* 'Incense'
トケイソウ［インセンス］

3 *Eremurus stenophyllus*
(Boiss. & Buhse) Baker
エルムレス

4 *Veronica* 'Caroline Blue'
ベロニカ［カロラインブルー］

5 *Agapanthus africanus* 'Royal Blue'
リプサリス・カスタ［ロイヤルブルー］

6 *Delphinium elatum*
'Aurora Deep Purple'
デルフィニウム
［オーロラディープパープル］

7 *Paeonia lactiflora* 'Yubae'
シャクヤク［夕映（ゆうばえ）］

8 *Zantedeschia aethiopica*
'Captain Durance'
カラー［キャプテンデュランス］

9 *Zantedeschia aethiopica*
'Captain Promise'
カラー［キャプテンプロミス］

10 *Dahlia* 'Namahage Magic'
ダリア［NAMAHAGEマジック
（なまはげまじっく）］

11   pp. 142–143

1 *Epidendrum secundum*
   'Orange Ball'
   エピデンドラム［オレンジボール］

2 *Vanda* 'Deep Purple Spots'
   バンダ［ディープパープルスポット］

3 *Chrysanthemum* × *morifolium*
   'Jenny Orange'
   キク［ジェニーオレンジ］

4 *Crocosmia* 'Lucifer'
   クロコスミア［ルシファー］

5 *Dahlia*
   'Peach Pie × Namahage Nuance'
   ダリア［ピーチパイ × NAMAHAGE
   ニュアンス（なまはげにゅあんす）］

6 *Tapeinochilos ananassae*
   'Wax Ginger'
   ジンジャー［ワックスジンジャー］

7 *Aechmea fasciata* (Lindl.) Baker
   エクメア・ファシアータ

8 *Helichrysum bracteatum*
   (Vent.) Andrews
   ヘリクリサム

9 *Paranomus reflexus* N. E. Br.
   パラノムス

10 *Phalaenopsis* 'Golden Beauty'
   ファレノプシス［ゴールデンビューティー］

11 *Corymbia ficifolia*
   'Flower Gum Orange'
   ユーカリ［フラワーガムオレンジ］

12 *Dianthus caryophyllus* 'Golem'
   カーネーション［ゴレム］

12   pp. 144–145

1 *Rhyncholaeliocattleya*
   Memoria Helen Brown
   'Sweet Afton'
   カトレヤ・リンコレリオカトレヤ・
   メモリアヘレンブラウン
   ［スウィートアフトン］

2 *Anthurium andreanum* 'Kalapana'
   アンスリウム［カラパナ］

3 *Gerbera* 'Terra Nova'
   ガーベラ［テラノバ］

4 *Kniphofia uvaria* 'Flamenco'
   トリトマ［フラメンコ］

5 *Nelumbo nucifera* 'Makotobasu'
   ハス［誠蓮（まことばす）］

6 *Ammi majus* 'Green Mist'
   レースフラワー［グリーンミスト］

7 *Lilium lancifolium*
   Thunb. var. *flaviflorum* Makino
   ユリ・オウゴンオニユリ

8 *Veronica* 'Pink Hunter'
   ベロニカ［ピンクハンター］

13   pp. 146–147

1 *Banksia coccinea* R. Br
   バンクシア・コッキネア

2 *Rubus fruitcosus* L.
   ルブス・ブラックベリー

3 *Gentiana triflora* var. *japonica*
   'Ashiro no Banshu'
   リンドウ［安代の晩秋（あしろのばんしゅう）］

4 *Buddleja davidii* 'Royal Red'
   ブッドレア［ロイヤルレッド］

5 *Curcuma alismatifolia* 'Old Rose'
   クルクマ［オールドローズ］

6 *Clematis florida* 'Magic Fountain'
   クレマチス［マジックフォンテーン］

7 *Dahlia* 'Namahage Magic'
   ダリア［NAMAHAGEマジック
   （なまはげまじっく）］

8 *Gerbera* 'Gio'
   ガーベラ［ジオ］

Names of Flowers │ WHOLE

December, 2014——August, 2016 in Tokyo

01　　　pp. 150–151

1　*Banksia integrifolia* L. f.
　バンクシア・インテグリフォリア

2　*Hyacinthus orientalis* 'Delft Blue'
　ヒヤシンス［デルフトブルー］

3　*Hydrangea macrophylla*
　'Sibylla Classic Blue'
　アジサイ［シビラクラシックブルー］

4　*Muscari aucheri* 'White Magic'
　ムスカリ［ホワイトマジック］

5　*Epidendrum* Wonder Valley
　'Noble Star'
　エピデンドラム・ワンダーバレー
　［ノーブルスター］

6　*Paphiopedilum insigne*
　(Wall. ex Lindl.) Pfitzer
　パフィオペディラム・インシグネ

7　*Anthurium andreanum* 'Safari'
　アンスリウム［サファリ］

8　*Dianthus barbatus* 'Green Trick'
　ナデシコ［グリーントリュフ］

9　*Gerbera* 'Voldemort'
　ガーベラ［ヴォルデモート］

10　*Gerbera* 'Red Trip'
　ガーベラ［レッドトリップ］

11　*Nerine bowdenii* 'Mr. John'
　ネリネ［ミスタージョン］

12　*Dianthus barbatus*
　'Breanthus Baron'
　ナデシコ［ブレアンサスバロン］

13　*Begonia venosa* Skan ex Hook. f.
　ベゴニア・ベノーサ

14　*Ammi majus* 'Green Mist'
　レースフラワー［グリーンミスト］

15　*Eustoma grandiflorum*
　'Corsage Pink'
　トルコキキョウ［コサージュピンク］

16　*Dahlia* 'Lalala'
　ダリア［ラ・ラ・ラ］

17　*Guzmania* 'Torch'
　グズマニア［トーチ］

18　*Paphiopedilum delenatii*
　Guillaumin
　パフィオペディラム・デレナティー

19　*Delphinium elatum*
　'Aurora Blue Imp'
　デルフィニウム［オーロラブルーインプ］

20　*Freesia refracta* 'Elegance'
　フリージア［エレガンス］

02　　　pp. 152–153

1　*Aechmea penduliflora* 'White Berry'
　エクメア［ホワイトベリー］

2　*Lilium longiflorum* 'Green Lily Alp'
　ユリ・テッポウユリ［グリーンリリアルプ］

3　*Dianthus barbatus* 'Green Trick'
　ナデシコ［グリーントリュフ］

4　*Haworthia cooperi* var. *obtusa*
　'Shizukuishi'
　ハオルチア［雫石（しずくいし）］

5　*Peperomia puteolata* Trel.
　ペペロミア・プテオラータ

6　*Echinacea purpurea* 'Pink Passion'
　エキナセア［ピンクパッション］

7　*Celosia argentea* var. *cristata*
　'Spring Green'
　ケイトウ［スプリンググリーン］

8　*Dionaea muscipula*
　'Dingleys Giant'
　ハエトリグサ［ディングレイズジャイアント］

9　*Rhipsalis teres* Steud.
　リプサリス・テレス

10　*Nepenthes sanguinea* Lindl.
　ネペンテス・サンギネア

11　*Cyathea spinulosa*
　Wall. ex Hook.
　ヘゴゼンマイ

12　*Clematis* L.
　クレマチスの実

13　*Curcuma alismatifolia*
　'Verdebianco'
　クルクマ［ヴェルデビアンコ］

14　*Mammillaria boolii* G. E. Linds.
　サボテン［ブーリー］

15　*Calathea cylindrica* 'Green Ice'
　カラテア［グリーンアイス］

16　*Allium giganteum* Regel
　アリウム・ギガンジュームの実

03   pp. 154–155

1 *Spathodea campanulata* P. Beauv.
カエンボク

2 *Anthurium andreanum* 'Burgundy'
アンスリウム［バーガンディ］

3 *Dahlia* 'Namahage Noir'
ダリア［NAMAHAGEノアール
（なまはげのあーる）］

4 *Chrysanthemum* × *morifolium*
'Lollipop Red'
キク［ロリポップレッド］

5 *Nepenthes* 'Dyeriana'
ネペンテス［ダイエリアナ］

6 *Cymbidium* 'Wine Shower'
シンビジューム［ワインシャワー］

7 *Zantedeschia aethiopica*
'Hot Chocolate'
カラー［ホットチョコレート］

8 *Tulipa turkestanica* (Regel) Regel
チューリップ・トルケスタニカ

9 *Paphiopedilum callosum* var. *vinicolor*
パフィオペディラム・カローサム・ビニカラー

10 *Cleistocactus winteri* D. Hunt
サボテン
［黄金紐綴化（おうごんちゅうてっか）］

11 *Dahlia* 'Kokucho'
ダリア［黒蝶（こくちょう）］

12 *Lilium orientalis* 'Firebolt'
ユリ［ファイヤーボルト］

13 *Vanilla planifolia*
Jacks. ex Andrews
バニラ

14 *Hyacinthus orientalis*
'Blue Jacket'
ヒヤシンス［ブルージャケット］

15 *Begonia rex* 'Morning Dew'
ベゴニア・レックスベゴニア
［モーニングデュー］

16 *Hippeastrum* × *hybridum*
'Black Baccara'
アマリリス［ブラックバッカラ］

17 *Faucaria bosscheana*
'Shiranami'
フォーカリア［白波（しらなみ）］

18 *Paphiopedilum spicerianum*
(Rchb. f) Pfitzer
パフィオペディラム・スピセリアナム

19 *Hedera rhombea*
Siebold & Zucc. ex Bean
ヘデラの実

04   pp. 156–157

1 *Sarracenia leucophylla* Raf.
サラセニア・レウコフィラ

2 *Tulipa* 'Largo'
チューリップ［ラルゴ］

3 *Nerine sarniensis* 'Berlioz'
ネリネ［ベルリッゾ］

4 *Paphiopedilum Sheerline* 'Rondo'
パフィオペディラム・シャーライン［ロンド］

5 *Freesia refracta* 'Aladdin'
フリージア［アラジン］

6 *Trametes versicolor* (L. Fr.) Quél.
カワラタケ

7 *Berzelia lanuginosa* (L.) Brongn.
バーゼリア・ラヌギノーサ

8 *Chrysanthemum* × *morifolium*
'Yo'
キク［陽（よう）］

9 *Muscari aucheri* 'White Magic'
ムスカリ［ホワイトマジック］

10 *Iris* × *hollandica* 'Blue Magic'
アヤメ・ダッチアイリス［ブルーマジック］

11 *Viola* 'Angel Rose Picotee'
ビオラ［エンジェルローズピコティ］

05   pp. 158–159

1 *Viola × wittrockiana*
'Frizzle Sizzle Passion Fruit'
パンジー［フリズルシズルパッションフルーツ］

2 *Dahlia* 'Koishigure'
ダリア［恋しぐれ（こいしぐれ）］

3 *Nerine humilis* (Jacq.) Herb.
ネリネ・フミリス

4 *Gerbera* 'Finesse'
ガーベラ［フィネッセ］

5 *Rosa* 'Sweet Avalanche'
バラ［スイートアバランチエ］

6 *Paeonia lactiflora*
'Sarah Bernhardt'
シャクヤク［サラベルナール］

7 *Epidendrum* Parasol Valley
'Hatsukoi'
エピデンドラム・パラソルバレー［ハツコイ］

8 *Ranunculus asiaticus* 'Charlotte'
ラナンキュラス［シャルロット］

9 *Bouvardia* 'Royal Roza'
ブバルディア［ロイヤルローザ］

10 *Rhyncholaeliocattleya*
Pamela Hetherington
'Coronation'
カトレヤ・リンコレリオカトレヤ・
パメラヘザリントン［コロネーション］

11 *Chrysanthemum × morifolium*
'Epoch'
キク［エポック］

12 *Phragmipedium* 'Rosy Charm'
フラグミペディウム［ロージーチャーム］

13 *Ranunculus asiaticus* 'Aurora'
ラナンキュラス［オーロラ］

14 *Phalaenopsis*
Happy Vivien 'Chunli'
ファレノプシス・ハッピーヴィヴィアン
［チュンリー］

15 *Serruria* 'Pretty n Pink'
セルリア［プリティピンク］

16 *Astilbe × arendsii* 'America'
アスチルベ［アメリカ］

17 *Lathyrus latifolius* 'Red Pearl'
スイートピー［レッドパール］

06   pp. 160–161

1 *Celosia argentea* var. *cristata*
'Sakata Pride'
ケイトウ［サカタプライド］

2 *Ranunculus asiaticus* 'Charlotte'
ラナンキュラス［シャルロット］

3 *Kalanchoe luciae* 'Flapjack'
カランコエ［フラップジャック］

4 *Skimmia japonica* 'Kew Green'
スキミア［キューグリーン］

5 *Dianthus caryophyllus*
'Crimson Tempo'
カーネーション［クリムゾンテンポ］

6 *Tulipa* 'Rococo'
チューリップ［ロココ］

7 *Rhipsalis ewaldiana*
Barthlott & N. P. Taylor
リプサリス・エワルディアナ

8 *Dianthus barbatus* 'Green Trick'
ナデシコ［グリーントリュフ］

9 *Banksia attenuata* R. Br.
バンクシア・アテナータ

10 *Dianthus barbatus*
'Breanthus Road'
ナデシコ［ブレアンサスロード］

11 *Rosa* 'Exciting Meilland'
バラ［エキサイティングメイアン］

12 *Dahlia* 'Iwaibana'
ダリア［祝花（いわいばな）］

13 *Adenanthos × cunninghamii*
Meisn.
アデナントス・キャニングハーミー

14 *Zantedeschia aethiopica*
'Red Charm'
カラー［レッドチャーム］

15 *Ranunculus asiaticus*
'Morocco Tantan'
ラナンキュラス［モロッコタンタン］

16 *Dianthus caryophyllus*
'Nobio Violet'
カーネーション［ノビオバイオレット］

07   pp. 162–163

1 *Centaurea cyanus* 'Blue Carpet'
ヤグルマソウ［ブルーカーペット］
2 *Myosotis* L.
ワスレナグサ
3 *Ageratum houstonianum*
'Top Blue'
アゲラタム［トップブルー］
4 *Echeveria lilacina*
Kimn. & Moran
エケベリア・リラシナ
5 *Pericallis* × *hybrida* 'Tear Blue'
シネラリア［ティアブルー］
6 *Hyacinthus orientalis* 'Delft Blue'
ヒヤシンス［デルフトブルー］
7 *Hydrangea macrophylla*
'Blue Fresh'
アジサイ［ブルーフレッシュ］
8 *Viola* × *wittrockiana*
'Frizzle Sizzle Blue'
パンジー［フリズルシズルブルー］

9 *Allium* 'Blue Perfume'
アリウム［ブルーパフューム］
10 *Hyacinthus orientalis*
'Pink Pearl'
ヒヤシンス［ピンクパール］
11 *Nigella damascena*
'Persian Jewels'
ニゲラ［ペルシャンジュエル］
12 *Muscari aucheri* 'Blue Magic'
ムスカリ［ブルーマジック］
13 *Echeveria* 'Hercules'
エケベリア［ヘラクレス］
14 *Delphinium grandiflorum*
'Super Grand Blue'
デルフィニウム［スーパーグランブルー］
15 *Leucocoryne coquimbensis*
F. Phil. ex Phil.
リューココリーネ・コキンベンシス

08   pp. 164–165

1 *Zantedeschia aethiopica*
'Captain Odeon'
カラー［キャプテンオデオン］
2 *Gymnocalycium anisitsii*
(K. Schumann) Britton & Rose
サボテン［翠晃冠錦（すいこうかんにしき）]
3 *Zingiber spectabile*
'Golden Shampoo'
ジンジャー［ゴールデンシャンプー］
4 *Epidendrum secundum*
'Orange Ball'
エピデンドラム［オレンジボール］
5 *Ixora coccinea* L.
サンタンカ
6 *Dahlia* Cav.
ダリアの球根
7 *Gerbera* 'Anacleto'
ガーベラ［アナクレート］

8 *Lilium concolor* Salisb.
ユリ・チョウセンヒメユリ
9 *Tagetes erecta*
'Moonsong Deep Orange'
マリーゴールド
［ムーンソングディープオレンジ］
10 *Kniphofia uvaria* 'First Sunrise'
トリトマ［ファーストサンライズ］
11 *Zinnia haageana* 'Aztec Sunset'
ジニア［アズテックサンセット］
12 *Alstroemeria* 'Sesame Orange'
アルストロメリア［セサミオレンジ］
13 *Banksia coccinea* R. Br
バンクシア・コッキネア
14 *Kalanchoe blossfeldiana* 'Holly'
カランコエ［ホリー］

09   pp. 166–167

1 *Clematis integrifolia* 'Hendersonii'
   クレマチス［ヘンダーソニー］

2 *Begonia rex* 'Super Curl'
   ベゴニア・レックスベゴニア［スーパーカール］

3 *Callistephus chinensis*
   'Azumi Rose Pink'
   アスター［あずみローズピンク］

4 *Phalaenopsis* Queen Beer 'Mantenko'
   ファレノプシス・クインビー
   ［満天紅（まんてんこう）］

5 *Zantedeschia aethiopica*
   'Garnet Glow'
   カラー［ガーネットグロー］

6 *Lilium orientalis* 'Casa Blanca'
   ユリ［カサブランカ］

7 *Delphinium elatum*
   'Aurora Blue Imp'
   デルフィニウム［オーロラブルーインプ］

8 *Anthurium andreanum* 'Previa'
   アンスリウム［プレビア］

9 *Nerine bowdenii* 'Mr. John'
   ネリネ［ミスタージョン］

10 *Dahlia* 'Rebecca Lynn'
   ダリア［レベッカリン］

11 *Zantedeschia aethiopica* 'Majestic Red'
   カラー［マジェスティックレッド］

12 *Dianthus barbatus* 'Green Trick'
   ナデシコ［グリーントリュフ］

13 *Hippeastrum × hybidum*
   'Magic Green'
   アマリリス［マジックグリーン］

14 *Gerbera* 'Petit Akane'
   ガーベラ［プチアカネ］

15 *Hydrangea macrophylla*
   'Marine Blue'
   アジサイ［マリンブルー］

16 *Paeonia lactiflora* 'Fuji'
   シャクヤク［富士（ふじ）］

17 *Banksia integrifolia* L. f.
   バンクシア・インテグリフォリア

18 *Lilium orientalis* 'Mambo'
   ユリ［マンボ］

19 *Kalanchoe humilis* Britten
   カランコエ・フミリス

20 *Gloriosa superba* 'Pearl White'
   グロリオサ［パールホワイト］

21 *Hyacinthus orientalis*
   'Anna Marie'
   ヒヤシンス［アンナマリー］

22 *Rosa* 'Splash Sensation'
   バラ［スプラッシュセンセーション］

23 *Phalaenopsis* Taida Salu
   'Morning Sun'
   ファレノプシス・タイダソリュー
   ［モーニングサン］

24 *Piper kadsura* Trel. & Yunck.
   フウトウカズラ

25 *Viburnum tinus* L.
   ビバーナム・ティナス

26 *Echeveria* 'Black Prince'
   エケベリア［ブラックプリンス］

10   pp. 168–169

1 *Kalanchoe humilis* Britten
   カランコエ・フミリス

2 *Dahlia* 'Malcom's White'
   ダリア［マルコムズホワイト］

3 *Zantedeschia aethiopica*
   'Captain Mirage'
   カラー［キャプテンミラージュ］

4 *Freesia enkelbloemig* 'Anouk'
   フリージア［アヌーク］

5 *Eustoma grandiflorum*
   'Reina White'
   トルコキョウ［レイナホワイト］

6 *Chrysanthemum × morifolium*
   'Super Ping Pong'
   キク［スーパーピンポン］

7 *Paphiopedilum* 'F. C. Puddle'
   パフィオペディラム
   ［F. C. パッドル（えふしーぱっどる）］

8 *Espostoa blossfeldiorum*
   (Vaupel) Borg
   サボテン［幻楽（げんらく）］

11 pp. 170–171

1 *Polygala myrtifolia* var. *grandiflora* 'Sweet Pea Shrub'
ポリガラ［スイートピーシュラブ］

2 *Pelargonium graveolens* 'Bourbon'
ペラルゴニウム［ブルボン］

3 *Aquilegia chrysantha* 'Yellow Queen'
アクイレギア［イエロークイーン］

4 *Protea barbigera* 'Niobe'
プロテア［ニオベ］

5 *Pleiospilos nelii* 'Teigyoku'
プレイオスピロス［帝玉（ていぎょく）］

6 *Zantedeschia aethiopica* 'Gold Crown'
カラー［ゴールドクラウン］

7 *Dahlia* 'Asahi Temari'
ダリア［朝日てまり（あさひてまり）］

8 *Gerbera* 'Tomahawk'
ガーベラ［トマホーク］

9 *Jatropha podagrica* Hook.
ヤトロファ

10 *Guzmania dissitiflora* (André) L. B. Sm.
グズマニア・ディシティフローラ

11 *Senecio rowleyanus* H. Jacobsen
グリーンネックレス

12 *Lilium maculatum* 'Apricot Fudge'
ユリ・スカシユリ［アプリコットファッジ］

13 *Fritillaria persica* 'Ivory Bells'
フリチラリア［アイボリーベル］

14 *Telopea speciosissima* 'Waratah'
テロペア［ワラタ］

15 *Tillandsia andreana* E. Morren ex André
チランジア・アンドレアナ

16 *Aechmea fulgens* 'Red Berry'
エクメア［レッドベリー］

17 *Moluccella laevis* L.
モルセラ・ラエヴィス

18 *Nepenthes* 'Rebecca Soper'
ネペンテス［レベッカソーパー］

19 *Ganoderma applanatum* (Pers.) Pat.
コフキサルノコシカケ

20 *Vriesea carinata* 'Christiane'
フリーセア［クリスティアーナ］

21 *Ferocactus macrodiscus* (Mart.) Britton & Rose
サボテン［赤城（あかぎ）］

22 *Guzmania* 'Orangeade'
グズマニア［オレンジエード］

23 *Chrysanthemum* × *morifolium* 'Sei Nadal'
キク［セイナダル］

24 *Iris* × *hollandica* 'Blue Magic'
アヤメ・ダッチアイリス［ブルーマジック］

25 *Tillandsia xerographica* Rohweder
チランジア・キセログラフィカ

26 *Tagetes erecta* 'Sovereign'
マリーゴールド［ソブリン］

27 *Epidendrum* Star Valley 'Violet Queen'
エピデンドラム・スターバレー［バイオレットクイーン］

28 *Rhipsalis cereuscula* Haw.
リプサリス・ケレウスクラ

29 *Tulipa* 'Tete a Tete'
チューリップ［ティタティタ］

30 *Fritillaria acmopetala* Boiss.
フリチラリア・アクモペタラ

12 pp. 172–173

1 *Gerbera* 'Double Date'
ガーベラ［ダブルデート］

2 *Tillandsia ionantha* Planchon
チランジア・イオナンタ

3 *Kniphofia uvaria* 'Flamenco'
トリトマ［フラメンコ］

4 *Epidendrum secundum* 'Orange Ball'
エピデンドラム［オレンジボール］

5 *Haworthia reinwardtii*
'Taka no Tsume'
ハオルチア［鷹の爪（たかのつめ）］

6 *Zantedeschia aethiopica* 'Hot Shot'
カラー［ホットショット］

7 *Passiflora caerulea* 'Clear Sky'
トケイソウ［クリアスカイ］

8 *Mangifera indica* L.
マンゴー

9 *Gerbera* 'Pasta di Mamma'
ガーベラ［パスタディママ］

10 *Dichelostemma ida-maia*
(Alph. Wood) Greene
ディケロステンマ・イダマイア

11 *Banksia hookeriana* Meisn.
バンクシア・フーケリアナ

12 *Dahlia* 'Biedermannsdorf'
ダリア［ビーデルマンズドルフ］

13 *Dahlia* 'Peach in Season'
ダリア［ピーチインシーズン］

14 *Strelitzia reginae* Aiton
ストレリチア・レギネ

15 *Cocos nucifera* L.
ココナッツ

16 *Rosa* 'Milva'
バラ［ミルバ］

17 *Zinnia haageana* 'Old Fashion'
ジニア［オールドファッション］

18 *Musa ornata* Roxb.
バショウ［オレンジオルナタバナナ］

19 *Kalanchoe blossfeldiana* 'Holly'
カランコエ［ホリー］

20 *Rudbeckia hirta*
'Cherokee Sunset'
ルドベキア［チェロキーサンセット］

21 *Musa velutina*
H. Wendl. & Drude
バショウ［ピンクバナナ］

13 pp. 174–175

1 *Tillandsia ionantha* Planchon
チランジア・イオナンタ

2 *Chrysanthemum* × *morifolium*
'Bomber Green'
キク［ボンバーグリーン］

3 *Cyclamen hederifolium* Aiton
シクラメン・ヘデリフォリウム

4 *Sarracenia rubra* subsp. *gulfensis*
サラセニア・ルブラ・ガルフェンシス

5 *Protea barbigera* 'Snow Queen'
プロテア［スノークイーン］

6 *Phylica plumosa* L.
フィリカ・プルモーサ

7 *Tillandsia caput-medusae*
E. Morren
チランジア・カプトメデューサ

8 *Daucus carota* L.
ノラニンジン

9 *Kalanchoe beharensis* Drake
カランコエ・ベハレンシス

10 *Nepenthes muluensis* M. Hotta
ネペンテス・ムルエンシス

11 *Hippeastrum* × *hybridum*
'Christmas Gift'
アマリリス［クリスマスギフト］

12 *Dendropanax trifidus*
(Thunb.) Makino ex. H. Hara
カクレミノ

13 *Viscum album* subsp.
coloratum Komar
ヤドリギ

14 *Pelargonium graveolens*
'Bourbon'
ペラルゴニウム［ブルボン］

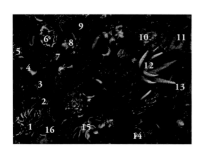

14   pp. 176–177

1 *Spathodea campanulata* P. Beauv.
カエンボク

2 *Lilium orientalis* 'Mambo'
ユリ [マンボ]

3 *Dahlia* 'Fidalgo Blacky'
ダリア [フィダルゴブラッキー]

4 *Zantedeschia aethiopica*
'Hot Chocolate'
カラー [ホットチョコレート]

5 *Viburnum tinus* L.
ビバーナム・ティナス

6 *Viola* × *wittrockiana*
'Frizzle Sizzle Burgundy Shade'
パンジー
[フリズルシズルバーガンディーシェード]

7 *Dianthus barbatus*
'Breanthus Queen'
ナデシコ [ブレアンサスクイーン]

8 *Heuchera* 'Midnight Rose'
ヒューケラ [ミッドナイトローズ]

9 *Dahlia* 'Kokucho'
ダリア [黒蝶 (こくちょう)]

10 *Brassica oleracea*
'Mitsuko Premium'
ハボタン
[光子プレミアム (みつこぷれみあむ)]

11 *Begonia masoniana*
Irmsch. ex Ziesenh.
ベゴニア・マソニアナ

12 *Aloe* 'Flamingo'
アロエ [フラミンゴ]

13 *Brassica oleracea* 'Silky Pearl'
ハボタン [シルキーパール]

14 *Phalaenopsis* 'Chocolate Disco'
ファレノプシス [チョコレートディスコ]

15 *Echeveria* 'Black Knight'
エケベリア [ブラックナイト]

16 *Scabiosa atropurpurea*
'Ace of Spades'
スカビオサ [エースオブスペード]

15   pp. 178–179

1 *Dahlia* 'Marron'
ダリア [マロン]

2 *Dianthus caryophyllus* 'Classico'
カーネーション [クラシコ]

3 *Gerbera* 'Knight Rider'
ガーベラ [ナイトライダー]

4 *Rosa* 'Halloween'
バラ [ハロウィン]

5 *Tulipa* L.
チューリップの実

6 *Digitalis parviflora* 'Milk Chocolate'
ジギタリス [ミルクチョコレート]

7 *Protea neriifolia* 'White Mink'
プロテア [ホワイトミンク]

8 *Cymbidium* 'Mocha'
シンビジューム [モカ]

9 *Peperomia caperata* 'Pink Lady'
ペペロミア [ピンクレディ]

10 *Daucus carota* 'Black Knight'
ダウカス [ブラックナイト]

11 *Nepenthes* 'Rebecca Soper'
ネペンテス [レベッカソーパー]

12 *Sarracenia rubra* subsp. *gulfensis*
サラセニア・ルブラ・ガルフェンシス

13 *Sarracenia leucophylla* Raf.
サラセニア・レウコフィラ

14 *Zinnia elegans*
'Queen Red Lime'
ジニア [クイーンレッドライム]

15 *Sempervivum tectorum* L.
センペルビウム・テクトラム

16 pp. 180–181
—

1 *Leucospermum cordifolium*
'Veldt Fire'
ピンクッション［ベルデファイヤー］

2 *Haemanthus albiflos* Jacq.
ハエマンサス・マユハケオモト

3 *Cycas revoluta* Thunb.
ソテツの実

4 *Agapanthus africanus*
(L.) Hoffmanns.
アガパンサスの実

5 *Banksia menziesii* R. Br.
バンクシア・メーンジーシー

6 *Dahlia* 'Tampico'
ダリア［タンピコ］

7 *Cynara scolymus* L.
アーティチョーク

8 *Epidendrum secundum*
'Pecan Orange'
エピデンドラム［ピーカンオレンジ］

9 *Guzmania* 'Torch'
グズマニア［トーチ］

10 *Zinnia elegans* 'Queen Lime'
ジニア［クイーンライム］

11 *Gerbera* 'Anacleto'
ガーベラ［アナクレート］

12 *Eucalyptus* 'Trumpet'
ユーカリ［トランペット］

13 *Tillandsia cyanea*
Linden ex K. Koch
チランジア・シアネア

14 *Kniphofia uvaria* 'Bees' Lemon'
トリトマ［ビーズレモン］

15 *Rhaphiolepis indica*
(L.) Lindl. ex Ker var. *umbellata*
(Thunb.) H. Ohashi
シャリンバイ

16 *Monstera friedrichsthalii* Schott
モンステラ・マドカズラ

17 *Clematis* L.
クレマチスの実

18 *Dahlia* 'Labella Piccolo Pink'
ダリア［ラベラピッコロピンク］

19 *Echinocactus grusonii* Hildm.
サボテン［金鯱（きんしゃち）］

20 *Rosa* 'Exciting Meilland'
バラ［エキサイティングメイアン］

21 *Paphiopedilum dianthum*
Tang & F. T. Wang
パフィオペディラム・ディアンサム

22 *Cyathea spinulosa*
Wall. ex Hook.
ヘゴゼンマイ

23 *Sarracenia leucophylla* Raf.
サラセニア・レイコフィラ

24 *Brassia* Eternal Wind
'Summer Dream'
ブラッシア・エターナルウィンド
［サマードリーム］

25 *Narcissus tazetta*
var. *chinensis* M. Roem.
スイセン・ニホンズイセン

26 *Phalaenopsis* Taida Salu
'Alisan'
ファレノプシス・タイダソリュー
［アリサン］

27 *Paphiopedilum spicerianum*
(Rchb. f) Pfitzer
パフィオペディラム・スピセリアナム

28 *Telopea speciosissima* 'Waratah'
テロペア［ワラタ］

29 *Chrysanthemum × morifolium*
'Yo'
キク［陽（よう）］

30 *Nigella damascena*
'Persian Jewels'
ニゲラ［ペルシャンジュエル］

17　　　pp. 182–183

1 *Zantedeschia aethiopica*
'Golden Giant'
カラー［ゴールデンジャイアント］

2 *Kniphofia uvaria* 'Bees' Lemon'
トリトマ［ビーズレモン］

3 *Leucospermum cordifolium*
'Veldt Fire'
ピンクッション［ベルデファイヤー］

4 *Chrysanthemum × morifolium*
'Golden Ping Pong'
キク［ゴールデンピンポン］

5 *Dahlia* 'Lemon Light'
ダリア［レモンライト］

6 *Tagetes erecta* 'Yellow Isis'
マリーゴールド［イエローアイシス］

7 *Cymbidiu* 'Crescent'
シンビジューム［クレッセント］

8 *Anigozanthos flavidus* 'Green'
カンガルーポー［グリーン］

9 *Epidendrum* Sunlight Valley
'Happy Moon'
エビデンドラム・サンライトバレー
［ハッピームーン］

10 *Fockea multiflora* K. Schum.
フォッケア・ムルチフローラ

11 *Rosa* 'Ilios'
バラ［イリオス］

12 *Achillea alpina* L.
ノコギリソウ

13 *Carthamus tinctorius*
(Mohler, Roth, Schmidt &
Boudreaux)
ベニバナ

14 *Gerbera* 'Terra Asahi'
ガーベラ［テラアサヒ］

15 *Phalaenopsis*
Brother Sara Gold 'Magical'
ファレノプシス・ブラザーサラゴールド
［マジカル］

18　　　pp. 184–185

1 *Tillandsia xerographica* Rohweder
チランジア・キセログラフィカ

2 *Echeveria lilacina* Kimn. & Moran
エケベリア・リラシナ

3 *Echinocereus subinermis* var. *luteus*
(Britton & Rose) F. M. Knuth
サボテン［大仏殿（だいぶつでん）］

4 *Agapanthus africanus* 'Blue Heaven'
アガパンサス［ブルーヘブン］

5 *Curcuma alismatifolia* 'Verdebianco'
クルクマ［ヴェルデビアンコ］

6 *Sedum spectabile* 'Autumn Joy'
セダム［オータムジョイ］

7 *Passiflora* 'Victoria'
トケイソウ［ビクトリア］

8 *Gentiana triflora* var. *japonica*
'My Fantasy'
リンドウ［マイファンタジー］

9 *Salvia farinacea* 'Strata'
サルビア・ファリナセア［ストラータ］

10 *Sarracenia leucophylla* Raf.
サラセニア・レウコフィラ

11 *Haworthia minima* 'Shutensei'
ハオルチア［秋天星（しゅうてんせい）］

12 *Tillandsia capitata* Grisebach
チランジア・カピタータ

13 *Phylica plumosa* L.
フィリカ・プルモーサ

14 *Veronica* 'Caroline Blue'
ベロニカ［カロラインブルー］

15 *Begonia venosa*
Skan ex Hook. f.
ベゴニア・ベノーサ

16 *Eriosyce senilis* (Backeb.) Katt.
サボテン［銀翁玉（ぎんおうぎょく）］

17 *Echeveria* 'Shichifukujin'
エケベリア［七福神（しちふくじん）］

18 *Aechmea fasciata* (Lindl.) Baker
エクメア・ファシアータ

19 *Piper nigrum* L.
コショウ

20 *Hydrangea macrophylla*
'Magical Revolution Blue'
アジサイ［マジカルレボリューションブルー］

19   pp. 186–187

1 *Tapeinochilos ananassae*
   'Wax Ginger'
   ジンジャー［ワックスジンジャー］

2 *Gerbera* 'Summer Time'
   ガーベラ［サマータイム］

3 *Celosia argentea* var. *cristata*
   'Sakata Pride'
   ケイトウ［サカタプライド］

4 *Rosa* 'Andalusia'
   バラ［アンダルシア］

5 *Costus woodsonii* Maas
   コスタス・ウッドソニー

6 *Epidendrum secundum* 'Red 5'
   エピデンドラム［赤5（あかご）］

7 *Dahlia* 'Red Star'
   ダリア［レッドスター］

8 *Gloriosa superba* 'Mesa'
   グロリオサ［メイサ］

9 *Peperomia caperata*
   'Burgundy Ripple'
   ペペロミア［バーガンディリップル］

10 *Anthurium andreanum*
   'Black Queen'
   アンスリウム［ブラッククイーン］

20   pp. 188–189

1 *Platycerium bifurcatum*
   (Cav.) C. Chr.
   ビカクシダ・コウモリラン

2 *Banksia integrifolia* L. f.
   バンクシア・インテグリフォリア

3 *Chrysanthemum* × *morifolium*
   'Green Shamrock'
   キク［グリーンシャムロック］

4 *Nepenthes maxima*
   Reinw. ex Nees
   ネペンテス・マキシマ

5 *Pieris japonica* (Thunb.) D.
   Don ex G. Don
   アセビ

6 *Calathea cylindrica* 'Green Ice'
   カラテア［グリーンアイス］

7 *Phalaenopsis* Sogo Vieker
   'Taida Little Monkey'
   ファレノプシス・ソゴバイカー
   ［タイダリトルモンキー］

8 *Agave potatorum* 'Raijin'
   アガベ［雷神（らいじん）］

9 *Dryopteris crassirhizoma* Nakai
   オシダ

10 *Nepenthes alata* Blanco
   ネペンテス・アラータ

11 *Moluccella laevis* L.
   モルセラ・ラエヴィス

12 *Neoregelia* 'Fireball Variegata'
   ネオレゲリア
   ［ファイヤーボールバリエガタ］

13 *Echeveria* 'White Ghost'
   エケベリア［ホワイトゴースト］

14 *Fritillaria persica* 'Ivory Bells'
   フリチラリア［アイボリーベル］

15 *Chrysanthemum* × *morifolium*
   'Pure Green'
   キク［ピュアグリーン］

16 *Rhipsalis cassutha* Gaertn.
   リプサリス・カスタ

17 *Gloriosa superba* 'Lime'
   グロリオサ［ライム］

21 pp. 190–191

1 *Veronica spicata* 'Younique Baby White'
ベロニカ［ユニークベイビーホワイト］

2 *Chrysanthemum × morifolium* 'Pink Bell'
キク［ピンクベル］

3 *Chrysanthemum × morifolium* 'Say Opera Pink'
キク［セイオペラピンク］

4 *Hydrangea macrophylla* 'Magical Green Fire'
アジサイ［マジカルグリーンファイヤー］

5 *Spiraea japonica* L. f.
シモツケ

6 *Dianthus* 'Raffine Lili'
ナデシコ［ラフィーネリリ］

7 *Gerbera* 'Lipstick'
ガーベラ［リップスティック］

8 *Physostegia virginiana* (L.) Benth.
ハナトラノオ

9 *Clematis texensis* 'Oshikiri'
クレマチス［押切（おしきり）］

10 *Epidendrum* Parasol Valley 'Music Box'
エピデンドラム・パラソルバレー［ミュージックボックス］

11 *Monarda fistulosa* var. *menthifolia*
モナルダ・メンシフォリア

12 *Astilbe × arendsii* 'Pastel Pink'
アスチルベ［パステルピンク］

13 *Bouvardia* 'White Supreme'
ブバルディア［ホワイトシュープリーム］

22 pp. 192–193

1 *Begonia × hiemalis* 'Borias'
ベゴニア・エラチオールベゴニア［ボリアス］

2 *Zantedeschia aethiopica* 'Captain Promise'
カラー［キャプテンプロミス］

3 *Kniphofia uvaria* 'First Sunrise'
トリトマ［ファーストサンライズ］

4 *Lilium orientalis* 'Casa Blanca'
ユリ［カサブランカ］

5 *Epidendrum secundum* 'Pecan Yellow'
エピデンドラム［ピーカンイエロー］

6 *Hippeastrum blossfeldiae* (Traub & J. L. Doran) Van Scheepen
アマリリス・ブロスフェルディアエ

7 *Gerbera* 'Petit Akane'
ガーベラ［プチアカネ］

8 *Dahlia* 'Arabian Night'
ダリア［アラビアンナイト］

9 *Cyrtanthus mackenii* 'King Yellow'
キルタンサス［キングイエロー］

10 *Notocactus apricus* (Arechavaleta) Berger ex Backeberg
サボテン［河内丸（かわちまる）］

11 *Hyacinthus orientalis* 'Anna Marie'
ヒヤシンス［アンナマリー］

12 *Epidendrum secundum* 'Red 5'
エピデンドラム［赤5（あかご）］

23   pp. 194-195
—

1　*Ageratum houstonianum*
　'Blue Hawaii'
　アゲラタム［ブルーハワイ］

2　*Ranunculus asiaticus* 'Pomerol'
　ラナンキュラス［ポムロール］

3　*Anthurium andreanum* 'Forest'
　アンスリウム［フォレスト］

4　*Lilium longiflorum* 'Hinomoto'
　ユリ・テッポウユリ［日の本（ひのもと）］

5　*Brunia albiflora* E. Phillips
　ブルニア・アルビフローラ

6　*Muscari aucheri* 'Blue Magic'
　ムスカリ［ブルーマジック］

7　*Brassica oleracea* var. *botrytis*
　'Romanesco'
　カリフラワー［ロマネスコ］

8　*Hyacinthus orientalis* 'Purple Star'
　ヒヤシンス［パープルスター］

9　*Dianthus caryophyllus* 'Prado Mint'
　カーネーション［プラドミント］

10　*Pelargonium graveolens* 'Snowflake'
　ペラルゴニウム［スノーフレーク］

11　*Skimmia japonica* 'Kew Green'
　スキミア［キューグリーン］

12　*Viola* × *wittrockiana*
　'Frizzle Sizzle Blue'
　パンジー［フリズルシズルブルー］

13　*Iris* × *hollandica* 'Blue Magic'
　アヤメ・ダッチアイリス［ブルーマジック］

14　*Viburnum tinus* L.
　ビバーナム・ティナス

15　*Opuntia lanceolata* f. *cristata*
　サボテン［青海波（せいがいは）］

16　*Tulipa* 'Super Parrot'
　チューリップ［スーパーパーロット］

17　*Cymbidium* Lovely Valley
　'Peace in the World'
　シンビジュウム・ラブリーバレー
　［ピースインザワールド］

18　*Faucaria tuberculosa* 'Doto'
　フォーカリア［怒濤（どとう）］

19　*Epiterantha micromeris*
　(Engelmann) F. A. C. Weber
　ex Britt. & Rose
　サボテン［月世界（つきせかい）］

20　*Lachenalia mutabilis*
　Lodd. ex Sweet
　ラケナリア・ムタビリス

21　*Papaver nudicaule* L.
　ポピー・アイスランドポピー

24   pp. 196-197
—

1　*Graptoveria* 'Opalina'
　グラプトベリア［オパリナ］

2　*Dianthus caryophyllus* 'Primero Pluto'
　カーネーション［プリメロプルート］

3　*Anthurium andreanum* 'Safari'
　アンスリウム［サファリ］

4　*Begonia bowerae* var. *nigramarga*
　Ziesenh.
　ベゴニア・ボウエレ・ニグラマルガ

5　*Epidendrum secundum* 'Red 5'
　エピデンドラム［赤5（あかご）］

6　*Eustoma grandiflorum* 'Celeb Blue'
　トルコキキョウ［セレブブルー］

7　*Lathyrus latifolius* 'Pink Pearl'
　スイートピー［ピンクパール］

8　*Dahlia* 'Edinburgh'
　ダリア［エジンバラ］

9　*Dianthus caryophyllus* 'Sharara'
　カーネーション［シャララ］

10　*Gerbera* 'Japio'
　ガーベラ［ジャピオ］

11　*Chrysanthemum* × *morifolium*
　'Pretty Rio'
　キク［プリティリオ］

12　*Bouvardia* 'Royal Daphne Fresco'
　ブバルディア［ロイヤルダフネフレスコ］

13　*Zantedeschia aethiopica*
　'Majestic Red'
　カラー［マジェスティックレッド］

14　*Hyacinthus orientalis* 'Blue Star'
　ヒヤシンス［ブルースター］

15　*Phalaenopsis* Sogo Pearl
　'Pine Ridge'
　ファレノプシス・ソゴパール
　［パインリッジ］

16　*Scabiosa atropurpurea*
　'Oxford Blue'
　スカビオサ［オクスフォードブルー］

17　*Alstroemeria* 'Scorpion'
　アルストロメリア［スコーピオン］

25 pp. 198–199

1 *Hydrangea macrophylla* 'Immaculata'
アジサイ［インマクラータ］

2 *Ammi majus* 'Green Mist'
レースフラワー［グリーンミスト］

3 *Tillandsia tectorum* E. Morren
チランジア・テクトラム

4 *Lilium orientalis* 'Casa Blanca'
ユリ［カサブランカ］

5 *Eustoma grandiflorum*
'Voyage White'
トルコキキョウ［ボヤージュホワイト］

6 *Freesia refracta* 'Elegance'
フリージア［エレガンス］

7 *Zantedeschia aethiopica*
'Crystal Blush'
カラー［クリスタルブラッシュ］

8 *Lathyrus latifolius* 'White Pearl'
スイートピー［ホワイトパール］

9 *Nigella damascena* 'Miss Jekyll'
ニゲラ［ミスジーキル］

10 *Dahlia* 'Yukiguni'
ダリア［雪国（ゆきぐに）］

11 *Tillandsia xerographica* Rohweder
チランジア・キセログラフィカ

12 *Dianthus barbatus*
'Breanthus Duke'
ナデシコ［ブレアンサスデューク］

13 *Epidendrum* Princess Valley
'White Castle'
エピデンドラム・プリンセスバレー
［ホワイトキャッスル］

14 *Allium neapolitanum* 'Cowanii'
アリウム［コワニー］

15 *Papaver nudicaule* L.
ポピー・アイスランドポピー

16 *Tulipa polychroma* Stapf
チューリップ・ポリクロマ

17 *Tulipa* 'White River Star'
チューリップ［ホワイトリバースター］

26 pp. 200–201

1 *Tagetes erecta* 'Yellow Isis'
マリーゴールド［イエローアイシス］

2 *Anthurium andreanum* 'Black Queen'
アンスリウム［ブラッククイーン］

3 *Dahlia* 'Asahi Temari'
ダリア［朝日てまり（あさひてまり）］

4 *Lilium orientalis* 'Siberia'
ユリ［シベリア］

5 *Narcissus* 'Tete a Tete'
スイセン［ティタティタ］

6 *Gentiana triflora* var. *japonica*
'Iwate Yume Aoi'
リンドウ
［いわて夢あおい（いわてゆめあおい）］

7 *Cymbidium* 'Soleil Levant'
シンビジューム［ソレイユルヴァン］

8 *Ixora coccinea* L.
サンタンカ

9 *Chrysanthemum* × *morifolium*
'Green Shamrock'
キク［グリーンシャムロック］

10 *Gerbera* 'Petit Akane'
ガーベラ［プチアカネ］

11 *Paphiopedilum* Satsuma
'Karajishi'
パフィオペディラム
［薩摩唐獅子（さつまからじし）］

12 *Chrysanthemum* × *morifolium*
'Pure Green'
キク［ピュアグリーン］

13 *Celosia argentea* var. *cristata*
'Bombay Orange'
ケイトウ［ボンベイオレンジ］

14 *Epidendrum secundum* 'Chidori'
エピデンドラム［チドリ］

15 *Rhyncholaeliocattleya*
Peggy O'Neill 'Royal Lady'
カトレヤ・リンコレリオカトレヤ・
ペギーオニール［ロイヤルレディー］

16 *Lycopodium clavatum* L.
ヒカゲノカズラ

17 *Lilium orientalis* 'Casa Blanca'
ユリ［カサブランカ］

18 *Chrysanthemum pacificum* Nakai
イソギク

27　　　　pp. 202–203

1　*Echeveria* 'Tsuki Kage'
　エケベリア［月影（つきかげ）］

2　*Celosia argentea* var. *cristata*
　'Bombay Green'
　ケイトウ［ボンベイグリーン］

3　*Mammillaria elongata* DC.
　サボテン［黄金丸（こがねまる）］

4　*Haworthia cooperi* var. *obtusa*
　'Shizukuishi'
　ハオルチア［雫石（しずくいし）］

5　*Neoregelia* 'Fireball Variegata'
　ネオレゲリア［ファイヤーボールバリエガタ］

6　*Nepenthes* 'Dyeriana'
　ネペンテス［ダイエリアナ］

7　*Cyathea spinulosa* Wall. ex Hook.
　ヘゴゼンマイ

8　*Nelumbo nucifera* Gaertn.
　ハス台

9　*Paphiopedilum* Maudiae
　'The Queen'
　パフィオペディラム・モーディエ
　［クイーン］

10　*Haworthia cymbiformis*
　'Kyo no Hana'
　ハオルチア［京の華（きょうのはな）］

11　*Echeveria* 'Gorgon's Grotto'
　エケベリア［ゴルゴンズグロット］

12　*Curcuma alismatifolia*
　'Emerald Choco Zebra'
　クルクマ［エメラルドチョコゼブラ］

13　*Bouvardia*
　'Royal Daphne Green Summer'
　ブバルディア
　［ロイヤルダフネグリーンサマー］

14　*Berzelia lanuginosa*
　(L.) Brongn.
　バーゼリア・ラヌギノーサ

28　　　　pp. 204–205

1　*Chrysanthemum* × *morifolium*
　'Anastasia Dark Lime'
　キク［アナスタシアダークライム］

2　*Dahlia* 'Glenplace'
　ダリア［グレンプレス］

3　*Dianthus caryophyllus* 'Nebo'
　カーネーション［ネボ］

4　*Narcissus* 'February Gold'
　スイセン［フェブラリーゴールド］

5　*Alstroemeria* 'Scorpion'
　アルストロメリア［スコーピオン］

6　*Rhaphiolepis indica*
　(L.) Lindl. ex Ker var. *umbellata*
　(Thunb.) H. Ohashi
　シャリンバイの実

7　*Serruria* 'Carmen'
　セルリア［カルメン］

8　*Lachenalia viridiflora* W. F. Barker
　ラケナリア・ビリディフローラ

9　*Zinnia elegans* 'Queen Lime'
　ジニア［クイーンライム］

10　*Leucocoryne purpurea* 'Caravel'
　リューココリーネ［カラベル］

11　*Dianthus caryophyllus*
　'Hurricane'
　カーネーション［ハリケーン］

12　*Eustoma grandiflorum*
　'Voyage Blue'
　トルコキキョウ［ボヤージュブルー］

13　*Gerbera* 'Voldemort'
　ガーベラ［ヴォルデモート］

14　*Paeonia lactiflora* 'Red Charm'
　シャクヤク［レッドチャーム］

15　*Rosa* 'All 4 Kiss+'
　バラ［オール4キス+（おーるふぉー
　きすぷらす）］

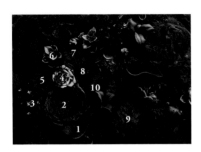

29　　pp. 206–207

1 *Zantedeschia aethiopica*
　'Hot Cherry'
　カラー［ホットチェリー］

2 *Rosa* 'Baronesse'
　バラ［バロネッセ］

3 *Epidendrum secundum* 'Red 5'
　エピデンドラム［赤5（あかご）］

4 *Rosa* 'Julio Iglesias'
　バラ［フリオイグレシアス］

5 *Rosa* 'Bell Rouge'
　バラ［ベルルージュ］

6 *Curcuma alismatifolia*
　'Saim Crown'
　クルクマ［サイアムクラウン］

7 *Dianthus barbatus*
　'Breanthus Road'
　ナデシコ［ブレアンサスロード］

8 *Gerbera* 'Petit Akane'
　ガーベラ［プチアカネ］

9 *Paeonia lactiflora* 'Red Baron'
　シャクヤク［レッドバロン］

10 *Tillandsia cyanea*
　Linden ex K. Koch
　チランジア・シアネア

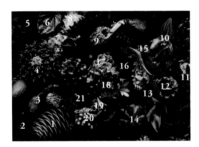

30　　pp. 208–209

1 *Zingiber spectabile*
　'Golden Shampoo'
　ジンジャー［ゴールデンシャンプー］

2 *Gerbera* 'Twister'
　ガーベラ［ツイスター］

3 *Dahlia* Cav.
　ダリアの球根

4 *Obregonia denegrii* Frič
　サボテン［帝冠（ていかん）］

5 *Rosa* 'Baronesse'
　バラ［バロネッセ］

6 *Peperomia caperata* 'Pink Lady'
　ペペロミア［ピンクレディ］

7 *Epidendrum secundum* 'Chidori'
　エピデンドラム［チドリ］

8 *Dianthus caryophyllus* 'Kiro'
　カーネーション［キロ］

9 *Banksia coccinea* R. Br
　バンクシア・コッキネア

10 *Paphiopedilum* 'St. Swithin'
　パフィオペディラム［セントスイシン］

11 *Lilium concolor* Salisb.
　ユリ・チョウセンヒメユリ

12 *Calathea cylindrica* 'Green Ice'
　カラテア［グリーンアイス］

13 *Heliconia rostrata* Ruiz & Pavon
　ヘリコニア・ロストラータ

14 *Gymnocalycium anisitsii*
　(K. Schumann) Britton & Rose
　サボテン
　［翠晃冠錦（すいこうかんにしき）］

15 *Monarda fistulosa* var.
　menthifolia
　モナルダ・メンシフォリア

16 *Rosa* 'Rote Rose'
　バラ［ローテローゼ］

17 *Hydrangea macrophylla*
　'Magical Green Fire'
　アジサイ［マジカルグリーンファイヤー］

18 *Passiflora* 'Incense'
　トケイソウ［インセンス］

19 *Agapanthus africanus*
　'Murasaki Shikibu'
　アガパンサス［紫式部（むらさきしきぶ）］

20 *Physostegia virginiana* (L.)
　Benth.
　ハナトラノオ

21 *Celosia argentea* var. *cristata*
　'Sakata Pride'
　ケイトウ［サカタプライド］

31   pp. 210–211

1 *Lathyrus odoratus* 'Blue Fragrance'
スイートピー［ブルーフレグランス］

2 *Hydrangea macrophylla* 'First Blue'
アジサイ［ファーストブルー］

3 *Hyacinthus orientalis* 'Blue Jacet'
ヒヤシンス［ブルージャケット］

4 *Nigella damascena* 'Persian Jewels'
ニゲラ［ペルシャンジュエル］

5 *Allium* 'Blue Perfume'
アリウム［ブルーパフューム］

6 *Myosotis* L.
ワスレナグサ

7 *Oxypetalum coeruleum* 'Pure Blue'
オキシペタルム［ピュアブルー］

8 *Delphinium grandiflorum* 'Grand Blue'
デルフィニウム［グランブルー］

9 *Dyckia* 'Nickel Silver'
ディッキア［ニッケルシルバー］

10 *Clematis socialis* Kral
クレマチス・ソシアリス

11 *Iris × hollandica* 'Blue Magic'
アヤメ・ダッチアイリス［ブルーマジック］

12 *Pachyphytum bracteosum* 'Hoshi Bijin'
パキフィツム［星美人（ほしびじん）］

32   pp. 212–213

1 *Aechmea fasciata* (Lindl.) Baker
エクメア・ファシアータ

2 *Lilium concolor* Salisb.
ユリ・チョウセンヒメユリ

3 *Epidendrum secundum* 'Red 5'
エビデンドラム［赤5（あかご）］

4 *Cirsium japonicum* Fisch. ex DC.
アザミ・ノアザミ

5 *Anthurium andreanum* 'Fesca'
アンスリウム［フェスカ］

6 *Hibiscus* 'Brilliant Red'
ハイビスカス［ブリリアントレッド］

7 *Phalaenopsis* 'Palermo'
ファレノプシス［パレルモ］

8 *Dianthus caryophyllus* 'Bizet'
カーネーション［ビゼー］

9 *Dahlia* 'Yuma'
ダリア［雄馬（ゆうま）］

10 *Clematis texensis* 'Scarlet'
クレマチス［スカーレット］

11 *Dianthus barbatus* 'Green Trick'
ナデシコ［グリーントリュフ］

12 *Dahlia* 'Micchan'
ダリア［ミッチャン］

13 *Allium hollandicum* 'Purple Sensation'
アリウム［パープルセンセーション］

14 *Astilbe × arendsii* 'Fanal'
アスチルベ［ファナル］

15 *Astilbe × arendsii* 'America'
アスチルベ［アメリカ］

16 *Paeonia lactiflora* 'Kirin Maru'
シャクヤク［麒麟丸（きりんまる）］

17 *Gloriosa superba* 'Precious Pearl'
グロリオサ［プレシャスパール］

18 *Echinacea purpurea* 'Eccentric'
エキナセア［エキセントリック］

19 *Protea barbigera* 'Niobe'
プロテア［ニオベ］

20 *Stephanotis floribunda* Brongn.
マダガスカルジャスミン

21 *Bouvardia* 'Green Magic'
ブバルディア［グリーンマジック］

22 *Nelumbo nucifera* Gaertn.
ハスの葉

23 *Zantedeschia aethiopica* 'Majestic Red'
カラー［マジェスティックレッド］

24 *Sedum spectabile* 'Autumn Joy'
セダム［オータムジョイ］

25 *Polygala myrtifolia* var. *grandiflora* 'Sweet Pea Shrub'
ポリガラ［スイートピーシュラブ］

26 *Dahlia* 'Asahitemari'
ダリア［朝日てまり（あさひてまり）］

27 *Begonia rex* 'African Jungle'
ベゴニア・レックスベゴニア
［アフリカンジャングル］

33   pp. 214–215

1 *Allium giganteum* Regel
アリウム・ギガンジューム

2 *Gerbera* 'Gio'
ガーベラ［ジオ］

3 *Ammi majus* 'Green Mist'
レースフラワー［グリーンミスト］

4 *Epidendrum secundum*
'Orange Ball'
エピデンドラム［オレンジボール］

5 *Hydrangea macrophylla* 'Bavaria'
アジサイ［ババリア］

6 *Dahlia* 'Dream Dance'
ダリア［ドリームダンス］

7 *Banksia ericifolia* L. f.
バンクシア・エリシフォリア

8 *Zantedeschia aethiopica*
'Garnet Glow'
カラー［ガーネットグロー］

9 *Bouvardia* 'Royal Daphne Nicollette'
ブバルディア［ロイヤルダフネニコレット］

10 *Dahlia* 'Nessho'
ダリア［熱唱（ねっしょう）］

11 *Fritillaria persica* L.
フリチラリア・ペルシカ

12 *Dahlia* 'Blue Peach'
ダリア［ブルーピーチ］

13 *Iris* × *hollandica* 'Blue Magic'
アヤメ・ダッチアイリス［ブルーマジック］

14 *Anthurium andreanum* 'Previa'
アンスリウム［プレビア］

15 *Chrysanthemum* × *morifolium*
'Zembla Brazil'
キク［ゼンブラブラジル］

16 *Sarracenia purpurea* L.
サラセニア・プルプレア

17 *Pisum sativum* L.
エンドウマメ

18 *Gerbera* 'Pasta di Mamma'
ガーベラ［パスタディママ］

19 *Polygala myrtifolia* var.
grandiflora 'Sweet Pea Shrub'
ポリガラ［スイートピーシュラブ］

20 *Tagetes erecta* 'Yellow Isis'
マリーゴールド［イエローアイシス］

34   pp. 216–217

1 *Anthurium andreanum* 'Alexia Jade'
アンスリウム［アレキシアジェイド］

2 *Dianthus caryophyllus* 'Prado Mint'
カーネーション［プラドミント］

3 *Sempervivum*
'Lavender and Old Lace'
センペルビウム
［ラベンダーアンドオールドレース］

4 *Gleichenia japonica* Spr.
ウラジロゼンマイ

5 *Ammi majus* 'Green Mist'
レースフラワー［グリーンミスト］

6 *Dianthus barbatus* 'Green Trick'
ナデシコ［グリーントリュフ］

7 *Haworthia fasciata* 'Juni no Maki'
ハオルチア［十二の巻（じゅうにのまき）］

8 *Dendrobium phalaenopsis*
'Lemon Green'
デンファレ［レモングリーン］

9 *Chrysanthemum* × *morifolium*
'Pure Green'
キク［ピュアグリーン］

10 *Neoregelia* 'Rio of Rio'
ネオレゲリア［リオ・オブ・リオ］

11 *Paphiopedilum Sheerline* 'Rondo'
パフィオペディラム・シャーライン
［ロンド］

12 *Sempervivum* 'Lobstum'
センペルビウム［ロブスツム］

13 *Fritillaria thunbergii* Miq.
フリチラリア・バイモユリ

14 *Silene vulgaris* 'Green Bell'
シレネ［グリーンベル］

15 *Pelargonium graveolens*
'Little Gem'
ペラルゴニウム［リトルジェム］

35 pp. 218–219
—

1 *Spathodea campanulata* P. Beauv.
カエンボク

2 *Cymbidium* Enzan Forest 'Majolica'
シンビジューム・エンザンフォレスト［マジョリカ］

3 *Dianthus barbatus* 'Green Trick'
ナデシコ［グリーントリュフ］

4 *Epidendrum secundum* 'Yellow Star'
エピデンドラム［イエロースター］

5 *Rosa* 'Flash Eye'
バラ［フラッシュアイ］

6 *Ranunculus asiaticus* 'Artemis'
ラナンキュラス［アルテミス］

7 *Bulbinella floribunda* (Aiton) T.
Durand & Schinz
バルビネラ・フロリバンダ

8 *Gerbera* 'Antique'
ガーベラ［アンティーク］

9 *Heliconia latispatha*
'Red Inazuma'
ヘリコニア［レッドイナズマ］

10 *Phaenocoma prolifera*
(L.) D. Don
フェノコマ

11 *Rosa* 'La Campanella'
バラ［ラ・カンパネラ］

12 *Rosa* 'K-Zebra'
バラ［K-ゼブラ（けーぜぶら）］

13 *Dianthus caryophyllus* 'Megan'
カーネーション［ミーガン］

14 *Tillandsia brachycaulos*
Schlechtendal
チランジア・ブラキカウロス

36 pp. 220–221
—

1 *Rubus fruticosus* L.
ルブス・ブラックベリー

2 *Obregonia denegrii* Frič
サボテン［帝冠（ていかん）］

3 *Sanguisorba hakusanensis* Makino
カライトソウ

4 *Dahlia* 'Yuki Tsubaki'
ダリア［雪椿（ゆきつばき）］

5 *Callistephus chinensis*
'Shaggy Deep Blue'
アスター［シャギーディープブルー］

6 *Gerbera* 'Gio'
ガーベラ［ジオ］

7 *Zantedeschia aethiopica*
'Hot Chocolate'
カラー［ホットチョコレート］

8 *Phalaenopsis* Taida Salu
'Azuki Chocolat'
ファレノプシス・タイダソリュー
［あずきしょこら］

9 *Nicandra physalodes* Schreb.
クロホオズキ

10 *Allium hollandicum*
'Purple Sensation'
アリウム［パープルセンセーション］

11 *Paphiopedilum* 'St. Swithin'
パフィオペディラム［セントスイシン］

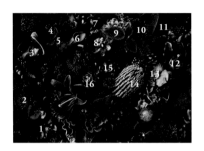

37 pp. 222–223

1 *Begonia bowerae* var. *nigramarga* Ziesenh.
ベゴニア・ボウエレ・ニグラマルガ

2 *Gerbera* 'Gio'
ガーベラ [ジオ]

3 *Paphiopedilum* 'Robin Hood'
パフィオペディラム [ロビンフッド]

4 *Dahlia* 'Kokucho'
ダリア [黒蝶 (こくちょう)]

5 *Sophrolaeliocattleya* Jewel Box 'Dark Waters'
カトレヤ・ソフロレリオカトレヤ・ジュエルボックス [ダークウォーターズ]

6 *Nepenthes* 'Rebecca Soper'
ネペンテス [レベッカソーパー]

7 *Aconitum japonicum* Thunb. var. *montanum* Nakai
ヤマトリカブト

8 *Passiflora* 'Incense'
トケイソウ [インセンス]

9 *Pilea involucrata* 'Moon Valley'
ピレア [ムーンバレー]

10 *Allium amethystinum* 'Red Mohican'
アリウム [レッドモヒカン]

11 *Dahlia* 'Glenplace'
ダリア [グレンプレス]

12 *Lilium orientalis* 'Mambo'
ユリ [マンボ]

13 *Echeveria lilacina* Kimn. & Moran
エケベリア・リラシナ

14 *Banksia menziesii* R. Br.
バンクシア・メーンジーシー

15 *Gentiana triflora* var. *japonica* 'Sky Blue Shinano'
リンドウ [スカイブルーシナノ]

16 *Cymbidium* 'Cha Cha'
シンビジューム [チャチャ]

38 pp. 224–225

1 *Dahlia* 'Lemon Card'
ダリア [レモンカード]

2 *Kniphofia uvaria* 'First Sunrise'
トリトマ [ファーストサンライズ]

3 *Strelitzia reginae* Aiton
ストレリチア・レギネ

4 *Lycoris aurea* (L'Hér.) Herb.
リコリス・オーレア

5 *Helianthus annuus* 'Van Gogh Sunflower'
ヒマワリ [ゴッホのひまわり]

6 *Phalaenopsis* Taida Smile 'Little Gold'
ファレノプシス・タイダスマイル [リトルゴールド]

7 *Gerbera* 'Terra Asahi'
ガーベラ [テラアサヒ]

8 *Guzmania* 'Orangeade'
グズマニア [オレンジエード]

9 *Rudbeckia hirta* 'Irish Eyes'
ルドベキア [アイリッシュアイ]

10 *Zinnia* 'Profusion Double Golden'
ジニア [プロフュージョンダブルゴールデン]

11 *Neoregelia spectabilis* (T. Moore) L. B. Sm.
ネオレゲリア・スペクタビリス

12 *Oncidium* Moon Shadow 'Tiger Tail'
オンシジューム・ムーンシャドウ [タイガーテイル]

39   pp. 226–227
—

1   *Dahlia* 'Junai no Kimi'
ダリア［純愛の君（じゅんあいのきみ）］

2   *Trollius chinensis* 'Golden Queen'
トロリウス［ゴールデンクイーン］

3   *Dahlia* 'Micchan'
ダリア［ミッチャン］

4   *Kalanchoe tomentosa* 'Tsukitoji'
カランコエ［月兎耳（つきとじ）］

5   *Banksia coccinea* R. Br
バンクシア・コッキネア

6   *Guzmania* 'Hilda'
グズマニア［ヒルダ］

7   *Nelumbo nucifera* Gaertn.
ハス台

8   *Nepenthes* 'Miranda'
ネペンテス［ミランダ］

9   *Tapeinochilos ananassae* 'Wax Ginger'
ジンジャー［ワックスジンジャー］

10   *Globba winitii* 'Pink Dragon'
グロッバ［ピンクドラゴン］

11   *Kniphofia uvaria* 'First Sunrise'
トリトマ［ファーストサンライズ］

12   *Cyathea spinulosa* Wall. ex Hook.
ヘゴゼンマイ

13   *Anthurium longifolium* (Hoffm.) G. Don
アンスリウム・ロンギフォリウム

14   *Rosa* 'Flash Eye'
バラ［フラッシュアイ］

15   *Paphiopedilum* 'Robin Hood'
パフィオペディラム［ロビンフッド］

16   *Anthurium andreanum* 'Maxima Verde'
アンスリウム［マキシマベルデ］

40   pp. 228–229
—

1   *Vanda falcata* 'Hakuunkaku'
フウラン［白雲閣（はくうんかく）］

2   *Hippeastrum × hybridum* 'Red Lion'
アマリリス［レッドライオン］

3   *Musa minor* Nakai
バショウ［キングバナナ］

4   *Zantedeschia aethiopica* 'Captain Durance'
カラー［キャプテンデュランス］

5   *Zantedeschia aethiopica* 'Captain Fuego'
カラー［キャプテンフエゴ］

6   *Heliconia xanthovillosa* 'Shogun'
ヘリコニア［ショウグン］

7   *Stephanotis floribunda* Brongn.
マダガスカルジャスミン

8   *Vriesea carinata* 'Christiane'
フリーセア［クリスティアーナ］

9   *Banksia menziesii* R. Br.
バンクシア・メーンジーシー

10   *Cymbidium* 'Akane'
シンビジューム［アカネ］

11   *Rosa* 'Shall Verse'
バラ［シュエルヴァーズ］

41   pp. 230–231

1 *Tillandsia xerographica* Rohweder
チランジア・キセログラフィカ

2 *Agapanthus africanus* 'Royal Blue'
アガパンサス［ロイヤルブルー］

3 *Clematis integrifolia* 'Rouguchi'
クレマチス［ロウグチ］

4 *Anthurium andreanum*
'ARCS Purple'
アンスリウム［ARCSパープル
（えーあーるしーえすぱーぷる）］

5 *Echeveria* 'Shichifukujin'
エケベリア［七福神（しちふくじん）］

6 *Trachelium caeruleum*
'Devotion Purple'
ユウギリソウ［ディボーションパープル］

7 *Viburnum tinus* L.
ビバーナム・ティナス

8 *Scabiosa caucasica* 'Fama'
スカビオサ［ファーマ］

9 *Graptoveria* 'Opalina'
グラプトベリア［オパリナ］

10 *Vanda* 'Yano Blue Spot'
バンダ［ヤノブルースポット］

11 *Veronica* 'Caroline Blue'
ベロニカ［カロラインブルー］

12 *Gentiana triflora* var. *japonica*
'Giovanni'
リンドウ［ジョバンニ］

13 *Haworthia cooperi* var. *obtusa*
'Shizukuishi'
ハオルチア［雫石（しずくいし）］

14 *Hydrangea* 'Arigato'
アジサイ［ありがとう］

42   pp. 232–233

1 *Dahlia* 'Nessho'
ダリア［熱唱（ねっしょう）］

2 *Epidendrum secundum* 'Red 5'
エピデンドラム［赤5（あかご）］

3 *Dahlia* 'Asahi Temari'
ダリア［朝日てまり（あさひてまり）］

4 *Celosia argentea* var. *cristata*
'Kurume Akajiku'
ケイトウ［クルメアカジク］

5 *Gerbera* 'Voldemort'
ガーベラ［ヴォルデモート］

6 *Jatropha podagrica* Hook.
ヤトロファ

7 *Doryanthes excelsa* Correa
ガイミアリリー

8 *Neoregelia* 'Zoe'
ネオレゲリア［ゾエ］

9 *Protea nana* (Berg.) Thunb.
プロテア・ナナ

10 *Protea cynaroides* 'Madiba'
プロテア・キングプロテア［マディバ］

11 *Cissus javana* DC.
シッサス・ジャバナ

12 *Paphiopedilum* 'Robin Hood'
パフィオペディラム［ロビンフッド］

13 *Anthurium longifolium*
(Hoffm.) G. Don
アンスリウム・ロンギフォリウム

14 *Bixa orellana* L.
ベニノキ

1 *Lilium hansonii* Leichtlin ex
   D. D. T. Moore
   ユリ・タケシマユリ

2 *Cinnamomum zeylanicum* J. Presl
   シナモン

3 *Cynara scolymus* L.
   アーティチョーク

4 *Laeliocattleya Quiseag* 'Mankaen'
   カトレヤ・レリオカトレヤ・クーシング
   [マンカエン]

5 *Dianthus barbatus* 'Green Trick'
   ナデシコ [グリーントリュフ]

6 *Calathea cylindrica* 'Green Ice'
   カラテア [グリーンアイス]

7 *Costus woodsonii* Maas
   コスタス・ウッドソニー

8 *Zingiber officinale* Roscoe
   ショウガ

9 *Celosia argentea* var. *cristata*
   'Melon Frill'
   ケイトウ [メロンフリル]

10 *Allium* 'Pinocchio'
   アリウム [ピノキオ]

11 *Pittosporum tobira* (Thunb.)
   W. T. Aiton
   トベラ

12 *Phlomis fruticosa* 'Green Star'
   フロミス [グリーンスター]

13 *Elettaria cardamomum* (L.) Maton
   カルダモン

14 *Euphorbia submamillaris*
   (A. Berger) A. Berger
   ユーフォルビア
   [姫キリン（ひめきりん）]

15 *Zantedeschia aethiopica*
   'Green Goddess'
   カラー [グリーンゴッデス]

16 *Curcuma alismatifolia*
   'Emerald Choco Zebra'
   クルクマ [エメラルドチョコゼブラ]

17 *Nepenthes bongso* Korth.
   ネペンテス・ボングソ

18 *Nepenthes alata* Blanco
   ネペンテス・アラータ

19 *Daucus carota* L.
   ノラニンジン

20 *Dipsacus fullonum* L.
   チーゼル

21 *Echeveria* 'Black Prince'
   エケベリア [ブラックプリンス]

22 *Anigozanthos flavidus* 'Green'
   カンガルーポー [グリーン]

23 *Curcuma gracillima*
   'Candy Cane'
   クルクマ [キャンディケーン]

24 *Clematis* L.
   クレマチスの実

List of Flower Names │ TONDO

December, 2014——August, 2016 in Tokyo

01   p. 238
——

1 *Dahlia* 'Lalala'
ダリア［ラ・ラ・ラ］
2 *Disa* Kewensis 'Artists Alba'
ディサ・キューエンシス［アーティストアルバ］

02   p. 239
——

1 *Dahlia* 'Sinbad'
ダリア［シンドバッド］
2 *Zinnia haageana* 'Persian Carpet'
ジニア［ペルシャンカーペット］

03   p. 240
——

1 *Dahlia* 'Jessica'
ダリア［ジェシカ］
2 *Disa* Kewensis 'Ann'
ディサ・キューエンシス［アン］

04   p. 241
——

1 *Dahlia* 'Junai no Kimi'
ダリア［純愛の君（じゅんあいのきみ）］
2 *Zinnia elegans* 'Red Sun'
ジニア［レッドサン］

05   p. 242
——

1 *Dahlia* 'Monaco S'
   ダリア［モナコS（もなこえす）］
2 *Epidendrum secundum* 'White Star'
   エピデンドラム［ホワイトスター］

06   p. 243
——

1 *Dahlia* 'Mrs. Eileen'
   ダリア［ミセスアイリーン］
2 *Epidendrum secundum* 'Red 5'
   エピデンドラム［赤5（あかご）］

07   p. 244
——

1 *Dahlia* 'Hinaarare'
   ダリア［雛あられ（ひなあられ）］
2 *Triteleia* 'Babylon'
   トリテレイア［バビロン］

08   p. 245
——

1 *Encyclia adenocaula* (Lex.) Schltr.
   エンシクリア・アデノカウラ
2 *Dahlia* 'Moon Stone'
   ダリア［ムーンストーン］

09   p. 246
—

1 *Phalaenopsis* 'Golden Beauty'
ファレノプシス［ゴールデンビューティー］
2 *Dahlia* 'Moon Waltz'
ダリア［ムーンワルツ］

10   p. 247
—

1 *Ascocenda* 'Muang Thong'
アスコセンダ［ムァントン］
2 *Dahlia* 'Eona G'
ダリア［エオナG（えおなじー）］

11   p. 248
—

1 *Echinacea purpurea* 'Hot Papaya'
エキナセア［ホットパパイヤ］
2 *Dahlia* 'Koto'
ダリア［古都（こと）］

12   p. 249
—

1 *Passiflora caerulea* 'Clear Sky'
トケイソウ［クリアスカイ］
2 *Dahlia* 'Murakingyo'
ダリア［群金魚（むらきんぎょ）］

13　　　　　p. 250
―

1　*Serruria* 'Pretty n Pink'
　　セルリア［プリティピンク］
2　*Dahlia* 'Sakuragai'
　　ダリア［桜貝（さくらがい）］

14　　　　　p. 251
―

1　*Disa* Kewensis 'Artists'
　　ディサ・キューエンシス［アーティスト］
2　*Dahlia* 'Gitt's Perfection'
　　ダリア［ギッツパーフェクション］

15　　　　　p. 252
―

1　*Passiflora* 'Incense'
　　トケイソウ［インセンス］
2　*Dahlia* 'Namahage Magic'
　　ダリア［NAMAHAGEマジック（なまはげまじっく）］

16　　　　　p. 253
―

1　*Phalaenopsis* 'Jaguar'
　　ファレノプシス［ジャガー］
2　*Dahlia* 'Hakusantemari'
　　ダリア［白山手まり（はくさんてまり）］

17   p. 254
——

1   *Dahlia* 'Namahage Swan'
    ダリア［NAMAHAGEスワン（なまはげすわん）］
2   *Passiflora caerulea* 'Constance Elliott'
    トケイソウ［コンスタンスエリオット］

18   p. 255
——

1   *Colmanara* Wildcat 'Bobcat'
    コルマナラ・ワイルドキャット［ボブキャット］
2   *Dahlia* 'Yuino'
    ダリア［結納（ゆいのう）］

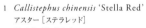

19   p. 256
——

1   *Zinnia elegans* 'Jersey Mix'
    ジニア［ジャジーミックス］
2   *Dahlia* 'Portlight Pair Beauty'
    ダリア［ポートライトペアビューティ］

20   p. 257
——

1   *Callistephus chinensis* 'Stella Red'
    アスター［ステラレッド］
2   *Dahlia* 'Lalala'
    ダリア［ラ・ラ・ラ］

21   pp. 258–259

1 *Viola* × *wittrockiana* 'Moulin Frill Golden'
   パンジー［ムーランフリルゴールデン］
2 *Dahlia* 'Yorokobi'
   ダリア［悦び（よろこび）］

List of Flower Names｜APPEARANCE

December, 2014——August, 2016 in Tokyo

01　　　　p. 263

1　Telopea speciosissima 'Waratah'
　テロペア［ワラタ］

2　Colmanara Wildcat 'Carmela'
　コルマナラ・ワイルドキャット［カルメラ］

3　Iris × hollandica 'Blue Magic'
　アヤメ・ダッチアイリス［ブルーマジック］

4　Leucospermum cordifolium
　'Veldt Fire'
　ピンクッション［ベルデファイヤー］

5　Dahlia 'Red Star'
　ダリア［レッドスター］

6　Polygala myrtifolia var. grandiflora
　'Sweet Pea Shrub'
　ポリガラ［スイートピーシュラブ］

7　Campanula medium
　'Champion Purple'
　カンパニュラ［チャンピオンパープル］

8　Epidendrum secundum 'Red 5'
　エピデンドラム［赤5（あかご）］

9　Allium giganteum Regel
　アリウム・ギガンジューム

10　Nepenthes 'Dyeriana'
　ネペンテス［ダイエリアナ］

11　Paphiopedilum Lebeau 'Bios King'
　パフィオペディラム・レボウ
　［ビオスキング］

12　Passiflora caerulea 'Clear Sky'
　トケイソウ［クリアスカイ］

13　Protea cynaroides 'Arctic Ice'
　プロテア・キングプロテア
　［アークティックアイス］

14　Fuchsia 'Hidcote Beauty'
　フクシア［ヒドコートビューティー］

15　Brassia Eternal Wind
　'Summer Dream'
　ブラッシア・エターナルウィンド
　［サマードリーム］

16　Nigella damascena
　'Persian Jewels'
　ニゲラ［ペルシャンジュエル］

17　Anigozanthos flavidus
　'Red and Green'
　カンガルーポー［レッドアンドグリーン］

18　Clematis florida
　'Crystal Fountain'
　クレマチス［クリスタルフォンテーン］

19　Clematis texensis 'Scarlet'
　クレマチス［スカーレット］

20　Viola × wittrockiana
　'Nature Yellow Broggi'
　パンジー［ナチュレイエローブロッチ］

21　Phalaenopsis
　'Wedding Promenade'
　ファレノプシス
　［ウェディングプロムナード］

22　Chrysanthemum × morifolium
　'Fuego'
　キク［フエゴ］

23　Neoregelia 'Fireball Variegata'
　ネオレゲリア
　［ファイヤーボールバリエガタ］

24　Tillandsia bulbosa Hook.
　チランジア・ブルボーサ

02　　　　p. 265

1　Hydrangea macrophylla 'Hot Red'
　アジサイ［ホットレッド］

2　Begonia rex 'Shirt Sleeves'
　ベゴニア・レックスベゴニア［シャツスリーブ］

3　Chrysanthemum × morifolium
　'Anastasia Green'
　キク［アナスタシアグリーン］

4　Rosa 'Red Elegance'
　バラ［レッドエレガンス］

5　Arpophyllum giganteum
　Hartw. ex Lindl.
　アーポフィラム・ギガンテウム

6　Dendrochilum dempoense J. J. Sm.
　デンドロキラム・デンポエンセ

7　Cymbidium 'Red Empress'
　シンビジューム［レッドエンプレス］

8　Hippeastrum × hybridum
　'Red Lion'
　アマリリス［レッドライオン］

9　Phalaenopsis 'Cacao'
　ファレノプシス［カカオ］

10　Chrysanthemum × morifolium
　'Epoch'
　キク［エポック］

11　Cymbidium tracyanum L. Castle
　シンビジューム・トラシアナム

12　Phalaenopsis Taida Salu 'Alisan'
　ファレノプシス・タイダソリュー
　［アリサン］

13　Anthurium andreanum
　'Black Queen'
　アンスリウム［ブラッククイーン］

03   p. 267

1 *Tillandsia xerographica* Rohweder
チランジア・キセログラフィカ

2 *Pinus parviflora* Sieb. & Zucc.
マツ［五葉松（ごようまつ）］

3 *Tulipa* 'Super Parrot'
チューリップ［スーパーパーロット］

4 *Hyacinthus orientalis* 'Blue Jacket'
ヒヤシンス［ブルージャケット］

5 *Paphiopedilum curtisii* var.
sanderae 'Fort Caroline'
パフィオペディラム・カーティシー・
サンデレー［フォートキャロライン］

6 *Viscum album* subsp. *coloratum*
Komar
ヤドリギ

7 *Helleborus foetidus* L.
クリスマスローズ・フェチダス

04   p. 269

1 *Aranda* 'Green Tiger'
アランダ［グリーンタイガー］

2 *Tulbaghia simmleri* Beauverd
ビオラセア・フレグランス

3 *Hyacinthus orientalis* 'Blue Jacket'
ヒヤシンス［ブルージャケット］

4 *Nepenthes rafflesiana* 'Koshikawa'
ネペンテス・ラフレシアナ［コシカワ］

5 *Lachenalia aloides* var. *quadricolor*
ラケナリア・アロイデス・クアドリカラー

6 *Sarracenia* 'Scarlet Bell'
サラセニア［スカーレットベル］

7 *Dahlia* 'Blue Peach'
ダリア［ブルーピーチ］

8 *Narcissus* 'Sweetness'
スイセン［スイートネス］

9 *Dahlia* 'Nessho'
ダリア［熱唱（ねっしょう）］

10 *Dendrochilum cobbianum* Rchb. f.
デンドロキラム・コビアナム

11 *Cymbidium*
'Nemureru Mori no Bijyo'
シンビジューム［眠れる森の美女
（ねむれるもりのびじょ）］

12 *Tulipa* 'Orange Princess'
チューリップ［オレンジプリンセス］

13 *Lachenalia viridiflora* W. F.
Barker
ラケナリア・ビリディフローラ

14 *Hyacinthus orientalis*
'Miss Saigon'
ヒヤシンス［ミスサイゴン］

05   p. 271

1 *Rhyncholaeliocattleya*
Red Crab 'Kuan-Miao #10'
カトレヤ・リンコレリオカトレヤ・レッドクラブ
［クァンミャオ#10（くぁんみゃおなんばーてん）］

2 *Epidendrum secundum* 'Pink Flamingo'
エビデンドラム［ピンクフラミンゴ］

3 *Viola* × *wittrockiana*
'Frizzle Sizzle Yellow'
パンジー［フリズルシズルイエロー］

4 *Narcissus tazetta* var. *chinensis*
M. Roem.
スイセン・ニホンズイセン

5 *Leucocoryne purpurea* 'Caravel'
リューココリーネ［カラベル］

6 *Dahlia* 'Red Marvelous'
ダリア［レッドマーベラス］

7 *Paphiopedilum spicerianum*
(Rchb. f) Pfitzer
パフィオペディラム・スピセリアナム

8 *Iris* × *hollandica* 'Blue Magic'
アヤメ・ダッチアイリス［ブルーマジック］

9 *Bessera elegans* Schult. f.
ベッセラ・エレガンス

10 *Blandfordia grandiflora*
'Christmas Bell'
ブランドフォルディア［クリスマスベル］

11 *Lomatophyllum prostratum*
H. Perrier
ロマトフィルム・プロストラツム

12 *Alstroemeria* 'Scorpion'
アルストロメリア［スコーピオン］

06   p. 273

1 *Tillandsia capitata* Grisebach
チランジア・カピタータ

2 *Gerbera* 'Crissing'
ガーベラ［クリッシング］

3 *Tagetes erecta* 'Perfection Orange'
マリーゴールド［パーフェクションオレンジ］

4 *Trachelium caeruleum*
'Devotion Purple'
ユウギリソウ［ディボーションパープル］

5 *Chrysanthemum × morifolium*
'Green Shamrock'
キク［グリーンシャムロック］

6 *Rosa* 'Red Elegance'
バラ［レッドエレガンス］

7 *Alpinia purpurata* 'Red Ginger'
ジンジャー［レッドジンジャー］

8 *Tulipa* 'Flaming Parrot'
チューリップ［フレミングパーロット］

9 *Dahlia* 'Asahi Temari'
ダリア［朝日てまり（あさひてまり）］

10 *Matteuccia struthiopteris*（L.）
Todaro
クサソテツ

11 *Paeonia lactiflora* 'Red Rose'
シャクヤク［レッドローズ］

12 *Rosa* 'Kanpai'
バラ［カンパイ］

13 *Grevillea* 'Honey Gem'
グレビレア［ハニージェム］

14 *Chrysanthemum × morifolium*
'Zembla Brazil'
キク［ゼンブラブラジル］

15 *Gerbera* 'Sun Glow'
ガーベラ［サングロー］

16 *Dahlia* 'Rose Quartz'
ダリア［ローズクォーツ］

07   pp. 274–275

1 *Tulipa* 'Flaming Parrot'
チューリップ［フレミングパーロット］

2 *Brassolaeliocattleya* Young-Min
Orange 'Jin Man 1'
カトレヤ・ブラッソレリオカトレヤ・
ヤンミンオレンジ［ジンマンワン］

3 *Phalaenopsis* 'Cacao'
ファレノプシス［カカオ］

4 *Tulipa* 'Mysterious Parrot'
チューリップ［ミステリアスパーロット］

5 *Tulipa* 'Monte Spider'
チューリップ［モンテスパイダー］

6 *Cattleya* Purple Cascade
'Fragrance Beauty'
カトレヤ・パープルキャスケイド
［フラグランスビューティ］

7 *Rosa* 'Gold Rush'
バラ［ゴールドラッシュ］

8 *Anthurium andreanum*
'Lady Jane'
アンスリウム［レディージェーン］

9 *Rosa* 'Amada+'
バラ［アマダ+（あまだぷらす）］

10 *Guzmania* 'Minor Variegata'
グズマニア［マイナーバリエガタ］

08   pp. 276–277

1 *Rhyncholaeliocattleya*
King of Taiwan 'Ta-Hsin'
カトレヤ・リンコレリオカトレヤ・キングオブ
タイワン［大新（たしん）］

2 *Cymbidium tracyanum* L. Castle
シンビジューム・トラシアナム

3 *Sarracenia flava* var. *rubricorpora*
サラセニア・フラバ・ルブリコーポラ

4 *Freesia refracta* 'Oberon'
フリージア［オベロン］

5 *Chrysanthemum* × *morifolium*
'Fuego'
キク［フエゴ］

6 *Paphiopedilum insigne*
(Wall. ex Lindl.) Pfitzer
パフィオペディラム・インシグネ

7 *Tulipa* 'Red Princess'
チューリップ［レッドプリンセス］

8 *Dendrobium* 'Sweet Candy'
デンドロビューム［スイートキャンディ］

9 *Phalaenopsis* 'Chian Xen Piano'
ファレノプシス［チャンシンピアノ］

10 *Paeonia lactiflora* 'Red Charm'
シャクヤク［レッドチャーム］

09   pp. 278–279

1 *Tillandsia caput–medusae* E. Morren
チランジア・カプトメデューサ

2 *Alocasia cucullata* (Lour.) G. Don
アロカシア・シマクワズイモ

3 *Rosa* 'Exciting Meilland'
バラ［エキサイティングメイアン］

4 *Anthurium andreanum* 'Jupiter'
アンスリウム［ジュピター］

5 *Epidendrum secundum* 'Red 5'
エピデンドラム［赤5（あかご）］

6 *Moluccella laevis* L.
モルセラ・ラエヴィス

7 *Epidendrum* Parasol Valley
'Music Box'
エピデンドラム・パラソルバレー
［ミュージックボックス］

8 *Dahlia* 'Asahi Temari'
ダリア［朝日てまり（あさひてまり）］

9 *Paphiopedilum delenatii*
Guillaumin
パフィオペディラム・デレナティー

10 *Tulipa* 'Monte Spider'
チューリップ［モンテスパイダー］

11 *Freesia refracta* 'Ancona'
フリージア［アンコナ］

12 *Tulipa* 'Hamilton'
チューリップ［ハミルトン］

13 *Chrysanthemum* × *morifolium*
'Elena'
キク［エレーナ］

14 *Hydrangea macrophylla*
'You and Me Together Pink'
アジサイ［ユーミートゥギャザーピンク］

15 *Gerbera* 'Sandy'
ガーベラ［サンディー］

16 *Rosa* 'Yves Piaget'
バラ［イヴピアッチェ］

17 *Syringa vulgaris*
'Madame Florent Stepman'
ライラック
［マダムフローレントステップマン］

18 *Tulipa* 'Purple Flag'
チューリップ［パープルフラッグ］

10   pp. 280–281

1 *Brassia* Eternal Wind
'Summer Dream'
ブラッシア・エターナルウィンド
[サマードリーム]

2 *Nepenthes tobaica* Danser
ネペンテス・トバイカ

3 *Fritillaria persica* L.
フリチラリア・ペルシカ

4 *Campanula medium*
'Champion Purple'
カンパニュラ [チャンピオンパープル]

5 *Potinara* Sweet Sugar 'Happy Field'
ポチナラ・スウィートシュガー
[ハッピーフィールド]

6 *Tillandsia bulbosa* Hook.
チランジア・ブルボーサ

7 *Paphiopedilum* Lebeau 'Bios King'
パフィオペディラム・レボウ [ビオスキング]

8 *Phalaenopsis* Sogo Ibis
'Little Maruko'
ファレノプシス・ソゴアイビス [リトルマルコ]

9 *Paphiopedilum callosum* var.
vinicolor
パフィオペディラム・カローサム・
ビニカラー

10 *Viola* 'Yellow Blotch'
ビオラ [イエローブロッチ]

11 *Fritillaria thunbergii* Miq.
フリチラリア・バイモユリ

12 *Iris* × *hollandica* 'Blue Magic'
アヤメ・ダッチアイリス [ブルーマジック]

13 *Leucospermum cordifolium*
'Veldt Fire'
ピンクッション [ベルデファイヤー]

14 *Anthurium andreanum*
'Tropical Red'
アンスリウム [トロピカルレッド]

15 *Passiflora caerulea* 'Clear Sky'
トケイソウ [クリアスカイ]

16 *Nigella damascena* 'Miss Jekyll'
ニゲラ「ミスジーキル」

11   pp. 282–283

1 *Hippeastrum* × *hybridum* 'Minerva'
アマリリス [ミネルヴァ]

2 *Hyacinthus orientalis* 'Blue Jacket'
ヒヤシンス [ブルージャケット]

3 *Cymbidium* 'Green Sour'
シンビジューム [グリーンサワー]

4 *Paphiopedilum* 'Lime Down'
パフィオペディラム [ライムドーン]

5 *Cymbidium floribundum* Lindl.
シンビジューム・キンリョウヘン

6 *Fritillaria camschatcensis* (L.)
Ker-Gawl.
フリチラリア・クロユリ

7 *Dryopteris crassirhizoma* Nakai
オシダ

8 *Papaver nudicaule* L.
ポピー・アイスランドポピー

9 *Leontochir ovallei* Phil.
レオントキール・オバレイ

10 *Allium schubertii* Zucc.
アリウム・シュベルティ

11 *Anthurium andreanum* 'Safari'
アンスリウム [サファリ]

12 *Hippeastrum* × *hybridum*
'Double Ribbon'
アマリリス [ダブルリボン]

13 *Chrysanthemum* × *morifolium*
'Green Shamrock'
キク [グリーンシャムロック]

14 *Rosa* 'Hanabi'
バラ [ハナビ]

15 *Begonia rex* 'Daisuke'
ベゴニア・レックスベゴニア
[大助 (だいすけ)]

16 *Brassica oleracea* var. *botrytis*
'Romanesco'
カリフラワー [ロマネスコ]

17 *Ageratum houstonianum*
'Top Blue'
アゲラタム [トップブルー]

12 pp. 284–285

1 *Hydrangea macrophylla* 'Blue Earth'
アジサイ［ブルーアース］

2 *Epidendrum secundum* 'Pecan Red'
エピデンドラム［ピーカンレッド］

3 *Chrysanthemum × morifolium*
'Sei Etude'
キク［セイエチュード］

4 *Dahlia* 'Nessho'
ダリア［熱唱（ねっしょう）］

5 *Strelitzia reginae* Aiton
ストリチア・レギネ

6 *Tillandsia andreana* E. Morren ex
André
チランジア・アンドレアナ

7 *Tulipa* 'Mysterious Parrot'
チューリップ［ミステリアスパーロット］

8 *Osmunda japonica* Thunb.
ゼンマイ

9 *Albuca spiralis* 'Frizzle Sizzle'
アルブカ・スピラリス［フリズルシズル］

10 *Tulipa* 'Barbados'
チューリップ［バルバドス］

11 *Freesia refracta* 'Aladdin'
フリージア［アラジン］

12 *Gerbera* 'Tomahawk'
ガーベラ［トマホーク］

13 *Ranunculus asiaticus* 'Ikaros'
ラナンキュラス［イカロス］

14 *Nigella damascena*
'Persian Jewels'
ニゲラ［ペルシャンジュエル］

15 *Chrysanthemum × morifolium*
'Delacroix'
キク［ドラクロワ］

16 *Tillandsia paleacea* Presl
チランジア・パレアセア

17 *Tillandsia seleriana* Mez
チランジア・セレリアナ

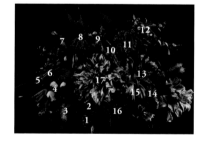

13 pp. 286–287

1 *Rohdea japonica* (Thunb.) Roth
オモトの実

2 *Anthurium andreanum* 'Safari'
アンスリウム［サファリ］

3 *Banksia spinulosa* Sm.
バンクシア・スピヌロサ

4 *Oncidium* Moon Shadow 'Tiger Tail'
オンシジューム・ムーンシャドウ
［タイガーテイル］

5 *Heliconia stricta* 'Firebird'
ヘリコニア［ファイヤーバード］

6 *Tulipa* 'Ballerina'
チューリップ［バレリーナ］

7 *Zantedeschia aethiopica*
'Captain Fuego'
カラー［キャプテンフエゴ］

8 *Bulbophyllum* Elizabeth Ann
'Buckleberry'
バルボフィラム・エリザベスアン
［バックルベリー］

9 *Paphiopedilum insigne*
(Wall. ex Lindl.) Pfitzer
パフィオペディラム・インシグネ

10 *Nepenthes* 'Dyeriana'
ネペンテス［ダイエリアナ］

11 *Dahlia* 'Hamilton Junior'
ダリア［ハミルトンジュニア］

12 *Cymbidium* 'Irohairo 01'
シンビジューム［いろはいろ01
（いろはいろぜろいち）］

13 *Aloe* 'Red Devil'
アロエ［レッドデビル］

14 *Leucospermum cordifolium*
'Succession'
ピンクッション［サクセション］

15 *Clivia gardenii* Hook.
クンシラン・ガルデニー

16 *Dahlia* 'Nessho'
ダリア［熱唱（ねっしょう）］

17 *Dahlia* 'Sabaku'
ダリア［砂漠（さばく）］

14   pp. 288–289

1 *Paeonia lactiflora*
'Kojima no Kagayaki'
シャクヤク [小島の輝き（こじまのかがやき）]

2 *Banksia spinulosa* Sm.
バンクシア・スピヌロサ

3 *Epidendrum secundum* 'Princess 8'
エピデンドラム
[プリンセス8（ぷりんせすえいと）]

4 *Tulipa* 'Flaming Flag'
チューリップ [フレミングフラッグ]

5 *Clematis × durandii*
クレマチス・デュランディ

6 *Chrysanthemum × morifolium* 'Yo'
キク [陽（よう）]

7 *Lachenalia aloides* var. *quadricolor*
ラケナリア・アロイデス・クアドリカラー

8 *Chrysanthemum × morifolium*
'Pretty Rio'
キク [プリティリオ]

9 *Tulipa* 'Palmyra'
チューリップ [パルミラ]

10 *Phalaenopsis*
'Ching Ann Diamond'
ファレノプシス [チンアンダイヤモンド]

11 *Hyacinthus orientalis*
'Blue Jacket'
ヒヤシンス [ブルージャケット]

12 *Kniphofia uvaria* 'Flamenco'
トリトマ [フラメンコ]

13 *Dahlia* 'Asahi Temari'
ダリア [朝日てまり（あさひてまり）]

14 *Lilium maculatum* 'Café Noir'
ユリ・スカシユリ [カフェノアール]

15 *Rosa* 'Flash Eye'
バラ [フラッシュアイ]

16 *Dahlia* 'Santa Claus'
ダリア [サンタクロース]

15   pp. 290–291

1 *Hippeastrum × hybidum* 'Susan'
アマリリス [スーザン]

2 *Ranunculus asiaticus* 'M Blue'
ラナンキュラス [エムブルー]

3 *Eustoma grandiflorum* 'Voyage Blue'
トルコキキョウ [ボヤージュブルー]

4 *Tulipa* 'Dolce Hess'
チューリップ [ドルチェヘス]

5 *Chrysanthemum × morifolium*
'Saffina'
キク [サフィーナ]

6 *Tulipa* 'Rococo'
チューリップ [ロココ]

7 *Hippeastrum papilio* (Ravenna)
Van Scheepen
アマリリス・パピリオ

8 *Anigozanthos flavidus*
'Red and Green'
カンガルーポー [レッドアンドグリーン]

9 *Euphorbia characias* L.
ユーフォルビア・カラキラス

10 *Paeonia lactiflora* 'Coral Charm'
シャクヤク [コーラルチャーム]

11 *Platycerium bifurcatum* (Cav.)
C. Chr.
ビカクシダ・コウモリラン

12 *Odontoglossum* Enzan Fantasy
'Rouge Magic'
オドントグロッサム・エンザンファンタジー
[ルージュマジック]

13 *Ranunculus asiaticus* 'M Pink'
ラナンキュラス [エムピンク]

14 *Dianthus caryophyllus*
'Dom Pedro'
カーネーション [ドンペドロ]

15 *Chrysanthemum × morifolium*
'Classic Cocoa'
キク [クラシックココア]

16   pp. 292–293

1 *Lilium maculatum* 'Black Out'
  ユリ・スカシユリ［ブラックアウト］
2 *Phalaenopsis* 'Cacao'
  ファレノプシス［カカオ］
3 *Hippeastrum × hybridum*
  'Red Peacock'
  アマリリス［レッドピーコック］
4 *Rhyncholaeliocattleya* Sophia Knot
  'Kayoko'
  カトレヤ・リンコレリオカトレヤ・ソフィアノット
  ［カヨコ］
5 *Iris × hollandica* 'Blue Diamond'
  アヤメ・ダッチアイリス［ブルーダイヤモンド］
6 *Cynara scolymus* L.
  アーティチョーク
7 *Anthurium crassinervium*
  'Jungle King'
  アンスリウム［ジャングルキング］
8 *Lilium orientalis* 'Carolina'
  ユリ［カロリーナ］

9 *Begonia rex* 'Stained Glass'
  ベゴニア・レックスベゴニア
  ［ステンドグラス］
10 *Gloriosa superba* 'Carsonii'
  グロリオサ［カルソニー］
11 *Nepenthes* 'Rebecca Soper'
  ネペンテス［レベッカソーパー］
12 *Rosa* 'Vague+'
  バラ［ヴァーグ+（ゔぁーぐぷらす）］
13 *Aeonium arboreum* 'Zwartkop'
  アエオニウム［黒法師（くろほうし）］
14 *Zantedeschia pentlandii* 'Odessa'
  カラー［オデッサ］
15 *Dahlia* 'Arabian Night'
  ダリア［アラビアンナイト］
16 *Paphiopedilum callosum* var.
  vinicolor
  パフィオペディラム・カローサム・
  ビニカラー

17   pp. 294–295

1 *Cynara scolymus* L.
  アーティチョーク
2 *Dianthus barbatus* 'Green Trick'
  ナデシコ［グリーントリュフ］
3 *Dianthus caryophyllus* 'Seychelles'
  カーネーション［セイシェル］
4 *Nepenthes alata* Blanco
  ネペンテス・アラータ
5 *Alpinia zerumbet* (Pers.) B. L. Burtt
  and R. M. Sm.
  ゲットウ
6 *Cyathea spinulosa* Wall. ex Hook.
  ヘゴゼンマイ
7 *Fritillaria thunbergii* Miq.
  フリチラリア・バイモユリ

8 *Protea barbigera* 'Niobe'
  プロテア［ニオベ］
9 *Vanda* 'Pakchong Blue'
  バンダ［パクチョンブルー］
10 *Aquilegia vulgaris* 'Winky Blue'
  アクイレギア［ウィンキーブルー］
11 *Zantedeschia aethiopica*
  'White Swan'
  カラー［エチオピカブレナ］
12 *Ranunculus asiaticus* 'Pomerol'
  ラナンキュラス［ポムロール］
13 *Lilium* 'Noble Lily'
  ユリ［ノーブルリリー］

18   pp. 296–297

1 *Dahlia* 'Murakingyo'
ダリア［群金魚（むらきんぎょ）］

2 *Paphiopedilum* Orchilla 'Chilton'
パフィオペディラム・オルチラ［チルトン］

3 *Narcissus* 'Grand Soleil d'Or'
スイセン［グランドソレドール］

4 *Phalaenopsis* 'Chocolate Pearl'
ファレノプシス［チョコレートパール］

5 *Begonia rex* 'Vista'
ベゴニア・レックスベゴニア［ヴィスタ］

6 *Dahlia* 'Agitato'
ダリア［アジタート］

7 *Hyacinthus orientalis* 'Blue Pearl'
ヒヤシンス［ブルーパール］

8 *Viola* × *wittrockiana* 'Chalon Giant'
パンジー［シャロンジャイアント］

9 *Cymbidium tracyanum* L. Castle
シンビジューム・トラシアナム

10 *Tulipa* 'Tete a Tete'
チューリップ［ティタティタ］

11 *Brassica oleracea*
'Versailles Black Lucien'
ハボタン
［ヴェルサイユブラックルシアン］

12 *Muscari aucheri* 'White Magic'
ムスカリ［ホワイトマジック］

13 *Anthurium andreanum*
'Black Queen'
アンスリウム［ブラッククイーン］

14 *Zantedeschia aethiopica*
'Schwarzwalder'
カラー［シュワルツワルダー］

15 *Nepenthes alata* Blanco
ネペンテス・アラータ

19   pp. 298–299

1 *Dahlia* 'Murakingyo'
ダリア［群金魚（むらきんぎょ）］

2 *Chrysanthemum* × *morifolium*
'Golden Ping Pong'
キク［ゴールデンピンポン］

3 *Agapanthus africanus* 'Ocean Blue'
アガパンサス［オーシャンブルー］

4 *Protea* 'Robyn'
プロテア［ロビン］

5 *Allium schubertii* Zucc.
アリウム・シュベルティ

6 *Passiflora* 'Belotii'
トケイソウ［ベロッティ］

7 *Fritillaria camschatcensis* (L.)
Ker-Gawl.
フリチラリア・クロユリ

8 *Nepenthes alata* Blanco
ネペンテス・アラータ

9 *Lilium longiflorum* 'Hinomoto'
ユリ・テッポウユリ［日の本（ひのもと）］

10 *Kalmia latifolia* 'Ostbo Red'
カルミア［オスボレッド］

11 *Allium giganteum* Regel
アリウム・ギガンジューム

12 *Tillandsia* 'Cotton Candy'
チランジア［コットンキャンディ］

13 *Freesia refracta* 'Aladdin'
フリージア［アラジン］

14 *Epidendrum secundum* 'Red 5'
エピデンドラム［赤5（あかご）］

15 *Paeonia lactiflora* 'Red Charm'
シャクヤク［レッドチャーム］

16 *Cymbidium* 'King Arthur'
シンビジューム［キングアーサー］

17 *Chrysanthemum* × *morifolium*
'Saba'
キク［サバ］

18 *Dichelostemma ida-maia*
'Pink Diamond'
ディケロステンマ［ピンクダイヤモンド］

20   pp. 300-301
—

1 *Hydrangea macrophylla*
'Marine Blue'
アジサイ［マリンブルー］

2 *Tephrocactus articulatus* (Pfeiff.)
Backeb.
サボテン［武蔵野（むさしの）］

3 *Narcissus* 'Tete a Tete'
スイセン［ティタティタ］

4 *Phalaenopsis* 'Cacao'
ファレノプシス［カカオ］

5 *Hippeastrum calyptratum*
(Ker Gawl.) Herb.
アマリリス・カリプトゥラタ

6 *Sarracenia* 'Dana's Delight'
サラセニア［ダナズデライト］

7 *Euphorbia lactea* Haw.
ユーフォルビア・ラクティア

8 *Paeonia lactiflora* 'Red Monarch'
シャクヤク［レッドモナーク］

9 *Tulipa* 'Rococo'
チューリップ［ロココ］

10 *Guzmania* 'Torch'
グズマニア［トーチ］

11 *Tillandsia aeranthos* (Loiseleur)
L. B. Sm.
チランジア・アエラントス

12 *Hippeastrum × hybridum*
'Royal Velvet'
アマリリス［ロイヤルベルベット］

13 *Neoregelia pauciflora* L. B. Sm.
ネオレゲリア・パウシフローラ

14 *Zamia furfuracea* L. f.
ザミア・フルフラケア

15 *Dahlia* 'Red Star'
ダリア［レッドスター］

16 *Echeveria* 'Fantasia Carol'
エケベリア［ファンタジアキャロル］

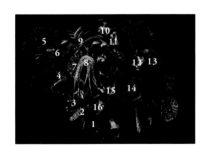

21   pp. 302-303
—

1 *Begonia negrosensis* 'Pink Dot'
ベゴニア［ピンクドット］

2 *Nepenthes* 'Dyeriana'
ネペンテス［ダイエリアナ］

3 *Hydrangea macrophylla*
'Magical Ruby Red'
アジサイ［マジカルルビーレッド］

4 *Anthurium andreanum* 'Emperor'
アンスリウム［エンペラー］

5 *Dahlia* 'Junai no Kimi'
ダリア［純愛の君（じゅんあいのきみ）］

6 *Lupinus nanus* 'Pixie Delight'
ルピナス［ピクシーデライト］

7 *Dahlia* 'Rose Quartz'
ダリア［ローズクォーツ］

8 *Dendrochilum magnum* Rchb. f.
デンドロキラム・マグナム

9 *Vanda falcata* 'Hakuunkaku'
フウラン［白雲閣（はくうんかく）］

10 *Helleborus*
'Double Rasberry Ripple'
クリスマスローズ
［ダブルラズベリーリップル］

11 *Tulipa polychroma* Stapf
チューリップ・ポリクロマ

12 *Lathyrus odoratus*
'Wiltshire Ripple'
スイートピー［シャーリップル］

13 *Rosa* 'Yves Red'
バラ［イヴレッド］

14 *Dianthus caryophyllus* 'Excellia'
カーネーション［エクセリア］

15 *Cymbidium tracyanum* L. Castle
シンビジューム・トラシアナム

16 *Anthurium andreanum*
'Black Queen'
アンスリウム［ブラッククイーン］

22   pp. 304–305

1 *Ranunculus asiaticus* 'Charlotte'
   ラナンキュラス［シャルロット］
2 *Grevillea* 'Golden Yu-Lo'
   グレビレア［ゴールデンユーロ］
3 *Lilium orientalis* 'Isabella'
   ユリ［イザベラ］
4 *Tulipa* 'Orange Monarch'
   チューリップ［オレンジモナーク］
5 *Cyathea spinulosa* Wall. ex Hook.
   ヘゴゼンマイ
6 *Argyranthemum frutescens* (L.)
   Sch. Bip.
   マーガレット
7 *Colmanara* Wildcat 'Bobcat'
   コルマナラ・ワイルドキャット［ボブキャット］
8 *Viora* × *wittrockiana*
   'Frizzle Sizzle Yellow Blue Swirl'
   パンジー
   ［フリズルシズルイエローブルースワール］
9 *Osmunda japonica* Thunb.
   ゼンマイ
10 *Cymbidium* Eastern Bunny
   'Tsuki no Hikari'
   シンビジューム・イースタンバニー
   ［月の光（つきのひかり）］

11 *Viola* × *wittrockiana*
   'Frizzle Sizzle Blue'
   パンジー［フリズルシズルブルー］
12 *Musa minor* Nakai
   バショウ［キングバナナ］
13 *Leucocoryne purpurea* 'Caravel'
   リューココリーネ［カラベル］
14 *Oxypetalum coeruleum*
   'Blue Star'
   オキシペタルム［ブルースター］
15 *Brassica oleracea* var. *botrytis*
   'Romanesco'
   カリフラワー［ロマネスコ］
16 *Rhyncholaeliocattleya*
   Rie's Orange Grove 'Harvest'
   カトレヤ・リンコレリオカトレヤ・
   リエズオレンジグローブ［ハーベスト］
17 *Tulipa* 'Barbados'
   チューリップ［バルバドス］
18 *Chrysanthemum* × *morifolium*
   'Saffina'
   キク［サフィーナ］
19 *Cyclamen persicum*
   'Happiness Mama'
   シクラメン［ハピネスママ］

23   pp. 306–307

1 *Phytolacca americana* L.
   ヨウシュヤマゴボウ
2 *Narcissus* 'Grand Soleil d'Or'
   スイセン［グランドソルドール］
3 *Dahlia* 'Micchan'
   ダリア［ミッチャン］
4 *Cymbidium floribundum* Lindl.
   シンビジューム・キンリョウヘン
5 *Gerbera* 'Stanza'
   ガーベラ［スタンザ］
6 *Gerbera* 'Voldemort'
   ガーベラ［ヴォルデモート］
7 *Dahlia* 'Lalala'
   ダリア［ラ・ラ・ラ］
8 *Anthurium andreanum* 'Jupiter'
   アンスリウム［ジュピター］
9 *Fritillaria persica* 'Ivory Bells'
   フリチラリア［アイボリーベル］
10 *Epidendrum secundum* 'Red 5'
   エピデンドラム［赤5（あかご）］

11 *Iris* × *hollandica* 'Blue Magic'
   アヤメ・ダッチアイリス
   ［ブルーマジック］
12 *Tulipa* 'Little Princess'
   チューリップ［リトルプリンセス］
13 *Osmunda japonica* Thunb.
   ゼンマイ
14 *Leontochir ovallei* Phil.
   レオントキール・オバレイ
15 *Tulipa* 'Monte Spider'
   チューリップ［モンテスパイダー］
16 *Ammi majus* 'Green Mist'
   レースフラワー［グリーンミスト］
17 *Lilium* 'Orange Art'
   ユリ［オレンジアート］
18 *Scabiosa columbaria* 'Blue Note'
   スカビオサ［ブルーノート］
19 *Tulipa* 'Yellow King'
   チューリップ［イエローキング］
20 *Tulipa* 'Purple Flag'
   チューリップ［パープルフラッグ］

24 pp. 308–309

1 *Anthurium andreanum* 'Emperor'
アンスリウム［エンペラー］

2 *Dahlia* 'Nessho'
ダリア［熱唱（ねっしょう）］

3 *Fuchsia* 'White Ann'
フクシア［ホワイトアン］

4 *Protea* 'Venus'
プロテア［ヴィーナス］

5 *Fritillaria persica* L.
フリチラリア・ペルシカ

6 *Arisaema urashima* Hara
ウラシマソウ

7 *Phalaenopsis* 'Cacao'
ファレノプシス［カカオ］

8 *Phalaenopsis* Sheena's Pearl
'Geisha Waltz'
ファレノプシス・シーナズパール
［ゲイシャワルツ］

9 *Paphiopedilum* 'Night Shadow'
パフィオペディラム［ナイトシャドウ］

10 *Helianthus annuus*
'Sunrich Orange'
ヒマワリ［サンリッチオレンジ］

11 *Gerbera* 'Pasta di Mamma'
ガーベラ［パスタディママ］

12 *Guzmania* 'Torch'
グズマニア［トーチ］

13 *Convallaria majalis* L.
スズラン

14 *Rosa* 'Red Ranunculus'
バラ［レッドラナンキュラ］

25 pp. 310–311

1 *Hyacinthus orientalis* 'Blue Jacket'
ヒヤシンス［ブルージャケット］

2 *Tillandsia xerographica* Rohweder
チランジア・キセログラフィカ

3 *Iris × hollandica* 'Blue Magic'
アヤメ・ダッチアイリス［ブルーマジック］

4 *Chrysanthemum × morifolium* 'Yo'
キク［陽（よう）］

5 *Epidendrum secundum* 'Red 5'
エピデンドラム［赤5（あかご）］

6 *Dahlia* 'Red Star'
ダリア［レッドスター］

7 *Neoregelia* 'Fireball Variegata'
ネオレゲリア［ファイヤーボールバリエガタ］

8 *Tulipa* 'Mon Amour'
チューリップ［モナムール］

9 *Dahlia* 'Nessho'
ダリア［熱唱（ねっしょう）］

10 *Oncidium Twinkle* 'Charm'
オンシジューム・トゥインクル［チャーム］

11 *Vande* 'Pat Delight'
バンダ［パットデライト］

12 *Camellia japonica* L.
ツバキ

13 *Narcissus* 'Tete a Tete'
スイセン［ティタティタ］

14 *Anthurium andreanum* 'Spice'
アンスリウム［スパイス］

15 *Paphiopedilum* Winston
Churchill 'Redoutable'
パフィオペディラム・
ウィンストンチャーチル［リダウタブル］

16 *Cymbidium tracyanum* L. Castle
シンビジューム・トラシアナム

26   pp. 312–313

1 *Dahlia* 'Fidalgo Blacky'
   ダリア [フィダルゴブラッキー]

2 *Cryptanthus fosterianus* 'Elaine'
   クリプタンサス [エレーヌ]

3 *Clematis integrifolia* 'Inspiration'
   クレマチス [インスピレーション]

4 *Phalaenopsis* Sogo Pearl 'Pine Ridge'
   ファレノプシス・ソゴパール [パインリッジ]

5 *Celosia argentea* var. *cristata*
   'Kurume Akajiku'
   ケイトウ [クルメアカジク]

6 *Eustoma grandiflorum* 'Voyage Blue'
   トルコキキョウ [ボヤージュブルー]

7 *Zantedeschia aethiopica* 'Picasso'
   カラー [ピカソ]

8 *Nerine sarniensis* 'Red Emperor'
   ネリネ [レッドエンペラー]

9 *Brassica oleracea* 'Black Swan'
   ハボタン [ブラックスワン]

10 *Gomphrena globosa* 'Rose Neon'
   センニチコウ [ローズネオン]

11 *Zingiber zerumbet*
   'Shampoo Ginger'
   ジンジャー [シャンプージンジャー]

27   pp. 314–315

1 *Anemone coronaria*
   'Saint Bridget Rose'
   アネモネ [セントブリジットローズ]

2 *Zantedeschia aethiopica* 'Fuka'
   カラー [風花 (ふうか)]

3 *Tulipa* 'Monte Carlo'
   チューリップ [モンテカルロ]

4 *Tulipa* 'Largo'
   チューリップ [ラルゴ]

5 *Anthurium andreanum* 'Rosa'
   アンスリウム [ローザ]

6 *Ranunculus asiaticus* 'Tanger'
   ラナンキュラス [タンジェ]

7 *Dahlia* 'Asahi Temari'
   ダリア [朝日てまり (あさひてまり)]

8 *Tillandsia* 'Cotton Candy'
   チランジア [コットンキャンディ]

9 *Dahlia* 'Matador'
   ダリア [マタドール]

10 *Aechmea gamosepala* Wittm.
   エクメア・ガモセパラ

11 *Papaver nudicaule* L.
   ポピー・アイスランドポピー

12 *Delphinium chinense*
   'Blue Candle'
   デルフィニウム [ブルーキャンドル]

13 *Tulipa* 'Acuminata'
   チューリップ [アクミナータ]

14 *Cyrtanthus mackenii*
   'King Yellow'
   キルタンサス [キングイエロー]

15 *Narcissus* 'Sweetness'
   スイセン [スイートネス]

16 *Phalaenopsis* Taida Salu 'Alisan'
   ファレノプシス・タイダソリュー [アリサン]

17 *Tulipa* 'White River Star'
   チューリップ [ホワイトリバースター]

Names of Flowers │ AUTOGENESIS

December, 2014——August, 2016 in Tokyo

01   p. 319

1 *Sarracenia* 'Scarlet Bell'
サラセニア［スカーレットベル］

2 *Protea magnifica* 'Queen'
プロテア［クイーン］

3 *Nepenthes* 'Rebecca Soper'
ネペンテス［レベッカソーパー］

4 *Phytolacca americama* L.
ヨウシュヤマゴボウ

5 *Dahlia* 'Pechka'
ダリア［ペチカ］

6 *Dahlia* 'Little Rosemary'
ダリア［リトルローズマリー］

7 *Tillandsia xerographica* Rohweder
チランジア・キセログラフィカ

8 *Dendrochilum magnum* Rchb. f.
デンドロキラム・マグナム

9 *Zantedeschia aethiopica* 'Picasso'
カラー［ピカソ］

10 *Leucospermum cordifolium*
'High Gold'
ピンクッション［ハイゴールド］

11 *Curcuma alismatifolia*
'Saim Crown'
クルクマ［サイアムクラウン］

12 *Tricyrtis formosana* Baker
タイワンホトトギス

13 *Tillandsia caput-medusae* E.
Morren
チランジア・カブトメデューサ

14 *Celosia argentea* var. *cristata*
'Sakata Pride'
ケイトウ［サカタプライド］

15 *Nelumbo nucifera* Gaertn.
ハス台

02   p. 321

1 *Dianthus caryophyllus* 'Clasico'
カーネーション［クラシコ］

2 *Nigella damascena* 'Persian Jewels'
ニゲラ［ペルシャンジュエル］

3 *Allium amethystinum* 'Red Mohican'
アリウム［レッドモヒカン］

4 *Leontopodium alpinum* Cass.
セイヨウウスユキソウ

5 *Daucus carota* L.
ノラニンジン

6 *Dianthus caryophyllus* 'Master'
カーネーション［マスター］

7 *Doryanthes excelsa* Correa
ガイミアリリー

8 *Celosia argentea* var. *cristata*
'Orange Queen'
ケイトウ［オレンジクイーン］

9 *Gerbera* 'Voldemort'
ガーベラ［ヴォルデモート］

10 *Anthurium longifolium*
(Hoffm.) G. Don
アンスリウム・ロンギフォリウム

11 *Calathea crotalifera* S. Watson
カラテア・クロタリフェラ

12 *Leucospermum cordifolium*
'High Gold'
ピンクッション［ハイゴールド］

13 *Tagetes erecta* 'Yellow Boy'
マリーゴールド［イエローボーイ］

14 *Echinacea purpurea*
'Harvest Moon'
エキナセア［ハーベストムーン］

15 *Serruria* 'Pretty n Pink'
セルリア［プリティピンク］

16 *Chrysanthemum × morifolium*
'Fuego'
キク［フエゴ］

17 *Strelitzia reginae* Aiton
ストレリチア・レギネ

03　　　　p. 323
—

1　*Medinilla magnifica* Lindl.
　メディニラ・マグニフィカ

2　*Echeveria* 'Melaco'
　エケベリア［メラコ］

3　*Paranomus reflexus* N. E. Br.
　パラノムス

4　*Paphiopedilum* 'St. Swithin'
　パフィオペディラム［セントスイシン］

5　*Haworthia fasciata* 'Juni no Maki'
　ハオルチア［十二の巻（じゅうにのまき）］

6　*Iris germanica* 'Stunning'
　アヤメ・ジャーマンアイリス［スタニング］

7　*Nepenthes alata* Blanco
　ネペンテス・アラータ

8　*Dahlia* 'Kokucho'
　ダリア［黒蝶（こくちょう）］

9　*Mammillaria elongata* f. *cristata*
　サボテン
　［金手毬綴化（きんてまりせっか）］

10　*Aloe jucunda* Reynolds
　アロエ・ジュクンダ

11　*Dianthus caryophyllus* 'Zurigo'
　カーネーション［ズリゴ］

12　*Sarracenia flava* L.
　サラセニア・フラバ

13　*Gerbera* 'Purple Springs'
　ガーベラ［パープルスプリングス］

04　　　　p. 325
—

1　*Dianthus caryophyllus* 'Hermès'
　カーネーション［エルメス］

2　*Tulipa* 'Exotic Sun'
　チューリップ［エキゾチックサン］

3　*Helianthus annuus*
　'Vincent Tangerine'
　ヒマワリ［ビンセントタンジェリン］

4　*Dendrochilum cobbianum* Rchb. f.
　デンドロキラム・コビアナム

5　*Osmunda japonica* Thunb.
　ゼンマイ

6　*Viola × wittrockiana*
　'Nature Yellow Broggi'
　パンジー［ナチュレイエローブロッチ］

7　*Conostylis setigera*
　'Joey Cat's Paw'
　コノスティリス［ジョーイキャッツポー］

8　*Ranunculus asiaticus* 'Gironde'
　ラナンキュラス［ジロンド］

9　*Viola × wittrockiana*
　'Chalon Giant'
　パンジー［シャロンジャイアント］

10　*Brassolaeliocattleya* Young-Min
　Orange 'Jin Man 1'
　カトレヤ・ブラッソレリオカトレヤ・
　ヤンミンオレンジ［ジンマンワン］

11　*Epidendrum secundum*
　'Yellow Star'
　エピデンドラム［イエロースター］

12　*Narcissus* 'Dick Wilden'
　スイセン［ディックウィルデン］

05   p. 327

1 *Phalaenopsis* Taida Salu 'Alisan'
   ファレノプシス・タイダソリュー［アリサン］

2 *Zantedeschia aethiopica* 'Hot Shot'
   カラー［ホットショット］

3 *Chrysanthemum × morifolium*
   'Saffina'
   キク［サフィーナ］

4 *Kniphofia uvaria* 'First Sunrise'
   トリトマ［ファーストサンライズ］

5 *Habenaria medusa* Kraenzl.
   ハベナリア・メドゥーサ

6 *Dahlia* 'Jessie Rita'
   ダリア［ジェシーリタ］

7 *Sarracenia purpurea* L.
   サラセニア・プルプレア

8 *Aechmea fasciata* (Lindl.) Baker
   エクメア・ファシアータ

9 *Cirsium purpuratum* (Maxim.)
   Matsum.
   アザミ・フジアザミ

10 *Heliconia vellerigera* 'She Kong'
    ヘリコニア［シーコング］

11 *Curcuma alismatifolia*
    'Saim Crown'
    クルクマ［サイアムクラウン］

12 *Nepenthes* 'Rebecca Soper'
    ネペンテス［レベッカソーパー］

13 *Phalaenopsis* 'Ringo White'
    ファレノプシス［リンゴホワイト］

14 *Dahlia* 'Namahage Purple'
    ダリア［NAMAHAGEパープル
    （なまはげぱーぷる）］

15 *Epidendrum secundum* 'Red 5'
    エピデンドラム［赤5（あかご）］

16 *Zinnia* 'Profusion Double Fire'
    ジニア［プロフュージョンダブルファイヤー］

17 *Ageratum houstonianum*
    'Top Blue'
    アゲラタム［トップブルー］

18 *Echinopsis tubiflora* (Pfeiff.)
    Zucc. ex K. Schum.
    サボテン［火星丸（かせいまる）］

19 *Protea cynaroides* 'Arctic Ice'
    プロテア・キングプロテア［アークティックアイス］

20 *Begonia bowerae* var. *nigramarga*
    Ziesenh.
    ベゴニア・ボウエレ・ニグラマルガ

06   p. 329

1 *Tulipa turkestanica* (Regel) Regel
   チューリップ・トルケスタニカ

2 *Muscari aucheri* 'Blue Magic'
   ムスカリ［ブルーマジック］

3 *Papaver nudicaule* L.
   ポピー・アイスランドポピー

4 *Smilax aspera* L.
   シオデ［イタリアンベリー］

5 *Cymbidium tracyanum* L. Castle
   シンビジューム・トラシアナム

6 *Gleichenia japonica* Spr.
   ウラジロゼンマイ

7 *Fritillaria camschatcensis* (L.)
   Ker-Gawl.
   フリチラリア・クロユリ

8 *Paphiopedilum* Maudiae
   'The Queen'
   パフィオペディラム・モーディエ
   ［クイーン］

9 *Moluccella laevis* L.
   モルセラ・ラエヴィス

10 *Anthurium andreanum* 'Midori'
    アンスリウム［ミドリ］

11 *Cyathea spinulosa* Wall. ex
    Hook.
    ヘゴゼンマイ

12 *Chrysanthemum × morifolium*
    'Amarantha'
    キク［アマランサ］

07　　　　p. 331
—

1　*Haworthia fasciata*
　'Juni no Maki'
　ハオルチア［十二の巻（じゅうにのまき）］

2　*Dahlia* 'Nekkyu'
　ダリア［熱球（ねっきゅう）］

3　*Begonia bowerae* var. *nigramarga*
　Ziesenh.
　ベゴニア・ボウエレ・ニグラマルガ

4　*Celosia argentea* var. *cristata*
　'Bombay Pink'
　ケイトウ［ボンベイピンク］

5　*Phytolacca americana* L.
　ヨウシュヤマゴボウ

6　*Zygopetalum* Redvale 'Fire Kiss'
　ジゴペタラム・レッドベイル［ファイヤーキス］

7　*Phalaenopsis* 'Wedding Promenade'
　ファレノプシス［ウェディングプロムナード］

8　*Tillandsia tectorum* E. Morren
　チランジア・テクトラム

9　*Aloe arborescens* Mill.
　アロエ・キダチアロエ

10　*Sarracenia* 'Juthatip Soper'
　サラセニア［ジュサティップソーパー］

11　*Kniphofia uvaria* 'First Sunrise'
　トリトマ［ファーストサンライズ］

12　*Cymbidium* 'Cappuccino'
　シンビジューム［カプチーノ］

13　*Dahlia* 'Jessie Rita'
　ダリア［ジェシーリタ］

14　*Gentiana triflora* var. *japonica*
　'Hatsukansetsu Love'
　リンドウ
　［初冠雪ラブ（はつかんせつらぶ）］

15　*Gerbera* 'Petit Akane'
　ガーベラ［プチアカネ］

16　*Scabiosa atropurpurea*
　'Ace of Spades'
　スカビオサ［エースオブスペード］

17　*Cirsium purpurayum* (Maxim.)
　Matsum.
　アザミ・フジアザミ

18　*Aranda* 'Green Tiger'
　アランダ［グリーンタイガー］

19　*Paphiopedilum*
　'Hsinying Rubyweb'
　パフィオペディラム
　［シンインルビーウェブ］

20　*Pilea involucrata* 'Moon Valley'
　ピレア［ムーンバレー］

21　*Dahlia* 'Pechka'
　ダリア［ペチカ］

22　*Lilium concolor* Salisb.
　ユリ・チョウセンヒメユリ

23　*Leycesteria formosa* Wall.
　レイシェステリア・フォルモーサ

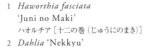

08　　　　p. 333
—

1　*Dahlia* 'Blue Peach'
　ダリア［ブルーピーチ］

2　*Cryptanthus bivittatus*
　'Pink Starlight'
　クリプタンサス［ピンクスターライト］

3　*Epidendrum secundum*
　'Pink Flamingo'
　エピデンドラム［ピンクフラミンゴ］

4　*Tillandsia tectorum* E. Morren
　チランジア・テクトラム

5　*Fritillaria meleagris* L.
　フリチラリア・メレアグリス

6　*Lachenalia aloides* var. *quadricolor*
　ラケナリア・アロイデス・クアドリカラー

7　*Tulipa polychroma* Stapf
　チューリップ・ポリクロマ

8　*Narcissus* 'Sweetness'
　スイセン［スイートネス］

9　*Papaver nudicaule* L.
　ポピー・アイスランドポピー

10　*Dendrobium* King Zip
　'Red Splash'
　デンドロビューム・キングジップ
　［レッドスプラッシュ］

11　*Anthurium andreanum*
　'ARCS Purple'
　アンスリウム［ARCSパープル
　（えーあーるしーえすぱーぷる）］

09   p. 335

1 *Nepenthes* 'Rebecca Soper'
   ネペンテス［レベッカソーパー］
2 *Aloe jucunda* Reynolds
   アロエ・ジュクンダ
3 *Passiflora caerulea* 'Clear Sky'
   トケイソウ［クリアスカイ］
4 *Rhipsalis ewaldiana*
   Barthlott & N. P. Taylor
   リプサリス・エワルディアナ
5 *Protea nana* (Berg.) Thunb.
   プロテア・ナナ
6 *Neoregelia* 'Fireball'
   ネオレゲリア［ファイヤーボール］
7 *Sarracenia purpurea* L.
   サラセニア・プルプレア
8 *Paeonia lactiflora* 'Paula Fay'
   シャクヤク［ポーラフェイ］
9 *Doryanthes excelsa* Correa
   ガイミアリリー
10 *Musa minor* Nakai
   バショウ［キングバナナ］
11 *Eremurus stenophyllus*
   (Boiss. & Buhse) Baker
   エルムレス

12 *Fittonia verschaffeltii*
   'Sunny Red'
   フィットニア［サニーレッド］
13 *Paphiopedilum lawrenceanum*
   (Rchb. f.) Pfitzer
   パフィオペディラム・ローレンセアナム
14 *Iris germanica* 'Miami Beach'
   アヤメ・ジャーマンアイリス
   ［マイアミビーチ］
15 *Disocactus flagelliformis* (L.)
   Barthlott
   サボテン［金紐（きんひも）］
16 *Strelitzia reginae* Aiton
   ストレリチア・レギネ
17 *Aphelandra squarrosa* 'Dania'
   アフェランドラ［ダニア］
18 *Paphiopedilum* 'St. Swithin'
   パフィオペディラム［セントスイシン］
19 *Asarum minamitanianum*
   'Ryokuho'
   オナガカンアオイ［緑鵬（りょくほう）］

10   pp. 336–337

1 *Tillandsia xerographica* Rohweder
   チランジア・キセログラフィカ
2 *Euphorbia lactea* Haw.
   ユーフォルビア・ラクティア
3 *Dianthus caryophyllus* 'Master'
   カーネーション［マスター］
4 *Gerbera* 'Petit Akane'
   ガーベラ［プチアカネ］
5 *Kniphofia uvaria* 'Bees' Lemon'
   トリトマ［ビーズレモン］
6 *Gentiana triflora* var. *japonica*
   'Ashiro no Banshu'
   リンドウ
   ［安代の晩秋（あしろのばんしゅう）］
7 *Paphiopedilum spicerianum*
   (Rchb. f) Pfitzer
   パフィオペディラム・スピセリアナム
8 *Sansevieria phillipsiae* N. E. Br.
   サンスベリア・フィリップシアエ
9 *Echeveria shaviana* Walther
   エケベリア・シャビアナ

10 *Epidendrum secundum* 'Red 5'
   エピデンドラム［赤5（あかご）］
11 *Curcuma alismatifolia* 'Pink Pearl'
   クルクマ［ピンクパール］
12 *Kniphofia uvaria* 'First Sunrise'
   トリトマ［ファーストサンライズ］
13 *Cereus jamacaru* DC.
   サボテン［ヤマカル柱（やまかるちゅう）］
14 *Sarracenia* 'Excellens'
   サラセニア［エクセレンス］
15 *Tagetes erecta* 'Zenith Red'
   マリーゴールド［ゼニスレッド］
16 *Celosia argentea* var. *cristata*
   'Kurume Akajiku'
   ケイトウ［クルメアカジク］
17 *Dianthus caryophyllus*
   'Lion King'
   カーネーション［ライオンキング］
18 *Eustoma grandiflorum*
   'Celeb Blue'
   トルコキキョウ［セレブブルー］

11   pp. 338–339

1 *Cyathea spinulosa* Wall. ex Hook.
   ヘゴゼンマイ
2 *Clematis* L.
   クレマチスの実
3 *Tillandsia caput-medusae* E. Morren
   チランジア・カプトメデューサ
4 *Banksia menziesii* R. Br.
   バンクシア・メーンジーシー
5 *Agapanthus africanus* (L.) Hoffmanns.
   アガパンサスの実
6 *Rhaphiolepis indica* (L.) Lindl. ex Ker
   var. *umbellata* (Thunb.) H.Ohashi
   シャリンバイの実

7 *Chrysanthemum × morifolium*
   'Feeling'
   キク［ヒーリング］
8 *Ornithogalum thyrsoides* Jacq.
   オーニソガラム・シルソイデス
9 *Eucalyptus* 'Trumpet'
   ユーカリ［トランペット］
10 *Zinnia elegans* 'Queen Lime'
   ジニア［クイーンライム］
11 *Leycesteria formosa* Wall.
   レイシェステリア・フォルモーサ

12   pp. 340–341

1 *Cynara scolymus* L.
   アーティチョーク
2 *Clematis integrifolia* 'Hendersonii'
   クレマチス［ヘンダーソニー］
3 *Paphiopedilum dianthum*
   Tang & F. T. Wang
   パフィオペディラム・ディアンサム
4 *Begonia venosa* Skan ex Hook. f.
   ベゴニア・ベノーサ

5 *Hydrangea macrophylla*
   'Glowing Alps Purple'
   アジサイ
   ［グローイングアルプスパープル］
6 *Nigella damascena*
   'Persian Jewels'
   ニゲラ［ペルシャンジュエル］

13   pp. 342–343

1 *Cymbidium* Enzan Forest 'Majolica'
   シンビジューム・エンザンフォレスト
   ［マジョリカ］
2 *Curcuma alismatifolia* 'Siam Crown'
   クルクマ［サイアムクラウン］
3 *Celosia argentea* var. *cristata*
   'Kurume Gold'
   ケイトウ［クルメゴールド］
4 *Lobelia sessilifolia* Lamb.
   サワギキョウ
5 *Anemone hupehensis*
   'Pretty Lady Diana'
   シュウメイギク［プリティーレディーダイアナ］
6 *Zingiber zerumbet*
   'Shampoo Ginger'
   ジンジャー［シャンプージンジャー］
7 *Dianthus caryophyllus* 'Anthony'
   カーネーション［アンソニー］

8 *Dahlia* 'Nekkyu'
   ダリア［熱球（ねっきゅう）］
9 *Lycoris incarnata*
   Comes ex Sprenger
   リコリス・インカルナータ
10 *Guzmania* 'Orangeade'
   グズマニア［オレンジエード］
11 *Paphiopedilum parishii*
   (Rchb. f.) Stein
   パフィオペディラム・パリシー
12 *Protea barbigera* 'Niobe'
   プロテア［ニオベ］
13 *Clivia miniata* (Lindl.)
   Verschaff.
   クンシラン・ミニアータ
14 *Cymbidium* 'Romance'
   シンビジウム［ロマンス］

14 pp. 344–345

1 *Gentiana triflora* var. *japonica*
'Hatsukansetsu Love'
リンドウ［初冠雪ラブ（はつかんせつらぶ）］
2 *Dahlia* 'Jessie Rita'
ダリア［ジェシーリタ］
3 *Haemanthus albiflos* Jacq.
ハエマンサス・マユハケオモト
4 *Chaenomeles speciosa* (Sweet)
Nakai
ボケ
5 *Dahlia* 'Wizard of Oz'
ダリア
［オズの魔法使い（おずのまほうつかい）］
6 *Celastrus orbiculatus* Thunb. var.
orbiculatus
ツルウメモドキ
7 *Nigella damascena* 'Persian Jewels'
ニゲラ［ペルシャンジュエル］
8 *Chrysanthemum* × *morifolium* 'Yo'
キク［陽（よう）］

9 *Dahlia* 'Lalala'
ダリア［ラ・ラ・ラ］
10 *Lilium orientalis* 'Asuka'
ユリ［明日香（あすか）］
11 *Dahlia* 'Fukuju'
ダリア［福寿（ふくじゅ）］
12 *Veronica* 'Smart Bizarre'
ベロニカ［スマートビザーレ］
13 *Chrysanthemum* × *morifolium*
'Feeling Green'
キク［フィーリンググリーン］
14 *Dianthus barbatus* 'Green Trick'
ナデシコ［グリーントリュフ］
15 *Narcissus tazetta* var. *chinensis*
M. Roem.
スイセン・ニホンズイセン

15 pp. 346–347

1 *Dahlia* 'Agitato'
ダリア［アジタート］
2 *Zinnia elegans* 'Dreamland Scarlet'
ジニア［ドリームランドスカーレット］
3 *Rosa* 'Samurai'
バラ［サムライ］
4 *Dahlia* 'Asahi Temari'
ダリア［朝日てまり（あさひてまり）］
5 *Epidendrum secundum* 'Red 5'
エピデンドラム［赤5（あかご）］
6 *Sterculia monosperma* Vent.
ピンポンノキの実
7 *Heliconia stricta* 'Firebird'
ヘリコニア［ファイヤーバード］

8 *Dahlia* 'Nekkyu'
ダリア［熱球（ねっきゅう）］
9 *Guzmania* 'Cherry'
グズマニア［チェリー］
10 *Sarracenia* 'Scarlet Bell'
サラセニア［スカーレットベル］
11 *Viburnum opulus* 'Compactum'
ビバーナム［コンパクタ］
12 *Begonia rex* 'Inca Night'
ベゴニア・レックスベゴニア
［インカナイト］

16   pp. 348–349

1 *Ganoderma applanatum*
  (Pers.) Pat.
  コフキサルノコシカケ

2 *Amaranthus cruentus* 'Shidare Keito'
  アマランサス [シダレケイトウ]

3 *Dahlia* 'Biedermannsdorf'
  ダリア [ビーデルマンズドルフ]

4 *Nepenthes alata* Blanco
  ネペンテス・アラータ

5 *Disporum sessile* (Thunb.) D. Don
  ex Schult. & Schult. f.
  キバナホウチャクソウ

6 *Zingiber spectabile* 'Golden Shampoo'
  ジンジャー [ゴールデンシャンプー]

7 *Chrysanthemum* × *morifolium*
  'Fuego'
  キク [フエゴ]

8 *Zinnia elegans*
  'Queen Red Lime'
  ジニア [クイーンレッドライム]

9 *Kniphofia uvaria*
  'First Sunrise'
  トリトマ [ファーストサンライズ]

10 *Celosia argentea* var. *cristata*
   'Brown Beauty'
   ケイトウ [ブラウンビューティー]

11 *Zantedeschia aethiopica* 'Mango'
   カラー [マンゴ]

12 *Sarracenia* 'Maroon'
   サラセニア [マルーン]

13 *Sedum telephium* 'Matrona'
   セダム [マトロナ]

17   pp. 350–351

1 *Dahlia* 'Show N Tell'
  ダリア [ショーンテル]

2 *Cycas revoluta* Thunb.
  ソテツの実

3 *Glycine max* (L.) Merr.
  セッカダイズ

4 *Gloriosa superba* 'Carsonii'
  グロリオサ [カルソニー]

5 *Dahlia* 'Beautiful Days'
  ダリア [ビューティフルデイズ]

6 *Guzmania* 'Torch'
  グズマニア [トーチ]

7 *Nerine sarniensis* 'Red Admiral'
  ネリネ [レッドアドミラル]

8 *Celosia argentea* var. *cristata*
  'Early Rose'
  ケイトウ [アーリーローズ]

9 *Kniphofia uvaria* 'Bees' Lemon'
  トリトマ [ビーズレモン]

10 *Rosa* 'Exciting Meilland'
   バラ [エキサイティングメイアン]

11 *Gentiana triflora* var.
   japonica 'Hakuju'
   リンドウ [白寿 (はくじゅ)]

12 *Dahlia* 'Strawberry Cream'
   ダリア [ストロベリークリーム]

13 *Veronica* 'Smart Bizarre'
   ベロニカ [スマートビザーレ]

14 *Gerbera* 'Dakar'
   ガーベラ [ダカール]

18　　pp. 352–353

1 *Anemone hupehensis* var. *japonica*
'Honorine Jobert'
シュウメイギク［オノリーヌジョベール］

2 *Dianthus caryophyllus* 'Siberia'
カーネーション［シベリア］

3 *Protea mundii* 'Little Lady White'
プロテア［リトルレディホワイト］

4 *Argyreia nervosa* (Burm. f.) Bojer
ギンヨウアサガオ

5 *Lilium longiflorum* 'Pure Horn'
ユリ・テッポウユリ［ピュアホルン］

6 *Zantedeschia aethiopica*
'Crystal Blush'
カラー［クリスタルブラッシュ］

7 *Milla biflora* Cav.
ミラビフローラ

8 *Dahlia* 'Kamakura'
ダリア［かまくら］

9 *Eucharis* × *grandiflora*
Planch. & Linden
ユーチャリス

10 *Schinus terebinthifolius*
'Pepper Berry'
サンショウモドキ［ペッパーベリー］

11 *Colchicum autumnale* 'Alba'
コルチカム［アルバ］

12 *Nerine bowdenii* 'Bianca Perla'
ネリネ［ビアンカパーラ］

13 *Mammillaria hahniana*
Werderm.
サボテン［玉翁（たまおきな）］

19　　pp. 354–355

1 *Phalaenopsis* 'Wedding Promenade'
ファレノプシス［ウェディングプロムナード］

2 *Anthurium andreanum* 'Sonata'
アンスリウム［ソナタ］

3 *Nerine bowdenii* 'Favourite'
ネリネ［フェイバリット］

4 *Phalaenopsis* Taida Salu
'Azuki Chocolat'
ファレノプシス・タイダソリュー
［あずきしょこら］

5 *Celosia argentea* var. *cristata*
'Rose Queen'
ケイトウ［ローズクイーン］

6 *Physostegia virginiana* (L.) Benth.
ハナトラノオ

7 *Protea cynaroides* 'Red Rex'
プロテア・キングプロテア
［レッドレックス］

8 *Dahlia* 'Ms. Zelda'
ダリア［ミスゼルダ］

9 *Aechmea fasciata* (Lindl.) Baker
エクメア・ファシャータ

10 *Hydrangea macrophylla* 'Rosita'
アジサイ［ロシタ］

11 *Gerbera* 'Petit Akane'
ガーベラ［プチアカネ］

20   pp. 356–357
—

1 *Platycerium bifurcatum*
(Cav.) C. Chr.
ビカクシダ・コウモリラン

2 *Synurus pungens* (Franch. et Sav.)
Kitam.
オヤマボクチ

3 *Zantedeschia aethiopica*
'Schwarzwalder'
カラー［シュワルツワルダー］

4 *Paphiopedilum* Maudiae
'Black Jack'
パフィオペディラム・モーディエ
［ブラックジャック］

5 *Echeveria* 'Black Prince'
エケベリア［ブラックプリンス］

6 *Cynara scolymus* L.
アーティチョーク

7 *Leucadendron rubrum*
'Plumosus'
リューカデントロン［プルモサス］

21   pp. 358–359
—

1 *Dianthus caryophyllus*
'Hermès Orange'
カーネーション［エルメスオレンジ］

2 *Albuca spiralis* 'Frizzle Sizzle'
アルブカ・スピラリス［フリズルシズル］

3 *Hyacinthus orientalis* 'Woodstock'
ヒヤシンス［ウッドストック］

4 *Tulipa* 'Alexandra'
チューリップ［アレキサンドラ］

5 *Tulipa* 'Tete a Tete'
チューリップ［ティタティタ］

6 *Narcissus tazetta* var. *chinensis*
M. Roem.
スイセン・ニホンズイセン

7 *Massonia pustulata* Jacq.
マッソニア・プスツラータ

8 *Anemone coronaria*
'Saint Bridget Rose'
アネモネ［セントブリジットローズ］

9 *Ranunculus asiaticus* 'Gironde'
ラナンキュラス［ジロンド］

10 *Cyrtanthus mackenii*
'Scarlet'
キルタンサス［スカーレット］

11 *Tulipa* 'Monte Spider'
チューリップ［モンテスパイダー］

12 *Hyacinthus orientalis*
'Purple Star'
ヒヤシンス［パープルスター］

13 *Hippeastrum papilio* (Ravenna)
Van Scheepen
アマリリス・パピリオ

14 *Gerbera* 'Voldemort'
ガーベラ［ヴォルデモート］

15 *Anthurium andreanum*
'Rock Set'
アンスリウム［ロックセット］

16 *Bessera elegans* Schult. f.
ベッセラ・エレガンス

17 *Ranunculus asiaticus* 'Sisteron'
ラナンキュラス［シストロン］

18 *Dendrochilum propinquum*
Ames
デンドロキラム・プロピンクューム

19 *Tulipa* 'Flash Point'
チューリップ［フラッシュポイント］

20 *Tulipa* 'Exotic Parrot'
チューリップ［エキゾチックパーロット］

22   pp. 360–361

1 *Anthurium andreanum* 'Midori'
アンスリウム［ミドリ］
2 *Dianthus barbatus* 'Green Trick'
ナデシコ［グリーントリュフ］
3 *Iris domestica* Goldblatt & Mabb.
ヒオウギの実
4 *Aloe arborescens* Mill.
アロエ・キダチアロエ
5 *Alocasia* 'Amazonica'
アロカシア［アマゾニカ］

6 *Amaranthus caudatus* 'Viridis'
アマランサス［ハンギンググリーン］
7 *Paphiopedilum druryi* (Bedd.)
Stein
パフィオペディラム・ドルーリ
8 *Globba winitii* 'Green Dragon'
グロッバ［グリーンドラゴン］
9 *Gymnocalycium saglionis* (Cels)
Britton et Rose.
サボテン［新天地（しんてんち）］
10 *Philodendron selloum* K. Koch
フィロデンドロン・セローム

23   pp. 362–363

1 *Hydrangea macrophylla*
'Frau Nobuko'
アジサイ［フラウノブコ］
2 *Allium schubertii* Zucc.
アリウム・シュベルティ
3 *Dahlia* 'Moon Stone'
ダリア［ムーンストーン］
4 *Phalaenopsis* 'Ching Ann Diamond'
ファレノプシス［チンアンダイヤモンド］
5 *Freesia enkelbloemig* 'Blue Heaven'
フリージア［ブルーヘブン］

6 *Euphorbia lactea* Haw.
ユーフォルビア・ラクティア
7 *Salvia leucantha* Cav.
サルビア・レウカンサ
8 *Gerbera* 'New Madness'
ガーベラ［ニューマッドネス］
9 *Eustoma grandiflorum*
'Voyage Blue'
トルコキキョウ［ボヤージュブルー］

Index of Flower Names

ア		掲載ページ
アーティチョーク	*Cynara scolymus* L.	33　115　122　180　234　292　294　340　357
アーポフィラム・ギガンテウム	*Arpophyllum giganteum* Hartw. ex Lindl.	21　265
アエオニウム［黒法師（くろほうし）］	*Aeonium arboreum* 'Zwartkop'	293
アガパンサス［オーシャンブルー］	*Agapanthus africanus* 'Ocean Blue'	298
アガパンサス［ジューンブライド］	*Agapanthus africanus* 'June Bride'	122
アガパンサス［ブルーヘブン］	*Agapanthus africanus* 'Blue Heaven'	184
アガパンサス［紫式部（むらさきしきぶ）］	*Agapanthus africanus* 'Murasaki Shikibu'	208
アガパンサス［ロイヤルブルー］	*Agapanthus africanus* 'Royal Blue'	141　230
アガパンサスの実	*Agapanthus africanus* (L.) Hoffmanns.	180　339
アガベ［雷神（らいじん）］	*Agave potatorum* 'Raijin'	189
アクイレギア［イエロークイーン］	*Aquilegia chrysantha* 'Yellow Queen'	170
アクイレギア［ウィンキーブルー］	*Aquilegia vulgaris* 'Winky Blue'	295
アゲラタム［トップブルー］	*Ageratum houstonianum* 'Top Blue'	162　282　327
アゲラタム［ブルーハワイ］	*Ageratum houstonianum* 'Blue Hawaii'	194
アザミ・ノアザミ	*Cirsium japonicum* Fisch. ex DC.	212
アザミ・フジアザミ	*Cirsium purpuratum* (Maxim.) Matsum.	327　331
アジサイ［ありがとう］	*Hydrangea* 'Arigato'	231
アジサイ［インマクラータ］	*Hydrangea macrophylla* 'Immaculata'	198
アジサイ［グローイングアルプスパープル］	*Hydrangea macrophylla* 'Glowing Alps Purple'	341
アジサイ［シビラクラシックブルー］	*Hydrangea macrophylla* 'Sibylla Classic Blue'	150
アジサイ［ババリア］	*Hydrangea macrophylla* 'Bavaria'	214
アジサイ［ハワイアンブルー］	*Hydrangea macrophylla* 'Hawaiian Blue'	130
アジサイ［ファーストブルー］	*Hydrangea macrophylla* 'First Blue'	210
アジサイ［フラウノブコ］	*Hydrangea macrophylla* 'Frau Nobuko'	362
アジサイ［ブルーアース］	*Hydrangea macrophylla* 'Blue Earth'	284
アジサイ［ブルーフレッシュ］	*Hydrangea macrophylla* 'Blue Fresh'	163
アジサイ［ヘイズスターバースト］	*Hydrangea arborescens* 'Hayes Starburst'	125
アジサイ［ホットレッド］	*Hydrangea macrophylla* 'Hot Red'	265
アジサイ［マジカルグリーンファイヤー］	*Hydrangea macrophylla* 'Magical Green Fire'	190　208
アジサイ［マジカルビーレッド］	*Hydrangea macrophylla* 'Magical Ruby Red'	302
アジサイ［マジカルレボリューションブルー］	*Hydrangea macrophylla* 'Magical Revolution Blue'	184
アジサイ［マリンブルー］	*Hydrangea macrophylla* 'Marine Blue'	167　300
アジサイ［ユーミートゥギャザーピンク］	*Hydrangea macrophylla* 'You and Me Together Pink'	279
アジサイ［ロシタ］	*Hydrangea macrophylla* 'Rosita'	355
アスコセンダ［ムァントン］	*Ascocenda* 'Muang Thong'	247
アスター［あずみローズピンク］	*Callistephus chinensis* 'Azumi Rose Pink'	166
アスター［シャギーディープブルー］	*Callistephus chinensis* 'Shaggy Deep Blue'	221
アスター［シャギーピンクフラッシュ］	*Callistephus chinensis* 'Shaggy Pink Flash'	124　134
アスター［ステラレッド］	*Callistephus chinensis* 'Stella Red'	257
アスチルベ［アメリカ］	*Astilbe* × *arendsii* 'America'	158　213
アスチルベ［パステルピンク］	*Astilbe* × *arendsii* 'Pastel Pink'	191
アスチルベ［ファナル］	*Astilbe* × *arendsii* 'Fanal'	213
アセビ	*Pieris japonica* (Thunb.) D. Don ex G. Don	189
アデナントス・キャニングハーミー	*Adenanthos* × *cunninghamii* Meisn.	161
アネモネ［セントブリジットローズ］	*Anemone coronaria* 'Saint Bridget Rose'	314　358
アフェランドラ［ダニア］	*Aphelandra squarrosa* 'Dania'	335
アマランサス［シダレケイトウ］	*Amaranthus cruentus* 'Shidare Keito'	348
アマランサス［ハンギンググリーン］	*Amaranthus caudatus* 'Viridis'	134　361
アマリリス［クリスマスギフト］	*Hippeastrum* × *hybridum* 'Christmas Gift'	175
アマリリス［スーザン］	*Hippeastrum* × *hybridum* 'Susan'	290
アマリリス［ダブルリボン］	*Hippeastrum* × *hybridum* 'Double Ribbon'	283
アマリリス［ブラックバッカラ］	*Hippeastrum* × *hybridum* 'Black Baccara'	154
アマリリス［マジックグリーン］	*Hippeastrum* × *hybridum* 'Magic Green'	166
アマリリス［ミネルヴァ］	*Hippeastrum* × *hybridum* 'Minerva'	282
アマリリス［レッドピーコック］	*Hippeastrum* × *hybridum* 'Red Peacock'	292
アマリリス［レッドライオン］	*Hippeastrum* × *hybridum* 'Red Lion'	93　228　265
アマリリス［ロイヤルベルベット］	*Hippeastrum* × *hybridum* 'Royal Velvet'	301

アマリリス・カリプトゥラタ	Hippeastrum calyptratum (Ker Gawl.) Herb.	300				
アマリリス・コリエンシス	Hippeastrum correiense (Bury) Worsley	33				
アマリリス・パピリオ	Hippeastrum papilio (Ravenna) Van Scheepen	290	359			
アマリリス・ブロスフェルディアエ	Hippeastrum blossfeldiae (Traub & J. L. Doran) Van Scheepen	192				
アヤメ・オクラレルカ	Iris spuria subsp. ochroleuca (L.) Dykes	37				
アヤメ・ジャーマンアイリス［ウエンチ］	Iris germanica 'Wench'	95				
アヤメ・ジャーマンアイリス［スタニング］	Iris germanica 'Stunning'	323				
アヤメ・ジャーマンアイリス［ダスキーチャレンジャー］	Iris germanica 'Dusky Challenger'	79				
アヤメ・ジャーマンアイリス［マイアミビーチ］	Iris germanica 'Miami Beach'	335				
アヤメ・ダッチアイリス［ブルーマジック］	Iris × hollandica 'Blue Magic'	156	170	195	210	215
		263	271	281	307	310
アヤメ・ダッチアイリス［ブルーダイヤモンド］	Iris × hollandica 'Blue Diamond'	45	292			
アランダ［グリーンタイガー］	Aranda 'Green Tiger'	269	331			
アリウム［コワニー］	Allium neapolitanum 'Cowanii'	199				
アリウム［パープルセンセーション］	Allium hollandicum 'Purple Sensation'	213	221			
アリウム［ピノキオ］	Allium 'Pinocchio'	71	234			
アリウム［ブルーパフューム］	Allium 'Blue Perfume'	163	210			
アリウム［レッドモヒカン］	Allium amethystinum 'Red Mohican'	113	141	223	321	
アリウム・ギガンジューム	Allium giganteum Regel	214	263	299		
アリウム・ギガンジュームの実	Allium giganteum Regel	152				
アリウム・シュベルティ	Allium schubertii Zucc.	283	298	362		
アルストロメリア［スコーピオン］	Alstroemeria 'Scorpion'	196	204	271		
アルストロメリア［セサミオレンジ］	Alstroemeria 'Sesame Orange'	165				
アルブカ・スピラリス［フリズルシズル］	Albuca spiralis 'Frizzle Sizzle'	285	358			
アロエ［フラミンゴ］	Aloe 'Flamingo'	25	177			
アロエ［レッドデビル］	Aloe 'Red Devil'	287				
アロエ・キダチアロエ	Aloe arborescens Mill.	331	360			
アロエ・ジュクンダ	Aloe jucunda Reynolds	323	335			
アロカシア［アマゾニカ］	Alocasia 'Amazonica'	360				
アロカシア・シマクワズイモ	Alocasia cucullata (Lour.) G. Don	278				
アンスリウム［アミーゴ］	Anthurium andreanum 'Amigo'	139				
アンスリウム［アルーラピンク］	Anthurium andreanum 'Alula Pink'	65				
アンスリウム［アレキシアジェイド］	Anthurium andreanum 'Alexia Jade'	216				
アンスリウム［ARCS パープル（えーあーるしーえすぱーぷる）］	Anthurium andreanum 'ARCS Purple'	127	230	333		
アンスリウム［エンペラー］	Anthurium andreanum 'Emperor'	302	308			
アンスリウム［カラパナ］	Anthurium andreanum 'Kalapana'	144				
アンスリウム［サファリ］	Anthurium andreanum 'Safari'	106	150	196	283	286
アンスリウム［シエラマジック］	Anthurium andreanum 'Sierra Magic'	101				
アンスリウム［ジャングルキング］	Anthurium crassinervium 'Jungle King'	292				
アンスリウム［ジュピター］	Anthurium andreanum 'Jupiter'	278	306			
アンスリウム［スパイス］	Anthurium andreanum 'Spice'	310				
アンスリウム［ソナタ］	Anthurium andreanum 'Sonata'	354				
アンスリウム［トリニダ］	Anthurium andreanum 'Trinidad'	133				
アンスリウム［トロピカルレッド］	Anthurium andreanum 'Tropical Red'	90	280			
アンスリウム［バーガンディ］	Anthurium andreanum 'Burgundy'	154				
アンスリウム［フェスカ］	Anthurium andreanum 'Fesca'	212				
アンスリウム［フォレスト］	Anthurium andreanum 'Forest'	194				
アンスリウム［フューシャグリーン］	Anthurium andreanum 'Fuchsia Green'	55				
アンスリウム［ブラッククイーン］	Anthurium andreanum 'Black Queen'	187	200	265	297	302
アンスリウム［プレビア］	Anthurium andreanum 'Previa'	166	215			
アンスリウム［マキシマベルデ］	Anthurium andreanum 'Maxima Verde'	226				
アンスリウム［ミドリ］	Anthurium andreanum 'Midori'	329	360			
アンスリウム［レディージェーン］	Anthurium andreanum 'Lady Jane'	274				
アンスリウム［ローザ］	Anthurium andreanum 'Rosa'	314				
アンスリウム［ロックセット］	Anthurium andreanum 'Rock Set'	359				
アンスリウム・クラリネルヴィウム	Anthurium clarinervium Matuda	129				
アンスリウム・ロンギフォリウム	Anthurium longifolium (Hoffm.) G. Don	227	232	321		

イ・ウ

イソギク	Chrysanthemum pacificum Nakai	200	
イブキ［真柏（しんぱく）］	Juniperus chinensis var. sargentii	24	45
ウラシマソウ	Arisaema urashima Hara	309	

| ウラシマソウの実 | *Arisaema urashima* Hara | 109 | | | | |
| ウラジロゼンマイ | *Gleichenia japonica* Spr. | 216 | 329 | | | |

エ

エキナセア［エキセントリック］	*Echinacea purpurea* 'Eccentric'	213				
エキナセア［ハーベストムーン］	*Echinacea purpurea* 'Harvest Moon'	321				
エキナセア［ピンクパッション］	*Echinacea purpurea* 'Pink Passion'	152				
エキナセア［ホットパパイヤ］	*Echinacea purpurea* 'Hot Papaya'	123	248			
エクメア［スカーレットベリー］	*Aechmea wittmackiana* 'Scarlet Berry'	129				
エクメア［デルマー］	*Aechmea fendleri* 'Del Mar'	34				
エクメア［ホワイトベリー］	*Aechmea penduliflora* 'White Berry'	152				
エクメア［レッドベリー］	*Aechmea fulgens* 'Red Berry'	171				
エクメア・ガモセパラ	*Aechmea gamosepala* Wittm.	314				
エクメア・ファシアータ	*Aechmea fasciata* (Lindl.) Baker	143	185	212	327	355
エケベリア［ゴルゴンズグロット］	*Echeveria* 'Gorgon's Grotto'	203				
エケベリア［七福神（しちふくじん）］	*Echeveria* 'Shichifukujin'	139	185	230		
エケベリア［相府蓮（そうふれん）］	*Echeveria* 'Sofuren'	53				
エケベリア［月影（つきかげ）］	*Echeveria* 'Tsuki Kage'	202				
エケベリア［ファンタジアキャロル］	*Echeveria* 'Fantasia Carol'	300				
エケベリア［ブラックナイト］	*Echeveria* 'Black Knight'	176				
エケベリア［ブラックプリンス］	*Echeveria* 'Black Prince'	167	235	357		
エケベリア［ヘラクレス］	*Echeveria* 'Hercules'	163				
エケベリア［ホワイトゴースト］	*Echeveria* 'White Ghost'	189				
エケベリア［メラコ］	*Echeveria* 'Melaco'	323				
エケベリア［大和美尼（やまとびに）］	*Echeveria* 'Yamatobini'	29				
エケベリア・シャビアナ	*Echeveria shaviana* Walther	337				
エケベリア・リラシナ	*Echeveria lilacina* Kimn. & Moran	162	184	223		
エピデンドラム［赤5（あかご）］	*Epidendrum secundum* 'Red 5'	186	192	196	206	212
		232	243	263	279	299
		306	310	327	337	346
エピデンドラム［イエロースター］	*Epidendrum secundum* 'Yellow Star'	218	325			
エピデンドラム［オレンジボール］	*Epidendrum secundum* 'Orange Ball'	142	164	172	214	
エピデンドラム［チドリ］	*Epidendrum secundum* 'Chidori'	201	208			
エピデンドラム［ピーカンイエロー］	*Epidendrum secundum* 'Pecan Yellow'	192				
エピデンドラム［ピーカンオレンジ］	*Epidendrum secundum* 'Pecan Orange'	180				
エピデンドラム［ピーカンレッド］	*Epidendrum secundum* 'Pecan Red'	284				
エピデンドラム［ピンクフラミンゴ］	*Epidendrum secundum* 'Pink Flamingo'	271	333			
エピデンドラム［プリンセス8（ぷりんせすえいと）］	*Epidendrum secundum* 'Princess 8'	288				
エピデンドラム［ホワイトスター］	*Epidendrum secundum* 'White Star'	242				
エピデンドラム・サンライトバレー［ハッピームーン］	*Epidendrum* Sunlight Valley 'Happy Moon'	182				
エピデンドラム・スターバレー［バイオレットクイーン］	*Epidendrum* Star Valley 'Violet Queen'	137	171			
エピデンドラム・パラソルバレー［ハツコイ］	*Epidendrum* Parasol Valley 'Hatsukoi'	158				
エピデンドラム・パラソルバレー［ミュージックボックス］	*Epidendrum* Parasol Valley 'Music Box'	190	279			
エピデンドラム・プリンセスバレー［ホワイトキャッスル］	*Epidendrum* Princess Valley 'White Castle'	199				
エピデンドラム・ワンダーバレー［ノーブルスター］	*Epidendrum* Wonder Valley 'Noble Star'	150				
エルムレス	*Eremurus stenophyllus* (Boiss. & Buhse) Baker	140	335			
エンシクリア・アデノカウラ	*Encyclia adenocaula* (Lex.) Schltr.	245				
エンドウマメ	*Pisum sativum* L.	215				

オ

オウゴンヤグルマギク	*Centaurea macrocephala* Muss. Puschk. ex Willd.	131		
オーニソガラム・シルソイデス	*Ornithogalum thyrsoides* Jacq.	339		
オキシペタルム［ピュアブルー］	*Oxypetalum coeruleum* 'Pure Blue'	210		
オキシペタルム［ブルースター］	*Oxypetalum coeruleum* 'Blue Star'	305		
オシダ	*Dryopteris crassirhizoma* Nakai	189	283	
オドントグロッサム・エンザンファンタジー［ルージュマジック］	*Odontoglossum* Enzan Fantasy 'Rouge Magic'	291		
オナガカンアオイ［緑鵬（りょくほう）］	*Asarum minamitanianum* 'Ryokuho'	335		
オモトの実	*Rohdea japonica* (Thunb.) Roth	286		
オヤマボクチ	*Synurus pungens* (Franch. et Sav.) Kitam.	357		
オンシジューム・トゥインクル［チャーム］	*Oncidium* Twinkle 'Charm'	311		
オンシジューム・ムーンシャドウ［タイガーテイル］	*Oncidium* Moon Shadow 'Tiger Tail'	134	224	286

カ

カーネーション [アンソニー]	Dianthus caryophyllus 'Anthony'	342				
カーネーション [エクセリア]	Dianthus caryophyllus 'Excellia'	303				
カーネーション [エルメス]	Dianthus caryophyllus 'Hermès'	325				
カーネーション [エルメスオレンジ]	Dianthus caryophyllus 'Hermès Orange'	358				
カーネーション [キロ]	Dianthus caryophyllus 'Kiro'	208				
カーネーション [クラシコ]	Dianthus caryophyllus 'Classico'	178	321			
カーネーション [クリムゾンテンポ]	Dianthus caryophyllus 'Crimson Tempo'	160				
カーネーション [ゴレム]	Dianthus caryophyllus 'Golem'	143				
カーネーション [シベリア]	Dianthus caryophyllus 'Siberia'	352				
カーネーション [シャララ]	Dianthus caryophyllus 'Sharara'	196				
カーネーション [ズリゴ]	Dianthus caryophyllus 'Zurigo'	323				
カーネーション [セイシェル]	Dianthus caryophyllus 'Seychelles'	294				
カーネーション [デュエロ]	Dianthus caryophyllus 'Duelo'	135				
カーネーション [ドンペドロ]	Dianthus caryophyllus 'Dom Pedro'	29	291			
カーネーション [ネボ]	Dianthus caryophyllus 'Nebo'	204				
カーネーション [ノビオバイオレット]	Dianthus caryophyllus 'Nobio Violet'	160				
カーネーション [ハリケーン]	Dianthus caryophyllus 'Hurricane'	205				
カーネーション [ビゼー]	Dianthus caryophyllus 'Bizet'	212				
カーネーション [プラドミント]	Dianthus caryophyllus 'Prado Mint'	194	216			
カーネーション [プリメロプルート]	Dianthus caryophyllus 'Primero Pluto'	196				
カーネーション [マスター]	Dianthus caryophyllus 'Master'	126	321	336		
カーネーション [ミーガン]	Dianthus caryophyllus 'Megan'	218				
カーネーション [ライオンキング]	Dianthus caryophyllus 'Lion King'	337				
ガーベラ [アナクレート]	Gerbera 'Anacleto'	164	180			
ガーベラ [アンティーク]	Gerbera 'Antique'	219				
ガーベラ [ヴォルデモート]	Gerbera 'Voldemort'	150	205	232	306	321
		359				
ガーベラ [クリッシング]	Gerbera 'Crissing'	273				
ガーベラ [サマータイム]	Gerbera 'Summer Time'	186				
ガーベラ [サングロー]	Gerbera 'Sun Glow'	273				
ガーベラ [サンディー]	Gerbera 'Sandy'	279				
ガーベラ [ジオ]	Gerbera 'Gio'	147	214	221	222	
ガーベラ [ジャピオ]	Gerbera 'Japio'	197				
ガーベラ [スタンザ]	Gerbera 'Stanza'	133	306			
ガーベラ [ダカール]	Gerbera 'Dakar'	351				
ガーベラ [ダブルデート]	Gerbera 'Double Date'	172				
ガーベラ [ツイスター]	Gerbera 'Twister'	208				
ガーベラ [テラアサヒ]	Gerbera 'Terra Asahi'	183	225			
ガーベラ [テラノバ]	Gerbera 'Terra Nova'	144				
ガーベラ [トマホーク]	Gerbera 'Tomahawk'	130	170	285		
ガーベラ [ナイトライダー]	Gerbera 'Knight Rider'	178				
ガーベラ [ニューマッドネス]	Gerbera 'New Madness'	363				
ガーベラ [パープルスプリングス]	Gerbera 'Purple Springs'	323				
ガーベラ [パスタディママ]	Gerbera 'Pasta di Mamma'	172	215	309		
ガーベラ [フィネッセ]	Gerbera 'Finesse'	158				
ガーベラ [プチアカネ]	Gerbera 'Petit Akane'	167	193	201	206	331
		336	355			
ガーベラ [ブラックパール]	Gerbera 'Black Pearl'	134				
ガーベラ [ミゲル]	Gerbera 'Miguel'	126				
ガーベラ [ラストダンス]	Gerbera 'Last Dance'	136				
ガーベラ [リップスティック]	Gerbera 'Lipstick'	190				
ガーベラ [レッドトリップ]	Gerbera 'Red Trip'	150				
ガイミアリリー	Doryanthes excelsa Correa	60	232	321	335	
カエンボク	Spathodea campanulata P. Beauv.	154	176	218		
カクレミノ	Dendropanax trifidus (Thunb.) Makino ex. H. Hara	175				
カトレヤ・ソフロレリオカトレヤ・ジュエルボックス [ダークウォーターズ]	Sophrolaeliocattleya Jewel Box 'Dark Waters'	222				
カトレヤ・パープルキャスケイド [フラグランスビューティ]	Cattleya Purple Cascade 'Fragrance Beauty'	275				
カトレヤ・ブラッソレリオカトレヤ・ヤンミンオレンジ [ジンマンワン]	Brassolaeliocattleya Young-Min Orange 'Jin Man 1'	274	325			
カトレヤ・リンコレリオカトレヤ・キングオブタイワン [大新 (たしん)]	Rhyncholaeliocattleya King of Taiwan 'Ta-Hsin'	276				
カトレヤ・リンコレリオカトレヤ・ソフィアノット [カヨコ]	Rhyncholaeliocattleya Sophia Knot 'Kayoko'	292				
カトレヤ・リンコレリオカトレヤ・パメラヘザリントン [コロネーション]	Rhyncholaeliocattleya Pamela Hetherington 'Coronation'	159				

カトレヤ・リンコレリオカトレヤ・ペギーオニール [ロイヤルレディー]	*Rhyncholaeliocattleya* Peggy O'Neill 'Royal Lady'	201			
カトレヤ・リンコレリオカトレヤ・メモリアヘレンブラウン [スウィートアフトン]	*Rhyncholaeliocattleya* Memoria Helen Brown 'Sweet Afton'	145			
カトレヤ・リンコレリオカトレヤ・リエズオレンジグローブ [ハーベスト]	*Rhyncholaeliocattleya* Rie's Orange Grove 'Harvest'	304			
カトレヤ・リンコレリオカトレヤ・レッドクラブ [クァンミャオ #10（くぁんみゃおなんばーてん）]	*Rhyncholaeliocattleya* Red Crab 'Kuan-Miao #10'	271			
カトレヤ・レリオカトレヤ・クーシング [マンカエン]	*Laeliocattleya* Quiseag 'Mankaen'	234			
カラー [アキーラ]	*Zantedeschia aethiopica* 'Aquila'	128			
カラー [エチオピカブレナ]	*Zantedeschia aethiopica* 'White Swan'	37	295		
カラー [オデッサ]	*Zantedeschia pentlandii* 'Odessa'	292			
カラー [ガーネットグロー]	*Zantedeschia aethiopica* 'Garnet Glow'	166	215		
カラー [キャプテンオデオン]	*Zantedeschia aethiopica* 'Captain Odeon'	164			
カラー [キャプテンデュランス]	*Zantedeschia aethiopica* 'Captain Durance'	117	141	228	
カラー [キャプテンフエゴ]	*Zantedeschia aethiopica* 'Captain Fuego'	228	286		
カラー [キャプテンプロミス]	*Zantedeschia aethiopica* 'Captain Promise'	113	141	192	
カラー [キャプテンミラージュ]	*Zantedeschia aethiopica* 'Captain Mirage'	168			
カラー [グリーンゴッデス]	*Zantedeschia aethiopica* 'Green Goddess'	23	235		
カラー [クリスタルブラッシュ]	*Zantedeschia aethiopica* 'Crystal Blush'	198	352		
カラー [ゴールデンジャイアント]	*Zantedeschia aethiopica* 'Golden Giant'	182			
カラー [ゴールドクラウン]	*Zantedeschia aethiopica* 'Gold Crown'	170			
カラー [シュワルツワルダー]	*Zantedeschia aethiopica* 'Schwarzwalder'	296	357		
カラー [ピカソ]	*Zantedeschia aethiopica* 'Picasso'	313	319		
カラー [風花（ふうか）]	*Zantedeschia aethiopica* 'Fuka'	314			
カラー [ホットショット]	*Zantedeschia aethiopica* 'Hot Shot'	172	327		
カラー [ホットチェリー]	*Zantedeschia aethiopica* 'Hot Cherry'	206			
カラー [ホットチョコレート]	*Zantedeschia aethiopica* 'Hot Chocolate'	154	176	221	
カラー [マジェスティックレッド]	*Zantedeschia aethiopica* 'Majestic Red'	166	197	212	
カラー [マンゴ]	*Zantedeschia aethiopica* 'Mango'	349			
カラー [レッドチャーム]	*Zantedeschia aethiopica* 'Red Charm'	160			
カライトソウ	*Sanguisorba hakusanensis* Makino	220			
カラジウム [スカーレットビューティー]	*Caladium* 'Scarlet Beauty'	119			
カラテア [グリーンアイス]	*Calathea cylindrica* 'Green Ice'	153	189	209	234
カラテア・クロタリフェラ	*Calathea crotalifera* S. Watson	321			
カランコエ [月兎耳（つきとじ）]	*Kalanchoe tomentosa* 'Tsukitoji'	226			
カランコエ [フラップジャック]	*Kalanchoe luciae* 'Flapjack'	160			
カランコエ [ホリー]	*Kalanchoe blossfeldiana* 'Holly'	164	172		
カランコエ・フミリス	*Kalanchoe humilis* Britten	167	168		
カランコエ・ベハレンシス	*Kalanchoe beharensis* Drake	175			
カリフラワー [ロマネスコ]	*Brassica oleracea* var. *botrytis* 'Romanesco'	194	282	305	
カルダモン	*Elettaria cardamomum* (L.) Maton	234			
カルミア [オスボレッド]	*Kalmia latifolia* 'Ostbo Red'	299			
カワラタケ	*Trametes versicolor* (L. Fr.) Quél.	157			
カンガルーポー [オレンジクロス]	*Anigozanthos flavidus* 'Orange Cross'	123			
カンガルーポー [グリーン]	*Anigozanthos flavidus* 'Green'	182	235		
カンガルーポー [レッドアンドグリーン]	*Anigozanthos flavidus* 'Red and Green'	263	291		
カンパニュラ [チャンピオンパープル]	*Campanula medium* 'Champion Purple'	263	280		

キ

キク [アナスタシアグリーン]	*Chrysanthemum* × *morifolium* 'Anastasia Green'	265				
キク [アナスタシアダークライム]	*Chrysanthemum* × *morifolium* 'Anastasia Dark Lime'	204				
キク [アマランサ]	*Chrysanthemum* × *morifolium* 'Amarantha'	329				
キク [エポック]	*Chrysanthemum* × *morifolium* 'Epoch'	159	265			
キク [エレーナ]	*Chrysanthemum* × *morifolium* 'Elena'	279				
キク [クラシックココア]	*Chrysanthemum* × *morifolium* 'Classic Cocoa'	290				
キク [グリーンシャムロック]	*Chrysanthemum* × *morifolium* 'Green Shamrock'	55	139	188	201	273 283
キク [ゴールデンピンポン]	*Chrysanthemum* × *morifolium* 'Golden Ping Pong'	182	298			
キク [サバ]	*Chrysanthemum* × *morifolium* 'Saba'	127	298			
キク [サフィーナ]	*Chrysanthemum* × *morifolium* 'Saffina'	127	290	305	327	
キク [ジェニーオレンジ]	*Chrysanthemum* × *morifolium* 'Jenny Orange'	142				
キク [スーパーピンポン]	*Chrysanthemum* × *morifolium* 'Super Ping Pong'	168				
キク [セイエチュード]	*Chrysanthemum* × *morifolium* 'Sei Etude'	284				

キク［セイオペラピンク］	Chrysanthemum × morifolium 'Say Opera Pink'	190
キク［セイナダル］	Chrysanthemum × morifolium 'Sei Nadal'	170
キク［ゼンブラブラジル］	Chrysanthemum × morifolium 'Zembla Brazil'	215　273
キク［ドラクロワ］	Chrysanthemum × morifolium 'Delacroix'	285
キク［ヒーリング］	Chrysanthemum × morifolium 'Feeling'	339
キク［ピュアグリーン］	Chrysanthemum × morifolium 'Pure Green'	188　201　217
キク［ピンクベル］	Chrysanthemum × morifolium 'Pink Bell'	190
キク［フィーリンググリーン］	Chrysanthemum × morifolium 'Feeling Green'	345
キク［フエゴ］	Chrysanthemum × morifolium 'Fuego'	263　276　321　349
キク［プリティリオ］	Chrysanthemum × morifolium 'Pretty Rio'	197　289
キク［ボンバーグリーン］	Chrysanthemum × morifolium 'Bomber Green'	174
キク［陽（よう）］	Chrysanthemum × morifolium 'Yo'	81　157　180　288　310 344
キク［ロリポップレッド］	Chrysanthemum × morifolium 'Lollipop Red'	154
キバナホウチャクソウ	Disporum sessile (Thunb.) D. Don ex Schult. & Schult. f.	348
キブシ	Stachyurus praecox Siebold et Zucc.	51
キルタンサス［キングイエロー］	Cyrtanthus mackenii 'King Yellow'	193　315
キルタンサス［スカーレット］	Cyrtanthus mackenii 'Scarlet'	358
ギンヨウアサガオ	Argyreia nervosa (Burm. f.) Bojer	352

ク

クサソテツ	Matteuccia struthiopteris (L.) Todaro	273
グズマニア［オレンジエード］	Guzmania 'Orangeade'	170　225　342
グズマニア［チェリー］	Guzmania 'Cherry'	346
グズマニア［トーチ］	Guzmania 'Torch'	151　180　301　309　351
グズマニア［ヒルダ］	Guzmania 'Hilda'	226
グズマニア［マイナーバリエガタ］	Guzmania 'Minor Variegata'	274
グズマニア・ディシティフローラ	Guzmania dissitiflora (André) L. B. Sm.	170
グラジオラス・ムリエラ	Gladiolus murielae Kelway	47
グラプトベリア［オパリナ］	Graptoveria 'Opalina'	196　231
グリーンネックレス	Senecio rowleyanus H. Jacobsen	170
クリスマスローズ［ダブルラズベリーリップル］	Helleborus 'Double Rasberry Ripple'	302
クリスマスローズ・フェチダス	Helleborus foetidus L.	267
クリプタンサス［エレーヌ］	Cryptanthus fosterianus 'Elaine'	312
クリプタンサス［ピンクスターライト］	Cryptanthus bivittatus 'Pink Starlight'	19　333
クルクマ［ヴェルデビアンコ］	Curcuma alismatifolia 'Verdebianco'	153　184
クルクマ［エターナルピンク］	Curcuma alismatifolia 'Eternal Pink'	139
クルクマ［エメラルドチョコゼブラ］	Curcuma alismatifolia 'Emerald Choco Zebra'	203　235
クルクマ［オールドローズ］	Curcuma alismatifolia 'Old Rose'	146
クルクマ［キャンディケーン］	Curcuma gracillima 'Candy Cane'	234
クルクマ［サイアムクラウン］	Curcuma alismatifolia 'Saim Crown'	206　319　327　342
クルクマ［ジュエルオブタイランド］	Curcuma cordata 'Jewel of Thailand'	34
クルクマ［ピンクパール］	Curcuma alismatifolia 'Pink Pearl'	119　337
グレビレア［ゴールデンユーロ］	Grevillea 'Golden Yu-Lo'	304
グレビレア［ハニージェム］	Grevillea 'Honey Gem'	273
クレマチス［アルバプレナ］	Clematis florida 'Alba Plena'	87
クレマチス［インスピレーション］	Clematis integrifolia 'Inspiration'	312
クレマチス［押切（おしきり）］	Clematis texensis 'Oshikiri'	190
クレマチス［クリスタルフォンテーン］	Clematis florida 'Crystal Fountain'	263
クレマチス［スカーレット］	Clematis texensis 'Scarlet'	122　131　212　263
クレマチス［ヘンダーソニー］	Clematis integrifolia 'Hendersonii'	166　341
クレマチス［マジックフォンテーン］	Clematis florida 'Magic Fountain'	147
クレマチス［ミススミレ］	Clematis integrifolia 'Miss Sumire'	130
クレマチス［ロウグチ］	Clematis integrifolia 'Rouguchi'	230
クレマチス・ソシアリス	Clematis socialis Kral	211
クレマチス・デュランディ	Clematis × durandii	288
クレマチスの実	Clematis L.	153　181　234　338
クロコスミア［ルシファー］	Crocosmia 'Lucifer'	135　142
グロッパ［グリーンドラゴン］	Globba winitii 'Green Dragon'	135　361
グロッパ［ピンクドラゴン］	Globba winitii 'Pink Dragon'	227
クロトン［曙（あけぼの）］	Codiaeum variegatum 'Akebono'	129
クロホオズキ	Nicandra physalodes Schreb.	221
グロリオサ［カルソニー］	Gloriosa superba 'Carsonii'	293　350

グロリオサ［パールホワイト］	*Gloriosa superba* 'Pearl White'	167				
グロリオサ［プレシャスパール］	*Gloriosa superba* 'Precious Pearl'	213				
グロリオサ［メイサ］	*Gloriosa superba* 'Mesa'	186				
グロリオサ［ライム］	*Gloriosa superba* 'Lime'	188				
クンシラン・ガルデニー	*Clivia gardenii* Hook.	287				
クンシラン・ミニアータ	*Clivia miniata* (Lindl.) Verschaff.	343				

ケ

ゲットウ	*Alpinia zerumbet* (Pers.) B. L. Burtt and R. M. Sm.	33	294			
ケイトウ［アーリーローズ］	*Celosia argentea* var. *cristata* 'Early Rose'	351				
ケイトウ［オレンジクイーン］	*Celosia argentea* var. *cristata* 'Orange Queen'	321				
ケイトウ［クルメアカジク］	*Celosia argentea* var. *cristata* 'Kurume Akajiku'	232	313	337		
ケイトウ［クルメゴールド］	*Celosia argentea* var. *cristata* 'Kurume Gold'	342				
ケイトウ［サカタプライド］	*Celosia argentea* var. *cristata* 'Sakata Pride'	128	160	186	208	319
ケイトウ［スプリンググリーン］	*Celosia argentea* var. *cristata* 'Spring Green'	152				
ケイトウ［ブラウンビューティー］	*Celosia argentea* var. *cristata* 'Brown Beauty'	349				
ケイトウ［ボンベイオレンジ］	*Celosia argentea* var. *cristata* 'Bombay Orange'	201				
ケイトウ［ボンベイグリーン］	*Celosia argentea* var. *cristata* 'Bombay Green'	202				
ケイトウ［ボンベイピンク］	*Celosia argentea* var. *cristata* 'Bombay Pink'	331				
ケイトウ［メロンフリル］	*Celosia argentea* var. *cristata* 'Melon Frill'	234				
ケイトウ［ローズクイーン］	*Celosia argentea* var. *cristata* 'Rose Queen'	355				

コ

コウゾリナ	*Picris hieracioides* L. subsp. *japonica* (Thunb.) Krylov	51				
ココナッツ	*Cocos nucifera* L.	173				
コショウ	*Piper nigrum* L.	184				
コスタス・ウッドソニー	*Costus woodsonii* Maas	186	234			
コノスティリス［ジョーイキャッツポー］	*Conostylis setigera* 'Joey Cat's Paw'	325				
コフキサルノコシカケ	*Ganoderma applanatum* (Pers.) Pat.	171	348			
コルチカム［アルバ］	*Colchicum autumnale* 'Alba'	353				
コルマナラ・ワイルドキャット［カルメラ］	*Colmanara* Wildcat 'Carmela'	263				
コルマナラ・ワイルドキャット［ゴールデンレッドスター］	*Colmanara* Wildcat 'Golden Red Star'	132				
コルマナラ・ワイルドキャット［ボブキャット］	*Colmanara* Wildcat 'Bobcat'	255	304			

サ

サザンカ	*Camellia sasanqua* Thunb.	49			
サボテン［赤城（あかぎ）］	*Ferocactus macrodiscus* (Mart.) Britton & Rose	171			
サボテン［黄金紐綴化（おうごんちゅうてっか）］	*Cleistocactus winteri* D. Hunt	155			
サボテン［火星丸（かせいまる）］	*Echinopsis tubiflora* (Pfeiff.) Zucc. ex K. Schum.	327			
サボテン［河内丸（かわちまる）］	*Notocactus apricus* (Arechavaleta) Berger ex Backeberg	193			
サボテン［希望丸（きぼうまる）］	*Mammillaria albilanata* Backeb.	105			
サボテン［銀翁玉（ぎんおうぎょく）］	*Eriosyce senilis* (Backeb.) Katt.	185			
サボテン［金鯱（きんしゃち）］	*Echinocactus grusonii* Hildm.	181			
サボテン［金手毬綴化（きんてまりせっか）］	*Mammillaria elongata* f. *cristata*	323			
サボテン［金紐（きんひも）］	*Disocactus flagelliformis* (L.) Barthlott	335			
サボテン［幻楽（げんらく）］	*Espostoa blossfeldiorum* (Vaupel) Borg	169			
サボテン［黄金丸（こがねまる）］	*Mammillaria elongata* DC.	202			
サボテン［新天地（しんてんち）］	*Gymnocalycium saglionis* (Cels) Britton et Rose.	361			
サボテン［翠晃冠錦（すいこうかんにしき）］	*Gymnocalycium anisitsii* (K. Schumann) Britton & Rose	164	209		
サボテン［青海波（せいがいは）］	*Opuntia lanceolata* f. *cristata*	195			
サボテン［大仏殿（だいぶつでん）］	*Echinocereus subinermis* var. *luteus* (Britton & Rose) F. M. Knuth	184			
サボテン［玉翁（たまおきな）］	*Mammillaria hahniana* Werderm.	353			
サボテン［月世界（つきせかい）］	*Epiterantha micromeris* (Engelmann) F. A. C. Weber ex Britt. & Rose	195			
サボテン［帝冠（ていかん）］	*Obregonia denegrii* Frič	77	208	220	
サボテン［ブーリー］	*Mammillaria boolii* G. E. Linds.	153			
サボテン［武蔵野（むさしの）］	*Tephrocactus articulatus* (Pfeiff.) Backeb.	300			

サボテン［ヤマカル柱（やまかるちゅう）］	Cereus jamacaru DC.	337				
ザミア・フルフラケア	Zamia furfuracea L. f.	301				
サラセニア［エクセレンス］	Sarracenia 'Excellens'	337				
サラセニア［ジュサティップソーパー］	Sarracenia 'Juthatip Soper'	331				
サラセニア［スカーレットベル］	Sarracenia 'Scarlet Bell'	269	319	346		
サラセニア［ダナズデライト］	Sarracenia 'Dana's Delight'	300				
サラセニア［ナイトスカイ］	Sarracenia 'Night Sky'	132				
サラセニア［マルーン］	Sarracenia 'Maroon'	349				
サラセニア・アラータ・オルナタ	Sarracenia alata var. ornata	117				
サラセニア・フラバ	Sarracenia flava L.	323				
サラセニア・フラバ・ルブリコーポラ	Sarracenia flava var. rubricorpora	276				
サラセニア・フラバ・ルブリコーポラ［レッドバーガンディ］	Sarracenia flava var. rubricorpora 'Red Burgundy'	101				
サラセニア・プルプレア	Sarracenia purpurea L.	34	136	215	327	335
サラセニア・ルブラ・ガルフェンシス	Sarracenia rubra subsp. gulfensis	174	178			
サラセニア・レウコフィラ	Sarracenia leucophylla Raf.	77	156	178	181	185
サルビア・ファリナセア［ストラータ］	Salvia farinacea 'Strata'	185				
サルビア・レウカンサ	Salvia leucantha Cav.	363				
サワギキョウ	Lobelia sessilifolia Lamb.	342				
サンショウモドキ［ペッパーベリー］	Schinus terebinthifolius 'Pepper Berry'	352				
サンスベリア・フィリップシアエ	Sansevieria phillipsiae N. E. Br.	337				
サンタンカ	Ixora coccinea L.	164	200			

シ

シイタケ	Lentinula edodes (Berk.) Pegler	42				
シオデ［イタリアンベリー］	Smilax aspera L.	329				
ジギタリス［ミルクチョコレート］	Digitalis parviflora 'Milk Chocolate'	178				
シクラメン・ヘデリフォリウム	Cyclamen hederifolium Aiton	174				
シクラメン［ハピネスママ］	Cyclamen persicum 'Happiness Mama'	304				
ジゴペタラム・レッドベイル［ファイヤーキス］	Zygopetalum Redvale 'Fire Kiss'	331				
シッサス・ジャバナ	Cissus javana DC.	233				
シナモン	Cinnamomum zeylanicum J. Presl	234				
ジニア［アズテックサンセット］	Zinnia haageana 'Aztec Sunset'	165				
ジニア［オールドファッション］	Zinnia haageana 'Old Fashion'	173				
ジニア［クイーンライム］	Zinnia elegans 'Queen Lime'	126	180	205	339	
ジニア［クイーンレッドライム］	Zinnia elegans 'Queen Red Lime'	178	349			
ジニア［ジャジーミックス］	Zinnia elegans 'Jersey Mix'	256				
ジニア［ドリームランドスカーレット］	Zinnia elegans 'Dreamland Scarlet'	346				
ジニア［プロフュージョンダブルゴールデン］	Zinnia 'Profusion Double Golden'	225				
ジニア［プロフュージョンダブルファイヤー］	Zinnia 'Profusion Double Fire'	327				
ジニア［ペルシャンカーペット］	Zinnia haageana 'Persian Carpet'	128	239			
ジニア［レッドサン］	Zinnia elegans 'Red Sun'	241				
シネラリア［ティアブルー］	Pericallis × hybrida 'Tear Blue'	162				
シモツケ	Spiraea japonica L. f.	190				
シャクヤク［小島の輝き（こじまのかがやき）］	Paeonia lactiflora 'Kojima no Kagayaki'	288				
シャクヤク［麒麟丸（きりんまる）］	Paeonia lactiflora 'Kirin Maru'	213				
シャクヤク［コーラルチャーム］	Paeonia lactiflora 'Coral Charm'	291				
シャクヤク［サラベルナール］	Paeonia lactiflora 'Sarah Bernhardt'	158				
シャクヤク［バンカーヒル］	Paeonia lactiflora 'Bunker Hill'	129	133			
シャクヤク［富士（ふじ）］	Paeonia lactiflora 'Fuji'	167				
シャクヤク［ポーラフェイ］	Paeonia lactiflora 'Paula Fay'	335				
シャクヤク［夕映（ゆうばえ）］	Paeonia lactiflora 'Yubae'	141				
シャクヤク［レッドチャーム］	Paeonia lactiflora 'Red Charm'	205	276	299		
シャクヤク［レッドバロン］	Paeonia lactiflora 'Red Baron'	207				
シャクヤク［レッドモナーク］	Paeonia lactiflora 'Red Monarch'	300				
シャクヤク［レッドローズ］	Paeonia lactiflora 'Red Rose'	273				
シャリンバイ	Rhaphiolepis indica (L.) Lindl. ex Ker var. umbellata (Thunb.) H. Ohashi	181				
シャリンバイの実	Rhaphiolepis indica (L.) Lindl. ex Ker var. umbellata (Thunb.) H. Ohashi	204	339			
シュウメイギク［オノリーヌジョベール］	Anemone hupehensis var. japonica 'Honorine Jobert'	352				
シュウメイギク［プリティーレディーダイアナ］	Anemone hupehensis 'Pretty Lady Diana'	342				
ショウガ	Zingiber officinale Roscoe	234				
シレネ［グリーンベル］	Silene vulgaris 'Green Bell'	216				
ジンジャー［ゴールデンシャンプー］	Zingiber spectabile 'Golden Shampoo'	111	139	164	208	349

ジンジャー [シャンプージンジャー]	*Zingiber zerumbet* 'Shampoo Ginger'	313 342
ジンジャー [レッドジンジャー]	*Alpinia purpurata* 'Red Ginger'	273
ジンジャー [ワックスジンジャー]	*Tapeinochilos ananassae* 'Wax Ginger'	142 186 227
シンビジューム [アカネ]	*Cymbidium* 'Akane'	229
シンビジューム [いろはいろ 01 (いろはいろぜろいち)]	*Cymbidium* 'Irohairo 01'	287
シンビジューム [カプチーノ]	*Cymbidium* 'Cappuccino'	331
シンビジューム [キングアーサー]	*Cymbidium* 'King Arthur'	298
シンビジューム [グリーンサワー]	*Cymbidium* 'Green Sour'	282
シンビジューム [クレッセント]	*Cymbidium* 'Crescent'	182
シンビジューム [ソレイユルヴァン]	*Cymbidium* 'Soleil Levant'	200
シンビジューム [チャチャ]	*Cymbidium* 'Cha Cha'	222
シンビジューム [眠れる森の美女 (ねむれるもりのびじょ)]	*Cymbidium* 'Nemureru Mori no Bijyo'	269
シンビジューム [モカ]	*Cymbidium* 'Mocha'	178
シンビジューム [レッドエンプレス]	*Cymbidium* 'Red Empress'	265
シンビジューム [ロマンス]	*Cymbidium* 'Romance'	343
シンビジューム [ワインシャワー]	*Cymbidium* 'Wine Shower'	154
シンビジューム・イースタンバニー [月の光 (つきのひかり)]	*Cymbidium* Eastern Bunny 'Tsuki no Hikari'	305
シンビジューム・エンザンフォレスト [マジョリカ]	*Cymbidium* Enzan Forest 'Majolica'	218 342
シンビジューム・キンリョウヘン	*Cymbidium floribundum* Lindl.	282 306
シンビジューム・トラシアナム	*Cymbidium tracyanum* L. Castle	265 276 297 303 311 329
シンビジューム・ラブリーバレー [ピースインザワールド]	*Cymbidium* Lovely Valley 'Peace in the World'	195

ス

スイートピー [シャーリップル]	*Lathyrus odoratus* 'Wiltshire Ripple'	303
スイートピー [ピンクパール]	*Lathyrus latifolius* 'Pink Pearl'	196
スイートピー [ブルーフレグランス]	*Lathyrus odoratus* 'Blue Fragrance'	210
スイートピー [ホワイトパール]	*Lathyrus latifolius* 'White Pearl'	199
スイートピー [レッドパール]	*Lathyrus latifolius* 'Red Pearl'	159
スイセン [グランドソレドール]	*Narcissus* 'Grand Soleil d'Or'	296 306
スイセン [スイートネス]	*Narcissus* 'Sweetness'	269 315 333
スイセン [白房スイセン (しろふさすいせん)]	*Narcissus tazetta* 'Shirofusa Suisen'	42
スイセン [ティタティタ]	*Narcissus* 'Tete a Tete'	200 300 311
スイセン [ディックウィルデン]	*Narcissus* 'Dick Wilden'	325
スイセン [フェブラリーゴールド]	*Narcissus* 'February Gold'	204
スイセン・ニホンズイセン	*Narcissus tazetta* var. *chinensis* M. Roem.	180 271 345 358
スカビオサ [エースオブスペード]	*Scabiosa atropurpurea* 'Ace of Spades'	176 331
スカビオサ [オクスフォードブルー]	*Scabiosa atropurpurea* 'Oxford Blue'	196
スカビオサ [ファーマ]	*Scabiosa caucasica* 'Fama'	230
スカビオサ [ブルーノート]	*Scabiosa columbaria* 'Blue Note'	307
スカビオサ [モコパープル]	*Scabiosa atropurpurea* 'Moco Purple'	123
スキミア [キューグリーン]	*Skimmia japonica* 'Kew Green'	160 194
スズラン	*Convallaria majalis* L.	23 308
ストレリチア・レギネ	*Strelitzia reginae* Aiton	173 224 284 321 335

セ・ソ

セイヨウスユキソウ	*Leontopodium alpinum* Cass.	321
セダム [オータムジョイ]	*Sedum spectabile* 'Autumn Joy'	139 184 212
セダム [マトロナ]	*Sedum telephium* 'Matrona'	349
セッカダイズ	*Glycine max* (L.) Merr.	350
セルリア [カルメン]	*Serruria* 'Carmen'	204
セルリア [プリティピンク]	*Serruria* 'Pretty n Pink'	123 158 250 321
センニチコウ [ローズネオン]	*Gomphrena globosa* 'Rose Neon'	312
センペルビウム [ロブスツム]	*Sempervivum* 'Lobstum'	217
センペルビウム [ラベンダーアンドオールドレース]	*Sempervivum* 'Lavender and Old Lace'	216
センペルビウム・テクトラム	*Sempervivum tectorum* L.	178
ゼンマイ	*Osmunda japonica* Thunb.	284 304 307 325
ソテツの実	*Cycas revoluta* Thunb.	180 350

タ

タイワンホトトギス	*Tricyrtis formosana* Baker	319				
ダウカス［ブラックナイト］	*Daucus carota* 'Black Knight'	179				
タケ	*Bambuseae* Kunth ex Dumort.	47	48			
タッカ・シャントリエリ	*Tacca chantrieri* André	93				
ダリア［朝日てまり（あさひてまり）］	*Dahlia* 'Asahi Temari'	170	200	212	232	273
		279	289	314	346	
ダリア［アジタート］	*Dahlia* 'Agitato'	296	346			
ダリア［アラビアンナイト］	*Dahlia* 'Arabian Night'	193	292			
ダリア［アンティークレッド × ピーチパイ］	*Dahlia* 'Antique Red × Peach Pie'	136				
ダリア［祝花（いわいばな）］	*Dahlia* 'Iwaibana'	161				
ダリア［エオナG（えおなじー）］	*Dahlia* 'Eona G'	247				
ダリア［エジンバラ］	*Dahlia* 'Edinburgh'	196				
ダリア［オズの魔法使い（おずのまほうつかい）］	*Dahlia* 'Wizard of Oz'	344				
ダリア［ガーネット］	*Dahlia* 'Garnet'	123				
ダリア［かまくら］	*Dahlia* 'Kamakura'	352				
ダリア［ギッツパーフェクション］	*Dahlia* 'Gitt's Perfection'	251				
ダリア［グレンプレス］	*Dahlia* 'Glenplace'	204	223			
ダリア［恋しぐれ（こいしぐれ）］	*Dahlia* 'Koishigure'	158				
ダリア［黒蝶（こくちょう）］	*Dahlia* 'Kokucho'	126	155	176	222	323
ダリア［古都（こと）］	*Dahlia* 'Koto'	248				
ダリア［桜貝（さくらがい）］	*Dahlia* 'Sakuragai'	250				
ダリア［砂漠（さばく）］	*Dahlia* 'Sabaku'	286				
ダリア［サンタクロース］	*Dahlia* 'Santa Claus'	133	288			
ダリア［ジェシーリタ］	*Dahlia* 'Jessie Rita'	327	331	344		
ダリア［ジェシカ］	*Dahlia* 'Jessica'	240				
ダリア［JyuJyu（じゅじゅ）］	*Dahlia* 'JyuJyu'	136				
ダリア［純愛の君（じゅんあいのきみ）］	*Dahlia* 'Junai no Kimi'	122	226	241	302	
ダリア［ショーンテル］	*Dahlia* 'Show N Tell'	350				
ダリア［シンドバッド］	*Dahlia* 'Sinbad'	124	239			
ダリア［ストロベリークリーム］	*Dahlia* 'Strawberry Cream'	351				
ダリア［タンピコ］	*Dahlia* 'Tampico'	180				
ダリア［ドリームダンス］	*Dahlia* 'Dream Dance'	215				
ダリア［NAMAHAGE スワン（なまはげすわん）］	*Dahlia* 'Namahage Swan'	254				
ダリア［NAMAHAGE ノアール（なまはげのあーる）］	*Dahlia* 'Namahage Noir'	154				
ダリア［NAMAHAGE パープル（なまはげぱーぷる）］	*Dahlia* 'Namahage Purple'	327				
ダリア［NAMAHAGE マジック（なまはげまじっく）］	*Dahlia* 'Namahage Magic'	141	147	252		
ダリア［熱球（ねっきゅう）］	*Dahlia* 'Nekkyu'	331	342	346		
ダリア［熱唱（ねっしょう）］	*Dahlia* 'Nessho'	215	232	269	284	287
		308	311			
ダリア［白山手まり（はくさんてまり）］	*Dahlia* 'Hakusantemari'	253				
ダリア［ハミルトンジュニア］	*Dahlia* 'Hamilton Junior'	287				
ダリア［ピーチインシーズン］	*Dahlia* 'Peach in Season'	173				
ダリア［ピーチパイ × NAMAHAGE ニュアンス（なまはげにゅあんす）］	*Dahlia* 'Peach Pie × Namahage Nuance'	142				
ダリア［ビーデルマンズドルフ］	*Dahlia* 'Biedermannsdorf'	130	173	348		
ダリア［雛あられ（ひなあられ）］	*Dahlia* 'Hinaarare'	244				
ダリア［ビューティフルデイズ］	*Dahlia* 'Beautiful Days'	350				
ダリア［フィダルゴブラッキー］	*Dahlia* 'Fidalgo Blacky'	176	312			
ダリア［福寿（ふくじゅ）］	*Dahlia* 'Fukuju'	344				
ダリア［ブルーピーチ］	*Dahlia* 'Blue Peach'	215	269	333		
ダリア［ペチカ］	*Dahlia* 'Pechka'	319	331			
ダリア［ポートライトペアビューティ］	*Dahlia* 'Portlight Pair Beauty'	256				
ダリア［マタドール］	*Dahlia* 'Matador'	125	314			
ダリア［マルコムズホワイト］	*Dahlia* 'Malcom's White'	168				
ダリア［マロン］	*Dahlia* 'Marron'	178				
ダリア［ミスゼルダ］	*Dahlia* 'Ms. Zelda'	355				
ダリア［ミセスアイリーン］	*Dahlia* 'Mrs. Eileen'	243				
ダリア［ミッチャン］	*Dahlia* 'Micchan'	39	212	226	306	
ダリア［ムーンストーン］	*Dahlia* 'Moon Stone'	245	362			
ダリア［ムーンワルツ］	*Dahlia* 'Moon Waltz'	246				
ダリア［群金魚（むらきんぎょ）］	*Dahlia* 'Murakingyo'	126	249	296	298	
ダリア［モナコS（もなこえす）］	*Dahlia* 'Monaco S'	242				
ダリア［結納（ゆいのう）］	*Dahlia* 'Yuino'	255				
ダリア［雄馬（ゆうま）］	*Dahlia* 'Yuma'	212				
ダリア［雪国（ゆきぐに）］	*Dahlia* 'Yukiguni'	199				

ダリア [雪椿 (ゆきつばき)]	*Dahlia* 'Yuki Tsubaki'	220			
ダリア [悦び (よろこび)]	*Dahlia* 'Yorokobi'	258			
ダリア [ラベラピッコロピンク]	*Dahlia* 'Labella Piccolo Pink'	181			
ダリア [ラ・ラ・ラ]	*Dahlia* 'Lalala'	151	238	257	306	344
ダリア [リトルローズマリー]	*Dahlia* 'Little Rosemary'	319			
ダリア [レッドスター]	*Dahlia* 'Red Star'	186	263	301	310
ダリア [レッドマーベラス]	*Dahlia* 'Red Marvelous'	271			
ダリア [レベッカリン]	*Dahlia* 'Rebecca Lynn'	166			
ダリア [レモンカード]	*Dahlia* 'Lemon Card'	224			
ダリア [レモンライト]	*Dahlia* 'Lemon Light'	182			
ダリア [ローズクォーツ]	*Dahlia* 'Rose Quartz'	273	302		
ダリアの球根	*Dahlia* Cav.	164	208		

チ

チーゼル	*Dipsacus fullonum* L.	235			
チューリップ [アクミナータ]	*Tulipa* 'Acuminata'	315			
チューリップ [アレキサンドラ]	*Tulipa* 'Alexandra'	358			
チューリップ [イエローキング]	*Tulipa* 'Yellow King'	307			
チューリップ [エキゾチックサン]	*Tulipa* 'Exotic Sun'	325			
チューリップ [エキゾチックパーロット]	*Tulipa* 'Exotic Parrot'	359			
チューリップ [オレンジプリンセス]	*Tulipa* 'Orange Princess'	269			
チューリップ [オレンジモナーク]	*Tulipa* 'Orange Monarch'	304			
チューリップ [スーパーパーロット]	*Tulipa* 'Super Parrot'	51	195	267	
チューリップ [ティタティタ]	*Tulipa* 'Tete a Tete'	170	297	358	
チューリップ [ドルチェヘス]	*Tulipa* 'Dolce Hess'	290			
チューリップ [パープルフラッグ]	*Tulipa* 'Purple Flag'	278	306		
チューリップ [ハミルトン]	*Tulipa* 'Hamilton'	279			
チューリップ [バルバドス]	*Tulipa* 'Barbados'	284	304		
チューリップ [パルミラ]	*Tulipa* 'Palmyra'	289			
チューリップ [バレリーナ]	*Tulipa* 'Ballerina'	286			
チューリップ [フラッシュポイント]	*Tulipa* 'Flash Point'	359			
チューリップ [フレミングスプリンググリーン]	*Tulipa* 'Flaming Spring Green'	69			
チューリップ [フレミングパーロット]	*Tulipa* 'Flaming Parrot'	273	274		
チューリップ [フレミングフラッグ]	*Tulipa* 'Flaming Flag'	288			
チューリップ [ホワイトリバースター]	*Tulipa* 'White River Star'	198	315		
チューリップ [ミステリアスパーロット]	*Tulipa* 'Mysterious Parrot'	274	284		
チューリップ [モナムール]	*Tulipa* 'Mon Amour'	311			
チューリップ [モンテカルロ]	*Tulipa* 'Monte Carlo'	314			
チューリップ [モンテスパイダー]	*Tulipa* 'Monte Spider'	275	279	307	358
チューリップ [ラルゴ]	*Tulipa* 'Largo'	156	314		
チューリップ [リトルプリンセス]	*Tulipa* 'Little Princess'	307			
チューリップ [レッドプリンセス]	*Tulipa* 'Red Princess'	277			
チューリップ [ロココ]	*Tulipa* 'Rococo'	160	290	301	
チューリップ・トルケスタニカ	*Tulipa turkestanica* (Regel) Regel	87	154	329	
チューリップ・ポリクロマ	*Tulipa polychroma* Stapf	198	303	333	
チューリップの実	*Tulipa* L.	178			
チランジア [コットンキャンディ]	*Tillandsia* 'Cotton Candy'	41	299	314	
チランジア・アエラントス	*Tillandsia aeranthos* (Loiseleur) L. B. Sm.	301			
チランジア・アンドレアナ	*Tillandsia andreana* E. Morren ex André	171	284		
チランジア・イオナンタ	*Tillandsia ionantha* Planchon	172	174		
チランジア・カピタータ	*Tillandsia capitata* Grisebach	185	273		
チランジア・カプトメデューサ	*Tillandsia caput-medusae* E. Morren	175	278	319	338
チランジア・キセログラフィカ	*Tillandsia xerographica* Rohweder	171	184	199	230	267
		310	319	336	
チランジア・シアネア	*Tillandsia cyanea* Linden ex K. Koch	180	206		
チランジア・セレリアナ	*Tillandsia seleriana* Mez	285			
チランジア・テクトラム	*Tillandsia tectorum* E. Morren	198	331	333	
チランジア・パレアセア	*Tillandsia paleacea* Presl	284			
チランジア・ブラキカウロス	*Tillandsia brachycaulos* Schlechtendal	218			
チランジア・ブルボーサ	*Tillandsia bulbosa* Hook.	263	280		

ツ・テ・ト

ツバキ	Camellia japonica L.	311					
ツルウメモドキ	Celastrus orbiculatus Thunb. var. orbiculatus	344					
ディケロステンマ［ピンクダイヤモンド］	Dichelostemma ida-maia 'Pink Diamond'	298					
ディケロステンマ・イダマイア	Dichelostemma ida-maia (Alph. Wood) Greene	172					
ディサ・キューエンシス［アーティスト］	Disa Kewensis 'Artists'	251					
ディサ・キューエンシス［アーティストアルバ］	Disa Kewensis 'Artists Alba'	238					
ディサ・キューエンシス［アン］	Disa Kewensis 'Ann'	240					
ディッキア［ニッケルシルバー］	Dyckia 'Nickel Silver'	211					
デルフィニウム［オーロラディープパープル］	Delphinium elatum 'Aurora Deep Purple'	141					
デルフィニウム［オーロラブルーインプ］	Delphinium elatum 'Aurora Blue Imp'	123	150	166			
デルフィニウム［グランブルー］	Delphinium grandiflorum 'Grand Blue'	211					
デルフィニウム［スーパーグランブルー］	Delphinium grandiflorum 'Super Grand Blue'	163					
デルフィニウム［スーパースカイブルー］	Delphinium grandiflorum 'Super Sky Blue'	125					
デルフィニウム［ブルーキャンドル］	Delphinium chinense 'Blue Candle'	314					
テロペア［ワラタ］	Telopea speciosissima 'Waratah'	171	180	263			
デンドロキラム・コビアナム	Dendrochilum cobbianum Rchb. f.	269	325				
デンドロキラム・デンポエンセ	Dendrochilum dempoense J. J. Sm.	265					
デンドロキラム・プロピンキュウム	Dendrochilum propinquum Ames	359					
デンドロキラム・マグナム	Dendrochilum magnum Rchb. f.	82	302	319			
デンドロビューム［スイートキャンディ］	Dendrobium 'Sweet Candy'	277					
デンドロビューム・キングジップ［レッドスプラッシュ］	Dendrobium King Zip 'Red Splash'	333					
デンファレ［レモングリーン］	Dendrobium phalaenopsis 'Lemon Green'	217					
トクサ	Equisetum hyemale L.	71	128				
トケイソウ［インセンス］	Passiflora 'Incense'	102	141	208	223	252	
トケイソウ［クリアスカイ］	Passiflora caerulea 'Clear Sky'	95	172	249	263	280	
		335					
トケイソウ［コンスタンスエリオット］	Passiflora caerulea 'Constance Elliott'	254					
トケイソウ［ビクトリア］	Passiflora 'Victoria'	184					
トケイソウ［ベロッティ］	Passiflora 'Belotii'	298					
トベラ	Pittosporum tobira (Thunb.) W. T. Aiton	234					
トリテレイア［バビロン］	Triteleia 'Babylon'	244					
トリトマ［ビーズレモン］	Kniphofia uvaria 'Bees' Lemon'	134	181	182	336	351	
トリトマ［ファーストサンライズ］	Kniphofia uvaria 'First Sunrise'	165	192	224	227	327	
		331	337	349			
トリトマ［フラメンコ］	Kniphofia uvaria 'Flamenco'	144	172	289			
ドリミオプシス・マクラータ	Drimiopsis maculata Lindl. & Paxton	96					
トルコキキョウ［コサージュピンク］	Eustoma grandiflorum 'Corsage Pink'	151					
トルコキキョウ［セレブブルー］	Eustoma grandiflorum 'Celeb Blue'	196	337				
トルコキキョウ［ボヤージュブルー］	Eustoma grandiflorum 'Voyage Blue'	205	290	313	363		
トルコキキョウ［ボヤージュホワイト］	Eustoma grandiflorum 'Voyage White'	198					
トルコキキョウ［レイナホワイト］	Eustoma grandiflorum 'Reina White'	168					
トロリウス［ゴールデンクイーン］	Trollius chinensis 'Golden Queen'	226					

ナ・ニ・ネ・ノ

ナデシコ［グリーントリュフ］	Dianthus barbatus 'Green Trick'	126	136	150	152	161	
		166	212	216	218	234	
		294	345	360			
ナデシコ［ブレアンサスロード］	Dianthus barbatus 'Breanthus Road'	161	206				
ナデシコ［ブレアンサスクイーン］	Dianthus barbatus 'Breanthus Queen'	176					
ナデシコ［ブレアンサスデューク］	Dianthus barbatus 'Breanthus Duke'	199					
ナデシコ［ブレアンサスバロン］	Dianthus barbatus 'Breanthus Baron'	150					
ナデシコ［ラフィーネリリ］	Dianthus 'Raffine Lili'	190					
ニゲラ［ペルシャンジュエル］	Nigella damascena 'Persian Jewels'	163	180	210	263	285	
		321	341	344			
ニゲラ［ミスジーキル］	Nigella damascena 'Miss Jekyll'	199	280				
ニゲラの実	Nigella damascena L.	55					
ネオレゲリア［ゾエ］	Neoregelia 'Zoe'	233					
ネオレゲリア［ファイヤーボール］	Neoregelia 'Fireball'	335					
ネオレゲリア［ファイヤーボールバリエガタ］	Neoregelia 'Fireball Variegata'	189	202	263	311		
ネオレゲリア［リオ・オブ・リオ］	Neoregelia 'Rio of Rio'	217					
ネオレゲリア・スペクタビリス	Neoregelia spectabilis (T. Moore) L. B. Sm.	224					
ネオレゲリア・パウシフローラ	Neoregelia pauciflora L. B. Sm.	301					

ネペンテス［ダイエリアナ］	*Nepenthes* 'Dyeriana'	99　154　202　263　287
		302
ネペンテス［チェルソニー］	*Nepenthes* 'Chelsonii'	132
ネペンテス［ミランダ］	*Nepenthes* 'Miranda'	227
ネペンテス［レベッカソーパー］	*Nepenthes* 'Rebecca Soper'	59　171　179　222　293
		319　327　335
ネペンテス・アラータ	*Nepenthes alata* Blanco	189　235　294　297　299
		323　348
ネペンテス・サンギネア	*Nepenthes sanguinea* Lindl.	153
ネペンテス・トバイカ	*Nepenthes tobaica* Danser	280
ネペンテス・ボングソ	*Nepenthes bongso* Korth.	235
ネペンテス・マキシマ	*Nepenthes maxima* Reinw. ex Nees	188
ネペンテス・ムルエンシア	*Nepenthes muluensis* M. Hotta	175
ネペンテス・ラフレシアナ・ギガンテア	*Nepenthes rafflesiana* var. *gigantea*	111
ネペンテス・ラフレシアナ［コシカワ］	*Nepenthes rafflesiana* 'Koshikawa'	82　269
ネリネ［ビアンカパーラ］	*Nerine bowdenii* 'Bianca Perla'	353
ネリネ［フェイバリット］	*Nerine bowdenii* 'Favourite'	354
ネリネ［ベルリッゾ］	*Nerine sarniensis* 'Berlioz'	156
ネリネ［ミスタージョン］	*Nerine bowdenii* 'Mr. John'	150　166
ネリネ［レッドアドミラル］	*Nerine sarniensis* 'Red Admiral'	351
ネリネ［レッドエンペラー］	*Nerine sarniensis* 'Red Emperor'	313
ネリネ・フミリス	*Nerine humilis* (Jacq.) Herb.	158
ノコギリソウ	*Achillea alpina* L.	183
ノラニンジン	*Daucus carota* L.	175　235　321

ハ

バーゼリア・ラヌギノーサ	*Berzelia lanuginosa* (L.) Brongn.	157　202
ハイビスカス［ブリリアントレッド］	*Hibiscus* 'Brilliant Red'	212
ハエトリグサ［クラスタートラップス］	*Dionaea muscipula* 'Cluster Traps'	35
ハエトリグサ［ディングレイズジャイアント］	*Dionaea muscipula* 'Dingleys Giant'	128　152
ハエマンサス・マユハケオモト	*Haemanthus albiflos* Jacq.	180　344
ハオルチア［京の華（きょうのはな）］	*Haworthia cymbiformis* 'Kyo no Hana'	203
ハオルチア［雫石（しずくいし）］	*Haworthia cooperi* var. *obtusa* 'Shizukuishi'	152　202　231
ハオルチア［秋天星（しゅうてんせい）］	*Haworthia minima* 'Shutensei'	185
ハオルチア［十二の巻（じゅうにのまき）］	*Haworthia fasciata* 'Juni no Maki'	114　216　323　331
ハオルチア［鷹の爪（たかのつめ）］	*Haworthia reinwardtii* 'Taka no Tsume'	172
パキフィツム［星美人（ほしびじん）］	*Pachyphytum bracteosum* 'Hoshi Bijin'	210
バショウ［オレンジオルナタバナナ］	*Musa ornata* Roxb.	172
バショウ［キングバナナ］	*Musa minor* Nakai	34　228　305　335
バショウ［ピンクバナナ］	*Musa velutina* H. Wendl. & Drude	172
ハス［桜蓮（おうれん）］	*Nelumbo nucifera* 'Ouren'	72
ハス［誠蓮（まことばす）］	*Nelumbo nucifera* 'Makotobasu'	144
ハス［大紅袍（だいこうほう）］	*Nelumbo nucifera* 'Daikouho'	119
ハス台	*Nelumbo nucifera* Gaertn.	202　227　319
ハスの葉	*Nelumbo nucifera* Gaertn.	212
ハナトラノオ	*Physostegia virginiana* (L.) Benth.	190　208　355
バニラ	*Vanilla planifolia* Jacks. ex Andrews	155
パフィオペディラム［F. C. パッドル（えふしーぱっどる）］	*Paphiopedilum* 'F. C. Puddle'	168
パフィオペディラム［薩摩唐獅子（さつまからじし）］	*Paphiopedilum* Satsuma 'Karajishi'	201
パフィオペディラム［シンインルビーウェブ］	*Paphiopedilum* 'Hsinying Rubyweb'	331
パフィオペディラム［セントスイシン］	*Paphiopedilum* 'St. Swithin'	79　209　221　323　335
パフィオペディラム［ナイトシャドウ］	*Paphiopedilum* 'Night Shadow'	309
パフィオペディラム［ライムドーン］	*Paphiopedilum* 'Lime Down'	282
パフィオペディラム［ロビンフッド］	*Paphiopedilum* 'Robin Hood'	222　227　233
パフィオペディラム・インシグネ	*Paphiopedilum insigne* (Wall. ex Lindl.) Pfitzer	150　277　286
パフィオペディラム・ウィンストンチャーチル［リダウタブル］	*Paphiopedilum* Winston Churchill 'Redoubtable'	310
パフィオペディラム・オルチラ［チルトン］	*Paphiopedilum* Orchilla 'Chilton'	296
パフィオペディラム・カーティシー・サンデレー［フォートキャロライン］	*Paphiopedilum curtisii* var. *sanderae* 'Fort Caroline'	267
パフィオペディラム・カローサム	*Paphiopedilum callosum* (Rchb. f.) Stein	93
パフィオペディラム・カローサム・ビニカラー	*Paphiopedilum callosum* var. *vinicolor*	155　281　292
パフィオペディラム・シャーライン［ロンド］	*Paphiopedilum* Sheerline 'Rondo'	156　217
パフィオペディラム・スピセリアナム	*Paphiopedilum spicerianum* (Rchb. f) Pfitzer	154　180　271　337
パフィオペディラム・ディアンサム	*Paphiopedilum dianthum* Tang & F. T. Wang	181　341

パフィオペディラム・デレナティー	*Paphiopedilum delenatii* Guillaumin	151 279
パフィオペディラム・ドルーリ	*Paphiopedilum druryi* (Bedd.) Stein	361
パフィオペディラム・ニベウム	*Paphiopedilum niveum* (Rchb. f.) Stein	85
パフィオペディラム・ノリトハセガワ［ゴールドラッシュ］	*Paphiopedilum* Norito Hasegawa 'Gold Rush'	27
パフィオペディラム・ハッサリー［セイントマリー］	*Paphiopedilum* Hassallii 'Saint Mary'	134
パフィオペディラム・パリシー	*Paphiopedilum parishii* (Rchb. f.) Stein	343
パフィオペディラム・プラティフィラム	*Paphiopedilum platyphyllum* T. Yukawa	89
パフィオペディラム・ベナスタム［プチライト］	*Paphiopedilum venustum* 'Petit Light'	27
パフィオペディラム・モーディエ［クイーン］	*Paphiopedilum* Maudiae 'The Queen'	99 102 202 329
パフィオペディラム・モーディエ［ブラックジャック］	*Paphiopedilum* Maudiae 'Black Jack'	357
パフィオペディラム・レボウ［ビオスキング］	*Paphiopedilum* Lebeau 'Bios King'	263 281
パフィオペディラム・ローレンセアナム	*Paphiopedilum lawrenceanum* (Rchb. f.) Pfitzer	335
ハベナリア・メドゥーサ	*Habenaria medusa* Kraenzl.	327
ハボタン［ヴェルサイユブラックルシアン］	*Brassica oleracea* 'Versailles Black Lucien'	297
ハボタン［シルキーパール］	*Brassica oleracea* 'Silky Pearl'	177
ハボタン［パープルポップ］	*Brassica oleracea* 'Purple Pop'	53
ハボタン［ブラックスワン］	*Brassica oleracea* 'Black Swan'	313
ハボタン［光子プレミアム（みつこぷれみあむ）］	*Brassica oleracea* 'Mitsuko Premium'	177
バラ［アバランチェ］	*Rosa* 'Avalanche'	125
バラ［アマダ+（あまだぷらす）］	*Rosa* 'Amada+'	274
バラ［アンダルシア］	*Rosa* 'Andalusia'	186
バラ［イヴピアッチェ］	*Rosa* 'Yves Piaget'	279
バラ［イヴレッド］	*Rosa* 'Yves Red'	303
バラ［イリオス］	*Rosa* 'Ilios'	183
バラ［ヴァーグ+（ゔぁーぐぷらす）］	*Rosa* 'Vague+'	293
バラ［エキサイティングメイアン］	*Rosa* 'Exciting Meilland'	161 181 278 351
バラ［オール4キス+（おーるふぉーきすぷらす）］	*Rosa* 'All 4 Kiss+'	204
バラ［オール4ラブ（おーるふぉーらぶ）］	*Rosa* 'All 4 Love'	124
バラ［カンパイ］	*Rosa* 'Kanpai'	273
バラ［K-ゼブラ（けーぜぶら）］	*Rosa* 'K-Zebra'	219
バラ［ゴールドラッシュ］	*Rosa* 'Gold Rush'	275
バラ［サムライ］	*Rosa* 'Samurai'	346
バラ［シュエルヴァーズ］	*Rosa* 'Shall Verse'	229
バラ［スイートアバランチェ］	*Rosa* 'Sweet Avalanche'	158
バラ［スプラッシュセンセーション］	*Rosa* 'Splash Sensation'	166
バラ［タマンゴ］	*Rosa* 'Tamango'	128
バラ［ハナビ］	*Rosa* 'Hanabi'	283
バラ［ハロウィン］	*Rosa* 'Halloween'	178
バラ［バロネッセ］	*Rosa* 'Baronesse'	206 208
バラ［フラッシュアイ］	*Rosa* 'Flash Eye'	218 226 289
バラ［フリーダム］	*Rosa* 'Freedom'	126
バラ［フリオイグレシアス］	*Rosa* 'Julio Iglesias'	206
バラ［ベルルージュ］	*Rosa* 'Bell Rouge'	206
バラ［ミルバ］	*Rosa* 'Milva'	173
バラ［ラ・カンパネラ］	*Rosa* 'La Campanella'	219
バラ［レッドエレガンス］	*Rosa* 'Red Elegance'	61 265 273
バラ［レッドポンポン］	*Rosa* 'Red Pompon'	107
バラ［レッドラナンキュラ］	*Rosa* 'Red Ranunculus'	308
バラ［ローテローゼ］	*Rosa* 'Rote Rose'	209
パラノムス	*Paranomus reflexus* N. E. Br.	143 323
バルビネラ・フロリバンダ	*Bulbinella floribunda* (Aiton) T. Durand & Schinz	219
バルボフィラム・エリザベスアン［バックルベリー］	*Bulbophyllum* Elizabeth Ann 'Buckleberry'	286
バンクシア・アテナータ	*Banksia attenuata* R. Br.	161
バンクシア・インテグリフォリア	*Banksia integrifolia* L. f.	150 167 188
バンクシア・エリシフォリア	*Banksia ericifolia* L. f.	215
バンクシア・コッキネア	*Banksia coccinea* R. Br	147 165 208 226
バンクシア・スピヌロサ	*Banksia spinulosa* Sm.	286 288
バンクシア・フーケリアナ	*Banksia hookeriana* Meisn.	173
バンクシア・メーンジーシー	*Banksia menziesii* R. Br.	180 223 229 339
パンジー［シャロンジャイアント］	*Viola* × *wittrockiana* 'Chalon Giant'	297 325
パンジー［ナチュレイエローブロッチ］	*Viola* × *wittrockiana* 'Nature Yellow Broggi'	263 325
パンジー［フリズルシズルイエロー］	*Viola* × *wittrockiana* 'Frizzle Sizzle Yellow'	271
パンジー［フリズルシズルイエローブルースワール］	*Viola* × *wittrockiana* 'Frizzle Sizzle Yellow Blue Swirl'	304
パンジー［フリズルシズルバーガンディーシェード］	*Viola* × *wittrockiana* 'Frizzle Sizzle Burgundy Shade'	176
パンジー［フリズルシズルパッションフルーツ］	*Viola* × *wittrockiana* 'Frizzle Sizzle Passion Fruit'	158
パンジー［フリズルシズルブルー］	*Viola* × *wittrockiana* 'Frizzle Sizzle Blue'	163 195 305
パンジー［ムーランフリルゴールデン］	*Viola* × *wittrockiana* 'Moulin Frill Golden'	258

バンダ [ディープパープルスポット]	*Vanda* 'Deep Purple Spots'	113 142	
バンダ [パクチョンブルー]	*Vanda* 'Pakchong Blue'	295	
バンダ [パチャラデライト]	*Vanda* 'Pachara Delight'	134	
バンダ [パットデライト]	*Vanda* 'Pat Delight'	127 311	
バンダ [バラエティ]	*Vanda* 'Variety'	130	
バンダ [ヤノブルースポット]	*Vanda* 'Yano Blue Spot'	231	
バンダ [ロバートデライトブルー]	*Vanda* 'Robert's Delight Blue'	125	

ヒ

ヒオウギの実	*Iris domestica* Goldblatt & Mabb.	360	
ビオラ [イエローブロッチ]	*Viola* 'Yellow Blotch'	281	
ビオラ [エンジェルローズピコティ]	*Viola* 'Angel Rose Picotee'	156	
ビオラセア・フレグランス	*Tulbaghia simmleri* Beauverd	269	
ビカクシダ・コウモリラン	*Platycerium bifurcatum* (Cav.) C. Chr.	188 291 356	
ヒカゲノカズラ	*Lycopodium clavatum* L.	201	
ピトカイルニア・ウェンドランディ	*Pitacairnia wendlandii* Baker	34	
ビバーナム [コンパクタ]	*Viburnum opulus* 'Compactum'	346	
ビバーナム・ティナス	*Viburnum tinus* L.	166 176 195 230	
ヒマワリ [ゴッホのひまわり]	*Helianthus annuus* 'Van Gogh Sunflower'	224	
ヒマワリ [サンリッチオレンジ]	*Helianthus annuus* 'Sunrich Orange'	309	
ヒマワリ [東北八重 (とうほくやえ)]	*Helianthus annuus* 'Tohoku Yae'	122	
ヒマワリ [ビンセントタンジェリン]	*Helianthus annuus* 'Vincent Tangerine'	325	
ヒヤシンス [アンナマリー]	*Hyacinthus orientalis* 'Anna Marie'	167 193	
ヒヤシンス [ウッドストック]	*Hyacinthus orientalis* 'Woodstock'	358	
ヒヤシンス [デルフトブルー]	*Hyacinthus orientalis* 'Delft Blue'	150 163	
ヒヤシンス [パープルスター]	*Hyacinthus orientalis* 'Purple Star'	194 358	
ヒヤシンス [ピンクパール]	*Hyacinthus orientalis* 'Pink Pearl'	163	
ヒヤシンス [ブルージャケット]	*Hyacinthus orientalis* 'Blue Jacket'	49 155 210 267 269 282 289 310	
ヒヤシンス [ブルースター]	*Hyacinthus orientalis* 'Blue Star'	197	
ヒヤシンス [ブルーパール]	*Hyacinthus orientalis* 'Blue Pearl'	297	
ヒヤシンス [ミスサイゴン]	*Hyacinthus orientalis* 'Miss Saigon'	269	
ヒューケラ [ミッドナイトローズ]	*Heuchera* 'Midnight Rose'	176	
ピレア [ムーンバレー]	*Pilea involucrata* 'Moon Valley'	223 331	
ピンクッション [サクセション]	*Leucospermum cordifolium* 'Succession'	111 287	
ピンクッション [ハイゴールド]	*Leucospermum cordifolium* 'High Gold'	63 319 321	
ピンクッション [ベルデファイヤー]	*Leucospermum cordifolium* 'Veldt Fire'	180 182 263 281	
ピンポンノキの実	*Sterculia monosperma* Vent.	346	

フ

ファレノプシス [ウェディングプロムナード]	*Phalaenopsis* 'Wedding Promenade'	263 331 354	
ファレノプシス [カカオ]	*Phalaenopsis* 'Cacao'	265 274 292 300 309	
ファレノプシス [ゴールデンビューティー]	*Phalaenopsis* 'Golden Beauty'	143 246	
ファレノプシス [ジャガー]	*Phalaenopsis* 'Jaguar'	253	
ファレノプシス [チャンシンピアノ]	*Phalaenopsis* 'Chian Xen Piano'	277	
ファレノプシス [チョコレートディスコ]	*Phalaenopsis* 'Chocolate Disco'	177	
ファレノプシス [チョコレートパール]	*Phalaenopsis* 'Chocolate Pearl'	296	
ファレノプシス [チンアンダイヤモンド]	*Phalaenopsis* 'Ching Ann Diamond'	289 363	
ファレノプシス [パレルモ]	*Phalaenopsis* 'Palermo'	137 212	
ファレノプシス [リンゴホワイト]	*Phalaenopsis* 'Ringo White'	327	
ファレノプシス・クインビー [満天紅 (まんてんこう)]	*Phalaenopsis* Queen Beer 'Mantenko'	166	
ファレノプシス・シーナズパール [ゲイシャワルツ]	*Phalaenopsis* Sheena's Pearl 'Geisha Waltz'	309	
ファレノプシス・タイダスマイル [リトルゴールド]	*Phalaenopsis* Taida Smile 'Little Gold'	224	
ファレノプシス・タイダソリュー [あずきしょこら]	*Phalaenopsis* Taida Salu 'Azuki Chocolat'	221 354	
ファレノプシス・タイダソリュー [アリサン]	*Phalaenopsis* Taida Salu 'Alisan'	180 265 315 327	
ファレノプシス・タイダソリュー [モーニングサン]	*Phalaenopsis* Taida Salu 'Morning Sun'	166	
ファレノプシス・ソゴアイビス [リトルマルコ]	*Phalaenopsis* Sogo Ibis 'Little Maruko'	281	
ファレノプシス・ソゴパール [パインリッジ]	*Phalaenopsis* Sogo Pearl 'Pine Ridge'	197 312	
ファレノプシス・ソゴバイカー [タイダリトルモンキー]	*Phalaenopsis* Sogo Vieker 'Taida Little Monkey'	189	
ファレノプシス・ソゴユキディアン [V3 (ぶいすりー)]	*Phalaenopsis* Sogo Yukidian 'V3'	47	

ファレノプシス・ハッピーヴィヴィアン［チュンリー］	Phalaenopsis Happy Vivien 'Chunli'	159				
ファレノプシス・ブラザーサラゴールド［マジカル］	Phalaenopsis Brother Sara Gold 'Magical'	182				
フィットニア［サニーレッド］	Fittonia verschaffeltii 'Sunny Red'	335				
フィリカ・プルモーサ	Phylica plumosa L.	175	185			
フィロデンドロン・セローム	Philodendron selloum K. Koch	361				
フウトウカズラ	Piper kadsura Trel. & Yunck.	166				
フウラン［白雲閣（はくうんかく）］	Vanda falcata 'Hakuunkaku'	228	302			
フェノコマ	Phaenocoma prolifera (L.) D. Don	219				
フォーカリア［白波（しらなみ）］	Faucaria bosscheana 'Shiranami'	154				
フォーカリア［怒濤（どとう）］	Faucaria tuberculosa 'Doto'	195				
フォッケア［火星人（かせいじん）］	Fockea edulis 'Kaseijin'	71				
フォッケア・ムルチフローラ	Fockea multiflora K. Schum.	182				
ブッシュカン	Citrus medica var. sarcodactylis	66				
ブッドレア［ロイヤルレッド］	Buddleja davidii 'Royal Red'	146				
ブバルディア［グリーンマジック］	Bouvardia 'Green Magic'	213				
ブバルディア［ホワイトシュープリーム］	Bouvardia 'White Supreme'	190				
ブバルディア［ロイヤルダフネグリーンサマー］	Bouvardia 'Royal Daphne Green Summer'	202				
ブバルディア［ロイヤルダフネニコレット］	Bouvardia 'Royal Daphne Nicollette'	215				
ブバルディア［ロイヤルダフネフレスコ］	Bouvardia 'Royal Daphne Fresco'	197				
ブバルディア［ロイヤルローザ］	Bouvardia 'Royal Roza'	159				
フペルジア・スクアローサ	Huperzia squarrosa (G. Forst.) Trev.	129				
フラグミペディウム［ロージーチャーム］	Phragmipedium 'Rosy Charm'	159				
ブラッシア・エターナルウインド［サマードリーム］	Brassia Eternal Wind 'Summer Dream'	181	263	280		
ブラッシア・ベルコーサ	Brassia verrucosa Bateman ex Lindl.	135				
ブランドフォルディア［クリスマスベル］	Blandfordia grandiflora 'Christmas Bell'	271				
フリージア［アヌーク］	Freesia enkelbloemig 'Anouk'	168				
フリージア［アラジン］	Freesia refracta 'Aladdin'	156	285	299		
フリージア［アンコナ］	Freesia refracta 'Ancona'	279				
フリージア［エレガンス］	Freesia refracta 'Elegance'	150	198			
フリージア［オベロン］	Freesia refracta 'Oberon'	276				
フリージア［ブルーヘブン］	Freesia enkelbloemig 'Blue Heaven'	363				
フリーセア［クリスティアーナ］	Vriesea carinata 'Christiane'	34	81	134	171	229
フリチラリア［アイボリーベル］	Fritillaria persica 'Ivory Bells'	31	170	188	306	
フリチラリア［ルブラマキシマ］	Fritillaria imperialis 'Rubra Maxima'	19				
フリチラリア・アクモペタラ	Fritillaria acmopetala Boiss.	170				
フリチラリア・ウバブルビス	Fritillaria uva-vulpis Rix	39				
フリチラリア・クロユリ	Fritillaria camschatcensis (L.) Ker-Gawl.	299	282	329		
フリチラリア・バイモユリ	Fritillaria thunbergii Miq.	69	216	281	294	
フリチラリア・ペルシカ	Fritillaria persica L.	215	280	309		
フリチラリア・メレアグリス	Fritillaria meleagris L.	21	333			
ブルニア・アルビフローラ	Brunia albiflora E. Phillips	194				
プレイオスピロス［帝玉（ていぎょく）］	Pleiospilos nelii 'Teigyoku'	170				
プロテア［ヴィーナス］	Protea 'Venus'	308				
プロテア［クイーン］	Protea magnifica 'Queen'	319				
プロテア［スノークイーン］	Protea barbigera 'Snow Queen'	174				
プロテア［ニオベ］	Protea barbigera 'Niobe'	77	96	127	170	213
		295	343			
プロテア［ピンクアイス］	Protea 'Pink Ice'	93				
プロテア［ホワイトミンク］	Protea neriifolia 'White Mink'	178				
プロテア［リトルレディホワイト］	Protea mundii 'Little Lady White'	352				
プロテア［ロビン］	Protea 'Robyn'	298				
プロテア・キングプロテア［アークティックアイス］	Protea cynaroides 'Arctic Ice'	41	263	327		
プロテア・キングプロテア［マディバ］	Protea cynaroides 'Madiba'	233				
プロテア・キングプロテア［レッドレックス］	Protea cynaroides 'Red Rex'	85	355			
プロテア・グランディケプス	Protea grandiceps Tratt.	81				
プロテア・ナナ	Protea nana (Berg.) Thunb.	233	335			
フロミス［グリーンスター］	Phlomis fruticosa 'Green Star'	234				

ヘ・ホ

ヘゴゼンマイ	Cyathea spinulosa Wall. ex Hook.	59	135	153	181	202
		227	294	304	329	338
ベゴニア［ピンクドット］	Begonia negrosensis 'Pink Dot'	302				

ベゴニア・エラチオールベゴニア［ボリアス］	*Begonia* × *hiemalis* 'Borias'	192
ベゴニア・ベノーサ	*Begonia venosa* Skan ex Hook. f.	151　185　341
ベゴニア・ボウエレ・ニグラマルガ	*Begonia bowerae* var. *nigramarga* Ziesenh.	196　222　327　331
ベゴニア・マソニアナ	*Begonia masoniana* Irmsch. ex Ziesenh.	177
ベゴニア・レックスベゴニア［アフリカンジャングル］	*Begonia rex* 'African Jungle'	213
ベゴニア・レックスベゴニア［インカナイト］	*Begonia rex* 'Inca Night'	346
ベゴニア・レックスベゴニア［ヴィスタ］	*Begonia rex* 'Vista'	296
ベゴニア・レックスベゴニア［シャツスリーブ］	*Begonia rex* 'Shirt Sleeves'	265
ベゴニア・レックスベゴニア［スーパーカール］	*Begonia rex* 'Super Curl'	166
ベゴニア・レックスベゴニア［ステンドグラス］	*Begonia rex* 'Stained Glass'	293
ベゴニア・レックスベゴニア［大助（だいすけ）］	*Begonia rex* 'Daisuke'	283
ベゴニア・レックスベゴニア［モーニングデュー］	*Begonia rex* 'Morning Dew'	155
ベッセラ・エレガンス	*Bessera elegans* Schult. f.	271　359
ヘデラの実	*Hedera rhombea* Siebold & Zucc. ex Bean	154
ベニノキ	*Bixa orellana* L.	232
ベニバナ	*Carthamus tinctorius* (Mohler, Roth, Schmidt & Boudreaux)	183
ペペロミア［バーガンディリップル］	*Peperomia caperata* 'Burgundy Ripple'	186
ペペロミア［ピンクレディ］	*Peperomia caperata* 'Pink Lady'	178　208
ペペロミア・プテオラータ	*Peperomia puteolata* Trel.	152
ペラルゴニウム［スノーフレーク］	*Pelargonium graveolens* 'Snowflake'	124　194
ペラルゴニウム［ブルボン］	*Pelargonium graveolens* 'Bourbon'	170　174
ペラルゴニウム［リトルジェム］	*Pelargonium graveolens* 'Little Gem'	216
ヘリクリサム	*Helichrysum bracteatum* (Vent.) Andrews	136　143
ヘリコニア［シーコング］	*Heliconia vellerigera* 'She Kong'	327
ヘリコニア［ショウグン］	*Heliconia xanthovillosa* 'Shogun'	89　228
ヘリコニア［ファイヤーバード］	*Heliconia stricta* 'Firebird'	286　346
ヘリコニア［レッドイナズマ］	*Heliconia latispatha* 'Red Inazuma'	138　219
ヘリコニア・マグニフィカ	*Heliconia magnifica* W. J. Kress	34
ヘリコニア・ロストラータ	*Heliconia rostrata* Ruiz & Pavon	99　209
ベレバリア［グリンパール］	*Bellevalia paradoxa* 'Green Pearl'	31
ベロニカ［カロラインブルー］	*Veronica* 'Caroline Blue'	141　185　231
ベロニカ［スマートビザーレ］	*Veronica* 'Smart Bizarre'	345　351
ベロニカ［ピンクハンター］	*Veronica* 'Pink Hunter'	145
ベロニカ［ユニークベイビーホワイト］	*Veronica spicata* 'Younique Baby White'	190
ベロニカ［レッドフォックス］	*Veronica spicata* 'Red Fox'	137
ボケ	*Chaenomeles speciosa* (Sweet) Nakai	344
ポチナラ・スウィートシュガー［ハッピーフィールド］	*Potinara* Sweet Sugar 'Happy Field'	280
ポピー・アイスランドポピー	*Papaver nudicaule* L.	27　87　91　194　198　282　314　329　333
ポピー・オリエンタルポピー	*Papaver orientale* (L.)	109
ポリガラ［スイートピーシュラブ］	*Polygala myrtifolia* var. *grandiflora* 'Sweet Pea Shrub'	170　212　215　263

マ・ミ・ム・メ・モ

マーガレット	*Argyranthemum frutescens* (L.) Sch. Bip.	304
マダガスカルジャスミン	*Stephanotis floribunda* Brongn.	213　228
マツ［五葉松（ごようまつ）］	*Pinus parviflora* Sieb. & Zucc.	47　66　267
マツソニア・ブスツラータ	*Massonia pustulata* Jacq.	358
マリーゴールド［イエローアイシス］	*Tagetes erecta* 'Yellow Isis'	182　200　214
マリーゴールド［イエローボーイ］	*Tagetes erecta* 'Yellow Boy'	321
マリーゴールド［ゼニスレッド］	*Tagetes erecta* 'Zenith Red'	337
マリーゴールド［ソブリン］	*Tagetes erecta* 'Sovereign'	130　171
マリーゴールド［パーフェクションオレンジ］	*Tagetes erecta* 'Perfection Orange'	273
マリーゴールド［ムーンソングディープオレンジ］	*Tagetes erecta* 'Moonsong Deep Orange'	165
マンゴー	*Mangifera indica* L.	172
ミラビフローラ	*Milla biflora* Cav.	352
ムスカリ［ブルーマジック］	*Muscari aucheri* 'Blue Magic'	163　194　329
ムスカリ［ホワイトマジック］	*Muscari aucheri* 'White Magic'	150　157　297
メディニラ・マグニフィカ	*Medinilla magnifica* Lindl.	323
モナルダ・メンシフォリア	*Monarda fistulosa* var. *menthifolia*	191　209
モルセラ・ラエヴィス	*Moluccella laevis* L.	126　171　189　279　329
モンステラ・マドカズラ	*Monstera friedrichsthalii* Schott	181

ヤ・ユ・ヨ

和名	学名	頁			
ヤグルマソウ［ブルーカーペット］	Centaurea cyanus 'Blue Carpet'	162			
ヤドリギ	Viscum album subsp. coloratum Komar	174	267		
ヤトロファ	Jatropha podagrica Hook.	170	232		
ヤマトリカブト	Aconitum japonicum Thunb. var. montanum Nakai	222			
ユーカリ［トランペット］	Eucalyptus 'Trumpet'	180	339		
ユーカリ［フラワーガムオレンジ］	Corymbia ficifolia 'Flower Gum Orange'	143			
ユーチャリス	Eucharis × grandiflora Planch. & Linden	352			
ユーフォルビア・カラキラス	Euphorbia characias L.	291			
ユーフォルビア・ラクティア	Euphorbia lactea Haw.	300	336	363	
ユーフォルビア［姫キリン（ひめきりん）］	Euphorbia submamillaris (A. Berger) A. Berger	235			
ユウギリソウ［ディボーションパープル］	Trachelium caeruleum 'Devotion Purple'	134	230	273	
ユリ［明日香（あすか）］	Lilium orientalis 'Asuka'	345			
ユリ［イザベラ］	Lilium orientalis 'Isabella'	304			
ユリ［オレンジアート］	Lilium 'Orange Art'	307			
ユリ［カサブランカ］	Lilium orientalis 'Casa Blanca'	166	192	198	201
ユリ［カロリーナ］	Lilium orientalis 'Carolina'	125	293		
ユリ［シベリア］	Lilium orientalis 'Siberia'	200			
ユリ［セーラ］	Lilium orientalis 'Sheila'	65			
ユリ［ノーブルリリー］	Lilium 'Noble Lily'	294			
ユリ［ファイヤーボルト］	Lilium orientalis 'Firebolt'	155			
ユリ［マンボ］	Lilium orientalis 'Mambo'	167	176	223	
ユリ・ウコンユリ	Lilium ochroleucum Wall. ex Baker	77			
ユリ・オウゴンオニユリ	Lilium lancifolium Thunb. var. flaviflorum Makino	145			
ユリ・スカシユリ［アプリコットファッジ］	Lilium maculatum 'Apricot Fudge'	57	170		
ユリ・スカシユリ［カフェノアール］	Lilium maculatum 'Café Noir'	289			
ユリ・スカシユリ［ブラックアウト］	Lilium maculatum 'Black Out'	292			
ユリ・タケシマユリ	Lilium hansonii Leichtlin ex D. D. T. Moore	105	234		
ユリ・チョウセンヒメユリ	Lilium concolor Salisb.	165	209	212	331
ユリ・テッポウユリ［グリーンリリアルブ］	Lilium longiflorum 'Green Lily Alp'	152			
ユリ・テッポウユリ［日の本（ひのもと）］	Lilium longiflorum 'Hinomoto'	194	299		
ユリ・テッポウユリ［ピュアホルン］	Lilium longiflorum 'Pure Horn'	127	352		
ヨウシュヤマゴボウ	Phytolacca americana L.	306	319	331	

ラ

和名	学名	頁		
ライラック［マダムフローレントステップマン］	Syringa vulgaris 'Madame Florent Stepman'	278		
ラケナリア・アロイデス・クアドリカラー	Lachenalia aloides var. quadricolor	269	288	333
ラケナリア・ビリディフローラ	Lachenalia viridiflora W. F. Barker	204	269	
ラケナリア・ムタビリス	Lachenalia mutabilis Lodd. ex Sweet	194		
ラナンキュラス［アルテミス］	Ranunculus asiaticus 'Artemis'	218		
ラナンキュラス［イカロス］	Ranunculus asiaticus 'Ikaros'	285		
ラナンキュラス［エムピンク］	Ranunculus asiaticus 'M Pink'	291		
ラナンキュラス［エムブルー］	Ranunculus asiaticus 'M Blue'	290		
ラナンキュラス［オーロラ］	Ranunculus asiaticus 'Aurora'	159		
ラナンキュラス［シストロン］	Ranunculus asiaticus 'Sisteron'	359		
ラナンキュラス［シャルロット］	Ranunculus asiaticus 'Charlotte'	158	160	304
ラナンキュラス［ジロンド］	Ranunculus asiaticus 'Gironde'	325	358	
ラナンキュラス［タンジェ］	Ranunculus asiaticus 'Tanger'	314		
ラナンキュラス［ポムロール］	Ranunculus asiaticus 'Pomerol'	194	294	
ラナンキュラス［モロッコタンタン］	Ranunculus asiaticus 'Morocco Tantan'	160		
ラナンキュラス［モロッコマーミド］	Ranunculus asiaticus 'Morocco Mhamid'	57		
ラムズイヤー［プリムローズヘロン］	Stachys byzantina 'Primrose Heron'	135		

リ・ル・レ・ロ

和名	学名	頁	
リキュウソウ	Stemona japonica (Blume) Miq.	82	
リコリス・インカルナータ	Lycoris incarnata Comes ex Sprenger	342	
リコリス・オーレア	Lycoris aurea (L'Hér.) Herb.	224	
リプサリス・エワルディアナ	Rhipsalis ewaldiana Barthlott & N. P. Taylor	160	335
リプサリス・カスタ	Rhipsalis cassutha Gaertn.	189	
リプサリス・ケレウスクラ	Rhipsalis cereuscula Haw.	170	

リブサリス・テレス	*Rhipsalis teres* Steud.	152				
リューカデントロン [プルモサス]	*Leucadendron rubrum* 'Plumosus'	357				
リューココリーネ [カラベル]	*Leucocoryne purpurea* 'Caravel'	205	271	305		
リューココリーネ・コキンベンシス	*Leucocoryne coquimbensis* F. Phil. ex Phil.	162				
リンドウ [安代の晩秋 (あしろのばんしゅう)]	*Gentiana triflora* var. *japonica* 'Ashiro no Banshu'	138	146	336		
リンドウ [いわて夢あおい (いわてゆめあおい)]	*Gentiana triflora* var. *japonica* 'Iwate Yume Aoi'	200				
リンドウ [ジョバンニ]	*Gentiana triflora* var. *japonica* 'Giovanni'	231				
リンドウ [スカイブルーシナノ]	*Gentiana triflora* var. *japonica* 'Sky Blue Shinano'	223				
リンドウ [白寿 (はくじゅ)]	*Gentiana triflora* var. *japonica* 'Hakuju'	351				
リンドウ [パステルベル]	*Gentiana triflora* var. *japonica* 'Pastel Bell'	129				
リンドウ [初冠雪ラブ (はつかんせつらぶ)]	*Gentiana triflora* var. *japonica* 'Hatsukansetsu Love'	331	344			
リンドウ [マイファンタジー]	*Gentiana triflora* var. *japonica* 'My Fantasy'	185				
ルドベキア [アイリッシュアイ]	*Rudbeckia hirta* 'Irish Eyes'	225				
ルドベキア [チェロキーサンセット]	*Rudbeckia hirta* 'Cherokee Sunset'	172				
ルピナス [黄花ルピナス (きばなるぴなす)]	*Lupinus luteus* 'Kibana Lupinus'	63				
ルピナス [ピクシーデライト]	*Lupinus nanus* 'Pixie Delight'	302				
ルブス・ブラックベリー	*Rubus fruticosus* L.	122	146	220		
ルリタマアザミ [ベッチーズブルー]	*Echinops ritro* 'Veitch's Blue'	136				
レイシェステリア・フォルモーサ	*Leycesteria formosa* Wall.	331	339			
レースフラワー [グリーンミスト]	*Ammi majus* 'Green Mist'	144	151	198	214	216
		307				
レオントキール・オバレイ	*Leontochir ovallei* Phil.	283	307			
ロマトフィルム・プロストラツム	*Lomatophyllum prostratum* H. Perrier	271				

ワ

| ワスレナグサ | *Myosotis* L. | 162 | 210 |

Index of Flowers by Name

A	Page
Achillea alpina L.	183
Aconitum japonicum Thunb. var. *montanum* Nakai	222
Adenanthos × cunninghamii Meisn.	161
Aechmea fasciata (Lindl.) Baker	143 185 212 327
	355
Aechmea fendleri 'Del Mar'	34
Aechmea fulgens 'Red Berry'	171
Aechmea gamosepala Wittm.	314
Aechmea penduliflora 'White Berry'	152
Aechmea wittmackiana 'Scarlet Berry'	129
Aeonium arboreum 'Zwartkop'	293
Agapanthus africanus 'Blue Heaven'	184
Agapanthus africanus 'June Bride'	122
Agapanthus africanus 'Murasaki Shikibu'	208
Agapanthus africanus 'Ocean Blue'	298
Agapanthus africanus 'Royal Blue'	141 230
Agapanthus africanus (L.) Hoffmanns.	180 339
Agave potatorum 'Raijin'	189
Ageratum houstonianum 'Blue Hawaii'	194
Ageratum houstonianum 'Top Blue'	162 282 327
Albuca spiralis 'Frizzle Sizzle'	285 358
Allium 'Blue Perfume'	163 210
Allium 'Pinocchio'	71 234
Allium amethystinum 'Red Mohican'	113 141 223 321
Allium giganteum Regel	152 214 263 299
Allium hollandicum 'Purple Sensation'	213 221
Allium neapolitanum 'Cowanii'	199
Allium schubertii Zucc.	283 298 362
Alocasia 'Amazonica'	360
Alocasia cucullata (Lour.) G. Don	278
Aloe 'Flamingo'	25 177
Aloe 'Red Devil'	287
Aloe arborescens Mill.	331 360
Aloe jucunda Reynolds	323 335
Alpinia purpurata 'Red Ginger'	273
Alpinia zerumbet (Pers.) B. L. Burtt and R. M. Sm.	33 294
Alstroemeria 'Scorpion'	196 204 271
Alstroemeria 'Sesame Orange'	165
Amaranthus caudatus 'Viridis'	134 361
Amaranthus cruentus 'Shidare Keito'	348
Ammi majus 'Green Mist'	144 151 198 214
	216 307
Anemone coronaria 'Saint Bridget Rose'	314 358
Anemone hupehensis 'Pretty Lady Diana'	342
Anemone hupehensis var. *japonica* 'Honorine Jobert'	352
Anigozanthos flavidus 'Green'	182 235
Anigozanthos flavidus 'Orange Cross'	123
Anigozanthos flavidus 'Red and Green'	263 291
Anthurium andreanum 'Alexia Jade'	216
Anthurium andreanum 'Alula Pink'	65
Anthurium andreanum 'Amigo'	139
Anthurium andreanum 'ARCS Purple'	127 230 333
Anthurium andreanum 'Black Queen'	187 200 265 297
	302
Anthurium andreanum 'Burgundy'	154
Anthurium andreanum 'Emperor'	302 308
Anthurium andreanum 'Fesca'	212
Anthurium andreanum 'Forest'	194

Anthurium andreanum 'Fuchsia Green'	55
Anthurium andreanum 'Jupiter'	278 306
Anthurium andreanum 'Kalapana'	144
Anthurium andreanum 'Lady Jane'	274
Anthurium andreanum 'Maxima Verde'	226
Anthurium andreanum 'Midori'	329 360
Anthurium andreanum 'Previa'	166 215
Anthurium andreanum 'Rock Set'	359
Anthurium andreanum 'Rosa'	314
Anthurium andreanum 'Safari'	106 150 196 283
	286
Anthurium andreanum 'Sierra Magic'	101
Anthurium andreanum 'Sonata'	354
Anthurium andreanum 'Spice'	310
Anthurium andreanum 'Trinidad'	133
Anthurium andreanum 'Tropical Red'	90 280
Anthurium clarinervium Matuda	129
Anthurium crassinervium 'Jungle King'	292
Anthurium longifolium (Hoffm.) G. Don	227 232 321
Aphelandra squarrosa 'Dania'	335
Aquilegia chrysantha 'Yellow Queen'	170
Aquilegia vulgaris 'Winky Blue'	295
Aranda 'Green Tiger'	269 331
Argyranthemum frutescens (L.) Sch. Bip.	304
Argyreia nervosa (Burm. f.) Bojer	352
Arisaema urashima Hara	109 309
Arpophyllum giganteum Hartw. ex Lindl.	21 265
Asarum minamitanianum 'Ryokuho'	335
Ascocenda 'Muang Thong'	247
Astilbe × *arendsii* 'America'	158 213
Astilbe × *arendsii* 'Fanal'	213
Astilbe × *arendsii* 'Pastel Pink'	191

B

Bambuseae Kunth ex Dumort.	47 48
Banksia attenuata R. Br.	161
Banksia coccinea R. Br	147 165 208 226
Banksia ericifolia L. f.	215
Banksia hookeriana Meisn.	173
Banksia integrifolia L. f.	150 167 188
Banksia menziesii R. Br.	180 223 229 339
Banksia spinulosa Sm.	286 288
Begonia × *hiemalis* 'Borias'	192
Begonia bowerae var. *nigramarga* Ziesenh.	196 222 327 331
Begonia masoniana Irmsch. ex Ziesenh.	177
Begonia negrosensis 'Pink Dot'	302
Begonia rex 'African Jungle'	213
Begonia rex 'Daisuke'	283
Begonia rex 'Inca Night'	346
Begonia rex 'Morning Dew'	155
Begonia rex 'Shirt Sleeves'	265
Begonia rex 'Stained Glass'	293
Begonia rex 'Super Curl'	166
Begonia rex 'Vista'	296
Begonia venosa Skan ex Hook. f.	151 185 341
Bellevalia paradoxa 'Green Pearl'	31
Berzelia lanuginosa (L.) Brongn.	157 202
Bessera elegans Schult. f.	271 359
Bixa orellana L.	232
Blandfordia grandiflora 'Christmas Bell'	271
Bouvardia 'Green Magic'	213
Bouvardia 'Royal Daphne Fresco'	197
Bouvardia 'Royal Daphne Green Summer'	202
Bouvardia 'Royal Daphne Nicollette'	215

Bouvardia 'Royal Roza'   159
Bouvardia 'White Supreme'   190
Brassia Eternal Wind 'Summer Dream'   181   263   280
Brassia verrucosa Bateman ex Lindl.   135
Brassica oleracea 'Mitsuko Premium'   177
Brassica oleracea 'Black Swan'   313
Brassica oleracea 'Purple Pop'   53
Brassica oleracea 'Silky Pearl'   177
Brassica oleracea 'Versailles Black Lucien'   297
Brassica oleracea var. *botrytis* 'Romanesco'   194   282   305
Brunia albiflora E. Phillips   194
Brassolaeliocattleya Young-Min Orange 'Jin Man 1'   274   325
Buddleja davidii 'Royal Red'   146
Bulbinella floribunda (Aiton) T. Durand & Schinz   219
Bulbophyllum Elizabeth Ann 'Buckleberry'   286

C

Caladium 'Scarlet Beauty'   119
Calathea crotalifera S. Watson   321
Calathea cylindrica 'Green Ice'   153   189   209   234
Callistephus chinensis 'Azumi Rose Pink'   166
Callistephus chinensis 'Shaggy Deep Blue'   221
Callistephus chinensis 'Shaggy Pink Flash'   124   134
Callistephus chinensis 'Stella Red'   257
Camellia japonica L.   311
Camellia sasanqua Thunb.   49
Campanula medium 'Champion Purple'   263   280
Carthamus tinctorius (Mohler, Roth, Schmidt & Boudreaux) 183
Cattleya Purple Cascade 'Fragrance Beauty'   275
Celastrus orbiculatus Thunb. var. *orbiculatus*   344
Celosia argentea var. *cristata* 'Bombay Green'   202
Celosia argentea var. *cristata* 'Bombay Orange'   201
Celosia argentea var. *cristata* 'Bombay Pink'   331
Celosia argentea var. *cristata* 'Brown Beauty'   349
Celosia argentea var. *cristata* 'Early Rose'   351
Celosia argentea var. *cristata* 'Kurume Akajiku'   232   313   337
Celosia argentea var. *cristata* 'Kurume Gold'   342
Celosia argentea var. *cristata* 'Melon Frill'   234
Celosia argentea var. *cristata* 'Orange Queen'   321
Celosia argentea var. *cristata* 'Rose Queen'   355
Celosia argentea var. *cristata* 'Sakata Pride'   128   160   186   208   319
Celosia argentea var. *cristata* 'Spring Green'   152
Centaurea cyanus 'Blue Carpet'   162
Centaurea macrocephala Muss. Puschk. ex Willd.   131
Cereus jamacaru DC.   337
Chaenomeles speciosa (Sweet) Nakai   344
Chrysanthemum × *morifolium* 'Amarantha'   329
Chrysanthemum × *morifolium* 'Anastasia Dark Lime'   204
Chrysanthemum × *morifolium* 'Anastasia Green'   265
Chrysanthemum × *morifolium* 'Bomber Green'   174
Chrysanthemum × *morifolium* 'Classic Cocoa'   290
Chrysanthemum × *morifolium* 'Delacroix'   285
Chrysanthemum × *morifolium* 'Elena'   279
Chrysanthemum × *morifolium* 'Epoch'   159   265
Chrysanthemum × *morifolium* 'Feeling'   339
Chrysanthemum × *morifolium* 'Feeling Green'   345
Chrysanthemum × *morifolium* 'Golden Ping Pong'   182   298
Chrysanthemum × *morifolium* 'Jenny Orange'   142
Chrysanthemum × *morifolium* 'Lollipop Red'   154
Chrysanthemum × *morifolium* 'Pretty Rio'   197   289
Chrysanthemum × *morifolium* 'Pure Green'   188   201   217
Chrysanthemum × *morifolium* 'Saba'   127   298
Chrysanthemum × *morifolium* 'Saffina'   127   290   305   327
Chrysanthemum × *morifolium* 'Sei Etude'   284

Chrysanthemum × *morifolium* 'Sei Nadal'	170
Chrysanthemum × *morifolium* 'Super Ping Pong'	168
Chrysanthemum × *morifolium* 'Yo'	81 157 180 288 310
Chrysanthemum × *morifolium* 'Fuego'	263 276 321 349
Chrysanthemum × *morifolium* 'Green Shamrock'	55 139 188 201
	273 283
Chrysanthemum × *morifolium* 'Zembla Brazil'	215 273
Chrysanthemum × *morifolium* 'Pink Bell'	190
Chrysanthemum × *morifolium* 'Say Opera Pink'	190
Chrysanthemum pacificum Nakai	200 344
Cinnamomum zeylanicum J. Presl	234
Cirsium japonicum Fisch. ex DC.	212
Cirsium purpuratum (Maxim.) Matsum.	327 331
Cissus javana DC.	233
Citrus medica var. *sarcodactylis*	66
Cleistocactus winteri D. Hunt	155
Clematis florida 'Alba Plena'	87
Clematis florida 'Crystal Fountain'	263
Clematis florida 'Magic Fountain'	147
Clematis integrifolia 'Hendersonii'	166 341
Clematis integrifolia 'Inspiration'	312
Clematis integrifolia 'Miss Sumire'	130
Clematis integrifolia 'Rouguchi'	230
Clematis L.	153 181 234 338
Clematis socialis Kral	211
Clematis texensis 'Oshikiri'	190
Clematis texensis 'Scarlet'	122 131 212 263
Clematis × *durandii*	288
Clivia gardenii Hook.	287
Clivia miniata (Lindl.) Verschaff.	343
Cocos nucifera L.	173
Codiaeum variegatum 'Akebono'	129
Colchicum autumnale 'Alba'	353
Colmanara Wildcat 'Bobcat'	255 304
Colmanara Wildcat 'Carmela'	263
Colmanara Wildcat 'Golden Red Star'	132
Conostylis setigera 'Joey Cat's Paw'	325
Convallaria majalis L.	23 308
Corymbia ficifolia 'Flower Gum Orange'	143
Costus woodsonii Maas	186 234
Crocosmia 'Lucifer'	135 142
Cryptanthus bivittatus 'Pink Starlight'	19 333
Cryptanthus fosterianus 'Elaine'	312
Curcuma alismatifolia 'Emerald Choco Zebra'	203 235
Curcuma alismatifolia 'Eternal Pink'	139
Curcuma alismatifolia 'Old Rose'	146
Curcuma alismatifolia 'Pink Pearl'	119 337
Curcuma alismatifolia 'Saim Crown'	206 319 327 342
Curcuma alismatifolia 'Verdebianco'	153 184
Curcuma cordata 'Jewel of Thailand'	34
Curcuma gracillima 'Candy Cane'	234
Cyathea spinulosa Wall. ex Hook.	59 135 153 181 202
	227 294 304 329
	338
Cycas revoluta Thunb.	180 350
Cyclamen hederifolium Aiton	174
Cyclamen persicum 'Happiness Mama'	304
Cymbidium 'Akane'	229
Cymbidium 'Cappuccino'	331
Cymbidium 'Cha Cha'	222
Cymbidium 'Crescent'	182
Cymbidium 'Green Sour'	282
Cymbidium 'Irohairo 01'	287
Cymbidium 'King Arthur'	298
Cymbidium 'Mocha'	178
Cymbidium 'Nemureru Mori no Bijyo'	269
Cymbidium 'Red Empress'	265

Cymbidium 'Romance'   343
Cymbidium 'Soleil Levant'   200
Cymbidium 'Wine Shower'   154
Cymbidium Eastern Bunny 'Tsuki no Hikari'   305
Cymbidium Enzan Forest 'Majolica'   218   342
Cymbidium floribundum Lindl.   282   306
Cymbidium Lovely Valley 'Peace in the World'   195
Cymbidium tracyanum L. Castle   265   276   297   303
                                                               311   329
Cynara scolymus L.   33   115   122   180
                                                               234   292   294   340
                                                               357
Cyrtanthus mackenii 'King Yellow'   193   315
Cyrtanthus mackenii 'Scarlet'   358

D

Dahlia 'Agitato'   296   346
Dahlia 'Antique Red × Peach Pie'   136
Dahlia 'Arabian Night'   193   292
Dahlia 'Asahi Temari'   170   200   212   232
                                                               273   279   289   314
                                                               346
Dahlia 'Beautiful Days'   350
Dahlia 'Biedermannsdorf'   130   173   348
Dahlia 'Blue Peach'   215   269   333
Dahlia 'Dream Dance'   215
Dahlia 'Edinburgh'   196
Dahlia 'Eona G'   247
Dahlia 'Fidalgo Blacky'   176   312
Dahlia 'Fukuju'   344
Dahlia 'Garnet'   123
Dahlia 'Gitt's Perfection'   251
Dahlia 'Glenplace'   204   223
Dahlia 'Hakusantemari'   253
Dahlia 'Hamilton Junior'   287
Dahlia 'Hinaarare'   244
Dahlia 'Iwaibana'   161
Dahlia 'Jessica'   240
Dahlia 'Jessie Rita'   327   331   344
Dahlia 'Junai no Kimi'   122   226   241   302
Dahlia 'JyuJyu'   136
Dahlia 'Kamakura'   352
Dahlia 'Koishigure'   158
Dahlia 'Kokucho'   126   155   176   222   323
Dahlia 'Koto'   248
Dahlia 'Labella Piccolo Pink'   181
Dahlia 'Lalala'   151   238   257   306
                                                               344
Dahlia 'Lemon Card'   224
Dahlia 'Lemon Light'   182
Dahlia 'Little Rosemary'   319
Dahlia 'Malcom's White'   168
Dahlia 'Marron'   178
Dahlia 'Matador'   125   314
Dahlia 'Micchan'   39   212   226   306
Dahlia 'Monaco S'   242
Dahlia 'Moon Stone'   245   362
Dahlia 'Moon Waltz'   246
Dahlia 'Mrs. Eileen'   243
Dahlia 'Ms. Zelda'   355
Dahlia 'Murakingyo'   126   249   296   298
Dahlia 'Namahage Magic'   141   147   252
Dahlia 'Namahage Noir'   154
Dahlia 'Namahage Purple'   327

Dahlia 'Namahage Swan'	254			
Dahlia 'Nekkyu'	331	342	346	
Dahlia 'Nessho'	215	232	269	284
	287	308	311	
Dahlia 'Peach in Season'	173			
Dahlia 'Peach Pie × Namahage Nuance'	142			
Dahlia 'Pechka'	319	331		
Dahlia 'Portlight Pair Beauty'	256			
Dahlia 'Rebecca Lynn'	166			
Dahlia 'Red Marvelous'	271			
Dahlia 'Red Star'	186	263	301	310
Dahlia 'Rose Quartz'	273	302		
Dahlia 'Sabaku'	286			
Dahlia 'Sakuragai'	250			
Dahlia 'Santa Claus'	133	288		
Dahlia 'Show N Tell'	350			
Dahlia 'Sinbad'	124	239		
Dahlia 'Strawberry Cream'	351			
Dahlia 'Tampico'	180			
Dahlia 'Wizard of Oz'	344			
Dahlia 'Yorokobi'	258			
Dahlia 'Yuino'	255			
Dahlia 'Yuki Tsubaki'	220			
Dahlia 'Yukiguni'	199			
Dahlia 'Yuma'	212			
Dahlia Cav.	164	208		
Daucus carota 'Black Knight'	179			
Daucus carota L.	175	235	321	
Delphinium chinense 'Blue Candle'	314			
Delphinium elatum 'Aurora Blue Imp'	123	150	166	
Delphinium elatum 'Aurora Deep Purple'	141			
Delphinium grandiflorum 'Grand Blue'	211			
Delphinium grandiflorum 'Super Grand Blue'	163			
Delphinium grandiflorum 'Super Sky Blue'	125			
Dendrobium 'Sweet Candy'	277			
Dendrobium King Zip 'Red Splash'	333			
Dendrobium phalaenopsis 'Lemon Green'	217			
Dendrochilum cobbianum Rchb. f.	269	325		
Dendrochilum dempoense J. J. Sm.	265			
Dendrochilum magnum Rchb. f.	82	302	319	
Dendrochilum propinquum Ames	359			
Dendropanax trifidus (Thunb.) Makino ex. H. Hara	175			
Dianthus 'Raffine Lili'	190			
Dianthus barbatus 'Breanthus Baron'	150			
Dianthus barbatus 'Breanthus Duke'	199			
Dianthus barbatus 'Breanthus Queen'	176			
Dianthus barbatus 'Breanthus Road'	161	206		
Dianthus barbatus 'Green Trick'	126	136	150	152
	161	166	212	216
	218	234	294	345
	360			
Dianthus caryophyllus 'Anthony'	342			
Dianthus caryophyllus 'Bizet'	212			
Dianthus caryophyllus 'Classico'	178	321		
Dianthus caryophyllus 'Crimson Tempo'	160			
Dianthus caryophyllus 'Dom Pedro'	29	291		
Dianthus caryophyllus 'Duelo'	135			
Dianthus caryophyllus 'Excellia'	303			
Dianthus caryophyllus 'Golem'	143			
Dianthus caryophyllus 'Hermès'	325			
Dianthus caryophyllus 'Hermès Orange'	358			
Dianthus caryophyllus 'Hurricane'	205			
Dianthus caryophyllus 'Kiro'	208			
Dianthus caryophyllus 'Lion King'	337			
Dianthus caryophyllus 'Master'	126	321	336	
Dianthus caryophyllus 'Megan'	218			
Dianthus caryophyllus 'Nebo'	204			

Dianthus caryophyllus 'Nobio Violet'	160			
Dianthus caryophyllus 'Prado Mint'	194	216		
Dianthus caryophyllus 'Primero Pluto'	196			
Dianthus caryophyllus 'Seychelles'	294			
Dianthus caryophyllus 'Sharara'	196			
Dianthus caryophyllus 'Siberia'	352			
Dianthus caryophyllus 'Zurigo'	323			
Dichelostemma ida-maia 'Pink Diamond'	298			
Dichelostemma ida-maia (Alph. Wood) Greene	172			
Digitalis parviflora 'Milk Chocolate'	178			
Dionaea muscipula 'Cluster Traps'	35			
Dionaea muscipula 'Dingleys Giant'	128	152		
Dipsacus fullonum L.	235			
Disa Kewensis 'Ann'	240			
Disa Kewensis 'Artists Alba'	238			
Disa Kewensis 'Artists'	251			
Disocactus flagelliformis (L.) Barthlott	335			
Disporum sessile (Thunb.) D. Don ex Schult. & Schult. f.	348			
Doryanthes excelsa Correa	60	232	321	335
Drimiopsis maculata Lindl. & Paxton	96			
Dryopteris crassirhizoma Nakai	189	283		
Dyckia 'Nickel Silver'	211			

E · F · G

Echeveria 'Black Knight'	176			
Echeveria 'Black Prince'	167	235	357	
Echeveria 'Fantasia Carol'	300			
Echeveria 'Gorgon's Grotto'	203			
Echeveria 'Hercules'	163			
Echeveria 'Melaco'	323			
Echeveria 'Shichifukujin'	139	185	230	
Echeveria 'Sofuren'	53			
Echeveria 'Tsuki Kage'	202			
Echeveria 'White Ghost'	189			
Echeveria 'Yamatobini'	29			
Echeveria lilacina Kimn. & Moran	162	184	223	
Echeveria shaviana Walther	337			
Echinacea purpurea 'Eccentric'	213			
Echinacea purpurea 'Harvest Moon'	321			
Echinacea purpurea 'Hot Papaya'	123	248		
Echinacea purpurea 'Pink Passion'	152			
Echinocactus grusonii Hildm.	181			
Echinocereus subinermis var. *luteus* (Britton & Rose)	184			
Echinops ritro 'Veitch's Blue'	136			
Echinopsis tubiflora (Pfeiff.) Zucc. ex K. Schum.	327			
Elettaria cardamomum (L.) Maton	234			
Encyclia adenocaula (Lex.) Schltr.	245			
Epidendrum Parasol Valley 'Hatsukoi'	158			
Epidendrum Parasol Valley 'Music Box'	190	279		
Epidendrum Princess Valley 'White Castle'	199			
Epidendrum secundum 'Chidori'	201	208		
Epidendrum secundum 'Orange Ball'	142	164	172	214
Epidendrum secundum 'Pecan Orange'	180			
Epidendrum secundum 'Pecan Red'	284			
Epidendrum secundum 'Pecan Yellow'	192			
Epidendrum secundum 'Pink Flamingo'	271	333		
Epidendrum secundum 'Princess 8'	288			
Epidendrum secundum 'Red 5'	186	192	196	206
	212	232	243	263
	279	299	306	310
	327	337	346	
Epidendrum secundum 'White Star'	242			
Epidendrum secundum 'Yellow Star'	218	325		
Epidendrum Star Valley 'Violet Queen'	137	171		

Epidendrum Sunlight Valley 'Happy Moon'	182			
Epidendrum Wonder Valley 'Noble Star'	150			
Epiterantha micromeris (Engelmann) F. A. C. Weber ex Britt. & Rose	195			
Equisetum hyemale L.	71	128		
Eremurus stenophyllus (Boiss. & Buhse) Baker	140	335		
Eriosyce senilis (Backeb.) Katt.	185			
Espostoa blossfeldiorum (Vaupel) Borg	169			
Eucalyptus 'Trumpet'	180	339		
Eucharis × *grandiflora* Planch. & Linden	352			
Euphorbia characias L.	291			
Euphorbia lactea Haw.	300	336	363	
Euphorbia submamillaris (A. Berger) A. Berger	235			
Eustoma grandiflorum 'Celeb Blue'	196	337		
Eustoma grandiflorum 'Corsage Pink'	151			
Eustoma grandiflorum 'Reina White'	168			
Eustoma grandiflorum 'Voyage Blue'	205	290	313	363
Eustoma grandiflorum 'Voyage White'	198			
Faucaria bosscheana 'Shiranami'	154			
Faucaria tuberculosa 'Doto'	195			
Ferocactus macrodiscus (Mart.) Britton & Rose	171			
Fittonia verschaffeltii 'Sunny Red'	335			
Fockea edulis 'Kaseijin'	71			
Fockea multiflora K. Schum.	182			
Freesia enkelbloemig 'Anouk'	168			
Freesia enkelbloemig 'Blue Heaven'	363			
Freesia refracta 'Aladdin'	156	285	299	
Freesia refracta 'Ancona'	279			
Freesia refracta 'Elegance'	150	198		
Freesia refracta 'Oberon'	276			
Fritillaria acmopetala Boiss.	170			
Fritillaria camschatcensis (L.) Ker-Gawl.	299	282	329	
Fritillaria imperialis 'Rubra Maxima'	19			
Fritillaria meleagris L.	21	333		
Fritillaria persica 'Ivory Bells'	31	170	188	306
Fritillaria persica L.	215	280	309	
Fritillaria thunbergii Miq.	69	216	281	294
Fritillaria uva-vulpis Rix	39			
Fuchsia 'Hidcote Beauty'	263			
Fuchsia 'White Ann'	308			
Ganoderma applanatum (Pers.) Pat.	171	348		
Gentiana triflora var. *japonica* 'Ashiro no Banshu'	138	146	336	
Gentiana triflora var. *japonica* 'Giovanni'	231			
Gentiana triflora var. *japonica* 'Hakuju'	351			
Gentiana triflora var. *japonica* 'Hatsukansetsu Love'	331	344		
Gentiana triflora var. *japonica* 'Iwate Yume Aoi'	200			
Gentiana triflora var. *japonica* 'My Fantasy'	185			
Gentiana triflora var. *japonica* 'Pastel Bell'	129			
Gentiana triflora var. *japonica* 'Sky Blue Shinano'	223			
Gerbera 'Anacleto'	164	180		
Gerbera 'Antique'	219			
Gerbera 'Black Pearl'	134			
Gerbera 'Crissing'	273			
Gerbera 'Dakar'	351			
Gerbera 'Double Date'	172			
Gerbera 'Finesse'	158			
Gerbera 'Gio'	147	214	221	222
Gerbera 'Japio'	197			
Gerbera 'Knight Rider'	178			
Gerbera 'Last Dance'	136			
Gerbera 'Lipstick'	190			
Gerbera 'Miguel'	126			
Gerbera 'New Madness'	363			
Gerbera 'Pasta di Mamma'	172	215	309	
Gerbera 'Petit Akane'	167	193	201	206
	331	336	355	
Gerbera 'Purple Springs'	323			
Gerbera 'Red Trip'	150			

Gerbera 'Sandy'	279			
Gerbera 'Stanza'	133	306		
Gerbera 'Summer Time'	186			
Gerbera 'Sun Glow'	273			
Gerbera 'Terra Asahi'	183	225		
Gerbera 'Terra Nova'	144			
Gerbera 'Tomahawk'	130	170	285	
Gerbera 'Twister'	208			
Gerbera 'Voldemort'	150	205	232	306
	321	359		
Gladiolus murielae Kelway	47			
Gleichenia japonica Spr.	216	329		
Globba winitii 'Green Dragon'	135	361		
Globba winitii 'Pink Dragon'	227			
Gloriosa superba 'Carsonii'	293	350		
Gloriosa superba 'Lime'	188			
Gloriosa superba 'Mesa'	186			
Gloriosa superba 'Pearl White'	167			
Gloriosa superba 'Precious Pearl'	213			
Glycine max (L.) Merr.	350			
Gomphrena globosa 'Rose Neon'	312			
Graptoveria 'Opalina'	196	231		
Grevillea 'Golden Yu-Lo'	304			
Grevillea 'Honey Gem'	273			
Guzmania 'Cherry'	346			
Guzmania 'Hilda'	226			
Guzmania 'Minor Variegata'	274			
Guzmania 'Orangeade'	170	225	342	
Guzmania 'Torch'	151	180	301	309
	351			
Guzmania dissitiflora (André) L. B. Sm.	170			
Gymnocalycium anisitsii (K. Schumann) Britton & Rose	164	209		
Gymnocalycium saglionis (Cels) Britton et Rose.	361			

H · I · J

Habenaria medusa Kraenzl.	327			
Haemanthus albiflos Jacq.	180	344		
Haworthia cooperi var. *obtusa* 'Shizukuishi'	152	202	231	
Haworthia cymbiformis 'Kyo no Hana'	203			
Haworthia fasciata 'Juni no Maki'	114	216	323	331
Haworthia minima 'Shutensei'	185			
Haworthia reinwardtii 'Taka no Tsume'	172			
Hedera rhombea Siebold & Zucc. ex Bean	154			
Helianthus annuus 'Sunrich Orange'	309			
Helianthus annuus 'Tohoku Yae'	122			
Helianthus annuus 'Van Gogh Sunflower'	224			
Helianthus annuus 'Vincent Tangerine'	325			
Helichrysum bracteatum (Vent.) Andrews	136	143		
Heliconia latispatha 'Red Inazuma'	138	219		
Heliconia magnifica W. J. Kress	34			
Heliconia rostrata Ruiz & Pavon	99	209		
Heliconia stricta 'Firebird'	286	346		
Heliconia vellerigera 'She Kong'	327			
Heliconia xanthovillosa 'Shogun'	89	228		
Helleborus 'Double Rasberry Ripple'	302			
Helleborus foetidus L.	267			
Heuchera 'Midnight Rose'	176			
Hibiscus 'Brilliant Red'	212			
Hippeastrum blossfeldiae (Traub & J. L. Doran) Van Scheepen	192			
Hippeastrum calyptratum (Ker Gawl.) Herb.	300			
Hippeastrum correiense (Bury) Worsley	33			
Hippeastrum papilio (Ravenna) Van Scheepen	290	359		
Hippeastrum × hybridum 'Black Baccara'	154			
Hippeastrum × hybridum 'Christmas Gift'	175			

Hippeastrum × *hybridum* 'Double Ribbon'	283			
Hippeastrum × *hybridum* 'Magic Green'	166			
Hippeastrum × *hybridum* 'Minerva'	282			
Hippeastrum × *hybridum* 'Red Lion'	93	228	265	
Hippeastrum × *hybridum* 'Red Peacock'	292			
Hippeastrum × *hybridum* 'Royal Velvet'	301			
Hippeastrum × *hybridum* 'Susan'	290			
Huperzia squarrosa (G. Forst.) Trev.	129			
Hyacinthus orientalis 'Anna Marie'	167	193		
Hyacinthus orientalis 'Blue Jacket'	49	155	210	267
	269	282	289	310
Hyacinthus orientalis 'Blue Pearl'	297			
Hyacinthus orientalis 'Blue Star'	197			
Hyacinthus orientalis 'Delft Blue'	150	163		
Hyacinthus orientalis 'Miss Saigon'	269			
Hyacinthus orientalis 'Pink Pearl'	163			
Hyacinthus orientalis 'Purple Star'	194	358		
Hyacinthus orientalis 'Woodstock'	358			
Hydrangea 'Arigato'	231			
Hydrangea arborescens 'Hayes Starburst'	125			
Hydrangea macrophylla 'Bavaria'	214			
Hydrangea macrophylla 'Blue Earth'	284			
Hydrangea macrophylla 'Blue Fresh'	163			
Hydrangea macrophylla 'First Blue'	210			
Hydrangea macrophylla 'Frau Nobuko'	362			
Hydrangea macrophylla 'Glowing Alps Purple'	341			
Hydrangea macrophylla 'Hawaiian Blue'	130			
Hydrangea macrophylla 'Hot Red'	265			
Hydrangea macrophylla 'Immaculata'	198			
Hydrangea macrophylla 'Magical Green Fire'	190	208		
Hydrangea macrophylla 'Magical Revolution Blue'	184			
Hydrangea macrophylla 'Magical Ruby Red'	302			
Hydrangea macrophylla 'Marine Blue'	167	300		
Hydrangea macrophylla 'Rosita'	355			
Hydrangea macrophylla 'Sibylla Classic Blue'	150			
Hydrangea macrophylla 'You and Me Together Pink'	279			
Iris domestica Goldblatt & Mabb.	360			
Iris germanica 'Dusky Challenger'	79			
Iris germanica 'Miami Beach'	335			
Iris germanica 'Stunning'	323			
Iris germanica 'Wench'	95			
Iris spuria subsp. *ochroleuca* (L.) Dykes	37			
Iris × *hollandica* 'Blue Diamond'	45	292		
Iris × *hollandica* 'Blue Magic'	156	170	195	210
	215	263	271	281
	307	310		
Ixora coccinea L.	164	200		
Jatropha podagrica Hook.	170	232		
Juniperus chinensis var. *sargentii*	24	45		

K · L · M

Kalanchoe beharensis Drake	175			
Kalanchoe blossfeldiana 'Holly'	164	172		
Kalanchoe humilis Britten	167	168		
Kalanchoe luciae 'Flapjack'	160			
Kalanchoe tomentosa 'Tsukitoji'	226			
Kalmia latifolia 'Ostbo Red'	299			
Kniphofia uvaria 'Bees' Lemon'	134	181	182	336
	351			
Kniphofia uvaria 'First Sunrise'	165	192	224	227
	327	331	337	349
Kniphofia uvaria 'Flamenco'	144	172	289	
Lachenalia aloides var. *quadricolor*	269	288	333	
Lachenalia mutabilis Lodd. ex Sweet	194			

Lachenalia viridiflora W. F. Barker 204 269
Laeliocattleya Quiseag 'Mankaen' 234
Lathyrus latifolius 'Pink Pearl' 196
Lathyrus latifolius 'Red Pearl' 159
Lathyrus latifolius 'White Pearl' 199
Lathyrus odoratus 'Blue Fragrance' 210
Lathyrus odoratus 'Wiltshire Ripple' 303
Lentinula edodes (Berk.) Pegler 42
Leontochir ovallei Phil. 283 307
Leontopodium alpinum Cass. 321
Leucadendron rubrum 'Plumosus' 357
Leucocoryne coquimbensis F. Phil. ex Phil. 162
Leucocoryne purpurea 'Caravel' 205 271 305
Leucospermum cordifolium 'High Gold' 63 319 321
Leucospermum cordifolium 'Succession' 111 287
Leucospermum cordifolium 'Veldt Fire' 180 182 263 281
Leycesteria formosa Wall. 331 339
Lilium 'Noble Lily' 294
Lilium 'Orange Art' 307
Lilium concolor Salisb. 165 209 212 331
Lilium hansonii Leichtlin ex D. D. T. Moore 105 234
Lilium lancifolium Thunb. var. *flaviflorum* Makino 145
Lilium longiflorum 'Green Lily Alp' 152
Lilium longiflorum 'Hinomoto' 194 299
Lilium longiflorum 'Pure Horn' 127 352
Lilium maculatum 'Apricot Fudge' 57 170
Lilium maculatum 'Black Out' 292
Lilium maculatum 'Café Noir' 289
Lilium ochroleucum Wall. ex Baker 77
Lilium orientalis 'Asuka' 345
Lilium orientalis 'Carolina' 125 293
Lilium orientalis 'Casa Blanca' 166 192 198 201
Lilium orientalis 'Firebolt' 155
Lilium orientalis 'Isabella' 304
Lilium orientalis 'Mambo' 167 176 223
Lilium orientalis 'Sheila' 65
Lilium orientalis 'Siberia' 200
Lobelia sessilifolia Lamb. 342
Lomatophyllum prostratum H. Perrier 271
Lupinus luteus 'Kibana Lupinus' 63
Lupinus nanus 'Pixie Delight' 302
Lycopodium clavatum L. 201
Lycoris aurea (L'Hér.) Herb. 224
Lycoris incarnata Comes ex Sprenger 342
Mammillaria albilanata Backeb. 105
Mammillaria boolii G. E. Linds. 153
Mammillaria elongata DC. 202
Mammillaria elongata f. *cristata* 323
Mammillaria hahniana Werderm. 353
Mangifera indica L. 172
Massonia pustulata Jacq. 358
Matteuccia struthiopteris (L.) Todaro 273
Medinilla magnifica Lindl. 323
Milla biflora Cav. 352
Moluccella laevis L. 126 171 189 279
329
Monarda fistulosa var. *menthifolia* 191 209
Monstera friedrichsthalii Schott 181
Musa minor Nakai 34 228 305 335
Musa ornata Roxb. 172
Musa velutina H. Wendl. & Drude 172
Muscari aucheri 'Blue Magic' 163 194 329
Muscari aucheri 'White Magic' 150 157 297
Myosotis L. 162 210

Narcissus 'Dick Wilden'	325				
Narcissus 'February Gold'	204				
Narcissus 'Grand Soleil d'Or'	296	306			
Narcissus 'Sweetness'	269	315	333		
Narcissus 'Tete a Tete'	200	300	311		
Narcissus tazetta 'Shirofusa Suisen'	42				
Narcissus tazetta var. *chinensis* M. Roem.	180	271	345	358	
Nelumbo nucifera 'Daikouho'	119				
Nelumbo nucifera 'Makotobasu'	144				
Nelumbo nucifera 'Ouren'	72				
Nelumbo nucifera Gaertn.	202	212	227	319	
Neoregelia 'Fireball'	335				
Neoregelia 'Fireball Variegata'	189	202	263	311	
Neoregelia 'Rio of Rio'	217				
Neoregelia 'Zoe'	233				
Neoregelia pauciflora L. B. Sm.	301				
Neoregelia spectabilis (T. Moore) L. B. Sm.	224				
Nepenthes 'Chelsonii'	132				
Nepenthes 'Dyeriana'	99	154	202	263	
	287	302			
Nepenthes 'Miranda'	227				
Nepenthes 'Rebecca Soper'	59	171	179	222	293
	319	327	335		
Nepenthes alata Blanco	189	235	294	297	
	299	323	348		
Nepenthes bongso Korth.	235				
Nepenthes maxima Reinw. ex Nees	188				
Nepenthes muluensis M. Hotta	175				
Nepenthes rafflesiana 'Koshikawa'	82	269			
Nepenthes rafflesiana var. *gigantea*	111				
Nepenthes sanguinea Lindl.	153				
Nepenthes tobaica Danser	280				
Nerine bowdenii 'Bianca Perla'	353				
Nerine bowdenii 'Favourite'	354				
Nerine bowdenii 'Mr. John'	150	166			
Nerine humilis (Jacq.) Herb.	158				
Nerine sarniensis 'Berlioz'	156				
Nerine sarniensis 'Red Admiral'	351				
Nerine sarniensis 'Red Emperor'	313				
Nicandra physalodes Schreb.	221				
Nigella damascena 'Miss Jekyll'	199	280			
Nigella damascena 'Persian Jewels'	163	180	210	263	
	285	321	341	344	
Nigella damascena L.	55				
Notocactus apricus (Arechavaleta) Berger ex Backeberg	193				
Obregonia denegrii Frič	77	208	220		
Odontoglossum Enzan Fantasy 'Rouge Magic'	291				
Oncidium Moon Shadow 'Tiger Tail'	134	224	286		
Oncidium Twinkle 'Charm'	311				
Opuntia lanceolata f. *cristata*	195				
Ornithogalum thyrsoides Jacq.	339				
Osmunda japonica Thunb.	284	304	307	325	
Oxypetalum coeruleum 'Blue Star'	305				
Oxypetalum coeruleum 'Pure Blue'	210				

P

Pachyphytum bracteosum 'Hoshi Bijin'	210	
Paeonia lactiflora 'Bunker Hill'	129	133
Paeonia lactiflora 'Coral Charm'	291	
Paeonia lactiflora 'Fuji'	167	
Paeonia lactiflora 'Kirin Maru'	213	
Paeonia lactiflora 'Kojima no Kagayaki'	288	

Paeonia lactiflora 'Paula Fay'	335
Paeonia lactiflora 'Red Baron'	207
Paeonia lactiflora 'Red Charm'	205 276 299
Paeonia lactiflora 'Red Monarch'	300
Paeonia lactiflora 'Red Rose'	273
Paeonia lactiflora 'Sarah Bernhardt'	158
Paeonia lactiflora 'Yubae'	141
Papaver nudicaule L.	27 87 91 194 198
	282 314 329 333
Papaver orientale (L.)	109
Paphiopedilum 'F. C. Puddle'	168
Paphiopedilum 'Hsinying Rubyweb'	331
Paphiopedilum 'Lime Down'	282
Paphiopedilum 'Night Shadow'	309
Paphiopedilum 'Robin Hood'	222 227 233
Paphiopedilum 'St. Swithin'	79 209 221 323
	335
Paphiopedilum callosum (Rchb. f.) Stein	93
Paphiopedilum callosum var. *vinicolor*	155 281 292
Paphiopedilum curtisii var. *sanderae* 'Fort Caroline'	267
Paphiopedilum delenatii Guillaumin	151 279
Paphiopedilum dianthum Tang & F. T. Wang	181 341
Paphiopedilum druryi (Bedd.) Stein	361
Paphiopedilum Hassallii 'Saint Mary'	134
Paphiopedilum insigne (Wall. ex Lindl.) Pfitzer	150 277 286
Paphiopedilum lawrenceanum (Rchb. f.) Pfitzer	335
Paphiopedilum Lebeau 'Bios King'	263 281
Paphiopedilum Maudiae 'Black Jack'	357
Paphiopedilum Maudiae 'The Queen'	99 102 202 329
Paphiopedilum niveum (Rchb. f.) Stein	85
Paphiopedilum Norito Hasegawa 'Gold Rush'	27
Paphiopedilum Orchilla 'Chilton'	296
Paphiopedilum parishii (Rchb. f.) Stein	343
Paphiopedilum platyphyllum T. Yukawa	89
Paphiopedilum Satsuma 'Karajishi'	201
Paphiopedilum Sheerline 'Rondo'	156 217
Paphiopedilum spicerianum (Rchb. f) Pfitzer	154 180 271 337
Paphiopedilum venustum 'Petit Light'	27
Paphiopedilum Winston Churchill 'Redoutable'	310
Paranomus reflexus N. E. Br.	143 323
Passiflora 'Belotii'	298
Passiflora 'Incense'	102 141 208 223
	252
Passiflora 'Victoria'	184
Passiflora caerulea 'Clear Sky'	95 172 249 263
	280 335
Passiflora caerulea 'Constance Elliott'	254
Pelargonium graveolens 'Bourbon'	170 174
Pelargonium graveolens 'Little Gem'	216
Pelargonium graveolens 'Snowflake'	124 194
Peperomia caperata 'Burgundy Ripple'	186
Peperomia caperata 'Pink Lady'	178 208
Peperomia puteolata Trel.	152
Pericallis × *hybrida* 'Tear Blue'	162
Phaenocoma prolifera (L.) D. Don	219
Phalaenopsis 'Cacao'	265 274 292 300
	309
Phalaenopsis 'Chian Xen Piano'	277
Phalaenopsis 'Ching Ann Diamond'	289 363
Phalaenopsis 'Chocolate Disco'	177
Phalaenopsis 'Chocolate Pearl'	296
Phalaenopsis 'Golden Beauty'	143 246
Phalaenopsis 'Jaguar'	253
Phalaenopsis 'Palermo'	137 212
Phalaenopsis 'Ringo White'	327
Phalaenopsis 'Wedding Promenade'	263 331 354

Phalaenopsis Brother Sara Gold 'Magical'   182
Phalaenopsis Happy Vivien 'Chunli'   159
Phalaenopsis Queen Beer 'Mantenko'   166
Phalaenopsis Sheena's Pearl 'Geisha Waltz'   309
Phalaenopsis Sogo Ibis 'Little Maruko'   281
Phalaenopsis Sogo Pearl 'Pine Ridge'   197   312
Phalaenopsis Sogo Vieker 'Taida Little Monkey'   189
Phalaenopsis Sogo Yukidian 'V3'   47
Phalaenopsis Taida Salu 'Alisan'   180   265   315   327
Phalaenopsis Taida Salu 'Azuki Chocolat'   221   354
Phalaenopsis Taida Salu 'Morning Sun'   166
Phalaenopsis Taida Smile 'Little Gold'   224
Philodendron selloum K. Koch   361
Phlomis fruticosa 'Green Star'   234
Phragmipedium 'Rosy Charm'   159
Phylica plumosa L.   175   185
Physostegia virginiana (L.) Benth.   190   208   355
Phytolacca americana L.   306   319   331
Picris hieracioides L. subsp. *japonica* (Thunb.) Krylov   51
Pieris japonica (Thunb.) D. Don ex G. Don   189
Pilea involucrata 'Moon Valley'   223   331
Pinus parviflora Sieb. & Zucc.   47   66   267
Piper kadsura Trel. & Yunck.   166
Piper nigrum L.   184
Pisum sativum L.   215
Pitacairnia wendlandii Baker   34
Pittosporum tobira (Thunb.) W. T. Aiton   234
Platycerium bifurcatum (Cav.) C. Chr.   188   291   356
Pleiospilos nelii 'Teigyoku'   170
Polygala myrtifolia var. *grandiflora* 'Sweet Pea Shrub'   170   212   215   263
Potinara Sweet Sugar 'Happy Field'   280
Protea 'Pink Ice'   93
Protea 'Robyn'   298
Protea 'Venus'   308
Protea barbigera 'Niobe'   77   96   127   170   213
                                   295   343
Protea barbigera 'Snow Queen'   174
Protea cynaroides 'Arctic Ice'   41   263   327
Protea cynaroides 'Madiba'   233
Protea cynaroides 'Red Rex'   85   355
Protea grandiceps Tratt.   81
Protea magnifica 'Queen'   319
Protea mundii 'Little Lady White'   352
Protea nana (Berg.) Thunb.   233   335
Protea neriifolia 'White Mink'   178

R

Ranunculus asiaticus 'Artemis'   218
Ranunculus asiaticus 'Aurora'   159
Ranunculus asiaticus 'Charlotte'   158   160   304
Ranunculus asiaticus 'Gironde'   325   358
Ranunculus asiaticus 'Ikaros'   285
Ranunculus asiaticus 'M Blue'   290
Ranunculus asiaticus 'M Pink'   291
Ranunculus asiaticus 'Morocco Mhamid'   57
Ranunculus asiaticus 'Morocco Tantan'   160
Ranunculus asiaticus 'Pomerol'   194   294
Ranunculus asiaticus 'Sisteron'   359
Ranunculus asiaticus 'Tanger'   314
Rhaphiolepis indica (L.) Lindl. ex Ker var. *umbellata* (Thunb.) H. Ohashi   181   204   339
Rhipsalis cassutha Gaertn.   189
Rhipsalis cereuscula Haw.   170
Rhipsalis ewaldiana Barthlott & N. P. Taylor   160   335
Rhipsalis teres Steud.   152

Rhyncholaeliocattleya King of Taiwan 'Ta-Hsin' 276
Rhyncholaeliocattleya Memoria Helen Brown 'Sweet Afton' 145
Rhyncholaeliocattleya Pamela Hetherington 'Coronation' 159
Rhyncholaeliocattleya Peggy O'Neill 'Royal Lady' 201
Rhyncholaeliocattleya Red Crab 'Kuan-Miao #10' 271
Rhyncholaeliocattleya Rie's Orange Grove 'Harvest' 304
Rhyncholaeliocattleya Sophia Knot 'Kayoko' 292
Rohdea japonica (Thunb.) Roth 286
Rosa 'All 4 Kiss+' 204
Rosa 'All 4 Love' 124
Rosa 'Amada+' 274
Rosa 'Andalusia' 186
Rosa 'Avalanche' 125
Rosa 'Baronesse' 206 208
Rosa 'Bell Rouge' 206
Rosa 'Exciting Meilland' 161 181 278 351
Rosa 'Flash Eye' 218 226 289
Rosa 'Freedom' 126
Rosa 'Gold Rush' 275
Rosa 'Halloween' 178
Rosa 'Hanabi' 283
Rosa 'Ilios' 183
Rosa 'Julio Iglesias' 206
Rosa 'K-Zebra' 219
Rosa 'Kanpai' 273
Rosa 'La Campanella' 219
Rosa 'Milva' 173
Rosa 'Red Elegance' 61 265 273
Rosa 'Red Pompon' 107
Rosa 'Red Ranunculus' 308
Rosa 'Rote Rose' 209
Rosa 'Samurai' 346
Rosa 'Shall Verse' 229
Rosa 'Splash Sensation' 166
Rosa 'Sweet Avalanche' 158
Rosa 'Tamango' 128
Rosa 'Vague+' 293
Rosa 'Yves Piaget' 279
Rosa 'Yves Red' 303
Rubus fruticosus L. 122 146 220
Rudbeckia hirta 'Cherokee Sunset' 172
Rudbeckia hirta 'Irish Eyes' 225

S

Salvia farinacea 'Strata' 185
Salvia leucantha Cav. 363
Sanguisorba hakusanensis Makino 220
Sansevieria phillipsiae N. E. Br. 337
Sarracenia 'Dana's Delight' 300
Sarracenia 'Excellens' 337
Sarracenia 'Juthatip Soper' 331
Sarracenia 'Maroon' 349
Sarracenia 'Night Sky' 132
Sarracenia 'Scarlet Bell' 269 319 346
Sarracenia alata var. *ornata* 117
Sarracenia flava L. 323
Sarracenia flava var. *rubricorpora* 276
Sarracenia flava var. *rubricorpora* 'Red Burgundy' 101
Sarracenia leucophylla Raf. 77 156 178 181
185
Sarracenia purpurea L. 34 136 215 327
335
Sarracenia rubra subsp. *gulfensis* 174 178

Scabiosa atropurpurea 'Ace of Spades' — 176 331
Scabiosa atropurpurea 'Moco Purple' — 123
Scabiosa atropurpurea 'Oxford Blue' — 196
Scabiosa caucasica 'Fama' — 230
Scabiosa columbaria 'Blue Note' — 307
Schinus terebinthifolius 'Pepper Berry' — 352
Sedum spectabile 'Autumn Joy' — 139 184 212
Sedum telephium 'Matrona' — 349
Sempervivum 'Lavender and Old Lace' — 216
Sempervivum 'Lobstum' — 217
Sempervivum tectorum L. — 178
Senecio rowleyanus H. Jacobsen — 170
Serruria 'Carmen' — 204
Serruria 'Pretty n Pink' — 123 158 250 321
Silene vulgaris 'Green Bell' — 216
Skimmia japonica 'Kew Green' — 160 194
Smilax aspera L. — 329
Sophrolaeliocattleya Jewel Box 'Dark Waters' — 222
Spathodea campanulata P. Beauv. — 154 176 218
Spiraea japonica L. f. — 190
Stachys byzantina 'Primrose Heron' — 135
Stachyurus praecox Siebold et Zucc. — 51
Stemona japonica (Blume) Miq. — 82
Stephanotis floribunda Brongn. — 213 228
Sterculia monosperma Vent. — 346
Strelitzia reginae Aiton — 173 224 284 321 335
Synurus pungens (Franch. et Sav.) Kitam. — 357
Syringa vulgaris 'Madame Florent Stepman' — 278

T

Tacca chantrieri André — 93
Tagetes erecta 'Moonsong Deep Orange' — 165
Tagetes erecta 'Perfection Orange' — 273
Tagetes erecta 'Sovereign' — 130 171
Tagetes erecta 'Yellow Boy' — 321
Tagetes erecta 'Yellow Isis' — 182 200 214
Tagetes erecta 'Zenith Red' — 337
Tapeinochilos ananassae 'Wax Ginger' — 142 186 227
Telopea speciosissima 'Waratah' — 171 180 263
Tephrocactus articulatus (Pfeiff.) Backeb. — 300
Tillandsia 'Cotton Candy' — 41 299 314
Tillandsia aeranthos (Loiseleur) L. B. Sm. — 301
Tillandsia andreana E. Morren ex André — 171 284
Tillandsia brachycaulos Schlechtendal — 218
Tillandsia bulbosa Hook. — 263 280
Tillandsia capitata Grisebach — 185 273
Tillandsia caput-medusae E. Morren — 175 278 319 338
Tillandsia cyanea Linden ex K. Koch — 180 206
Tillandsia ionantha Planchon — 172 174
Tillandsia paleacea Presl — 284
Tillandsia seleriana Mez — 285
Tillandsia tectorum E. Morren — 198 331 333
Tillandsia xerographica Rohweder — 171 184 199 230 267 310 319 336
Trachelium caeruleum 'Devotion Purple' — 134 230 273
Trametes versicolor (L. Fr.) Quél. — 157
Tricyrtis formosana Baker — 319
Triteleia 'Babylon' — 244
Trollius chinensis 'Golden Queen' — 226
Tulbaghia simmleri Beauverd — 269
Tulipa 'Acuminata' — 315
Tulipa 'Alexandra' — 358
Tulipa 'Ballerina' — 286

Tulipa 'Barbados' 284 304
Tulipa 'Dolce Hess' 290
Tulipa 'Exotic Parrot' 359
Tulipa 'Exotic Sun' 325
Tulipa 'Flaming Flag' 288
Tulipa 'Flaming Parrot' 273 274
Tulipa 'Flaming Spring Green' 69
Tulipa 'Flash Point' 359
Tulipa 'Hamilton' 279
Tulipa 'Largo' 156 314
Tulipa 'Little Princess' 307
Tulipa 'Mon Amour' 311
Tulipa 'Monte Carlo' 314
Tulipa 'Monte Spider' 275 279 307 358
Tulipa 'Mysterious Parrot' 274 284
Tulipa 'Orange Monarch' 304
Tulipa 'Orange Princess' 269
Tulipa 'Palmyra' 289
Tulipa 'Purple Flag' 278 306
Tulipa 'Red Princess' 277
Tulipa 'Rococo' 160 290 301
Tulipa 'Super Parrot' 51 195 267
Tulipa 'Tete a Tete' 170 297 358
Tulipa 'White River Star' 198 315
Tulipa 'Yellow King' 307
Tulipa L. 178
Tulipa polychroma Stapf 198 303 333
Tulipa turkestanica (Regel) Regel 87 154 329

V · X · Z

Vanda 'Deep Purple Spots' 113 142
Vanda 'Pachara Delight' 134
Vanda 'Pakchong Blue' 295
Vanda 'Pat Delight' 127 311
Vanda 'Robert's Delight Blue' 125
Vanda 'Variety' 130
Vanda 'Yano Blue Spot' 231
Vanda falcata 'Hakuunkaku' 228 302
Vanilla planifolia Jacks. ex Andrews 155
Veronica 'Caroline Blue' 141 185 231
Veronica 'Pink Hunter' 145
Veronica 'Smart Bizarre' 345 351
Veronica spicata 'Red Fox' 137
Veronica spicata 'Younique Baby White' 190
Viburnum opulus 'Compactum' 346
Viburnum tinus L. 166 176 195 230
Viola 'Angel Rose Picotee' 156
Viola 'Yellow Blotch' 281
Viola × *wittrockiana* 'Chalon Giant' 297 325
Viola × *wittrockiana* 'Frizzle Sizzle Blue' 163 195 305
Viola × *wittrockiana* 'Frizzle Sizzle Burgundy Shade' 176
Viola × *wittrockiana* 'Frizzle Sizzle Passion Fruit' 158
Viola × *wittrockiana* 'Frizzle Sizzle Yellow' 271
Viola × *wittrockiana* 'Moulin Frill Golden' 258
Viola × *wittrockiana* 'Nature Yellow Broggi' 263 325
Viora × *wittrockiana* 'Frizzle Sizzle Yellow Blue Swirl' 304
Viscum album subsp. *coloratum* Komar 174 267
Vriesea carinata 'Christiane' 34 81 134 171
229
Zamia furfuracea L. f. 301
Zantedeschia aethiopica 'Aquila' 128
Zantedeschia aethiopica 'Captain Durance' 117 141 228
Zantedeschia aethiopica 'Captain Fuego' 228 286
Zantedeschia aethiopica 'Captain Mirage' 168

Zantedeschia aethiopica 'Captain Odeon' 164

Zantedeschia aethiopica 'Captain Promise' 113 141 192

Zantedeschia aethiopica 'Crystal Blush' 198 352

Zantedeschia aethiopica 'Fuka' 314

Zantedeschia aethiopica 'Garnet Glow' 166 215

Zantedeschia aethiopica 'Gold Crown' 170

Zantedeschia aethiopica 'Golden Giant' 182

Zantedeschia aethiopica 'Green Goddess' 23 235

Zantedeschia aethiopica 'Hot Cherry' 206

Zantedeschia aethiopica 'Hot Chocolate' 154 176 221

Zantedeschia aethiopica 'Hot Shot' 172 327

Zantedeschia aethiopica 'Majestic Red' 166 197 212

Zantedeschia aethiopica 'Mango' 349

Zantedeschia aethiopica 'Picasso' 313 319

Zantedeschia aethiopica 'Red Charm' 160

Zantedeschia aethiopica 'Schwarzwalder' 296 357

Zantedeschia aethiopica 'White Swan' 37 295

Zantedeschia pentlandii 'Odessa' 292

Zingiber officinale Roscoe 234

Zingiber spectabile 'Golden Shampoo' 111 139 164 208
  349

Zingiber zerumbet 'Shampoo Ginger' 313 342

Zinnia 'Profusion Double Fire' 327

Zinnia 'Profusion Double Golden' 225

Zinnia elegans 'Dreamland Scarlet' 346

Zinnia elegans 'Jersey Mix' 256

Zinnia elegans 'Queen Lime' 126 180 205 339

Zinnia elegans 'Queen Red Lime' 178 349

Zinnia elegans 'Red Sun' 241

Zinnia haageana 'Aztec Sunset' 165

Zinnia haageana 'Old Fashion' 173

Zinnia haageana 'Persian Carpet' 128 239

Zygopetalum Redvale 'Fire Kiss' 331

Profiles　略歴

東 信　　あずま・まこと
フラワーアーティスト

2002年、椎木俊介と共同し、注文に合わせてデッサンを起こし、花材を仕入れ、花束をつくるオートクチュールの花屋「JARDINS des FLEURS」を銀座に構える（現在は南青山所在）。

2005年頃から、こうした花屋としての活動に加え、植物による表現の可能性を探求し、彫刻作品ともいえる造形表現＝Botanical Sculptureを開始し、海外から注目を集めはじめる。ニューヨークでの個展を皮切りに、ヨーロッパを中心に先鋭的な作品を数多く発表するほか、2009年より実験的植物集団「東信、花樹研究所（AMKK）」を立ち上げ、世界各地の美術館やアートギャラリー、パブリックスペースなどで作品発表を重ねる。

近年では人と花の接点を模索するプロジェクトも精力的に展開。独自の視点から植物の美を追求し続けている。

Makoto AZUMA
Flower Artist

Azuma teamed up with Shunsuke Shiinoki in 2002 to open JARDINS des FLEURS, a "haute couture" flower shop offering bouquets designed on-demand using flowers purchased for the respective order, in the Ginza area (now located in Minami-Aoyama) in Tokyo.

In addition to the flower shop business, Azuma began to explore the expressive potential of plants in 2005. He invented the genre of the "botanical sculpture," creating works for which he soon received orders also from outside Japan. Following a solo exhibition in New York, his audacious works have been repeatedly shown in Europe. While launching the experimental botanical lab Azuma Makoto Kaju Kenkyujo (AMKK) in 2009, he went on to exhibit his works at art museums, galleries and public spaces in all over the world.

In recent years, Azuma has been focusing on projects that explore the connections between human beings and flowers. He continues to pursue the beauty of plants from his distinctive point of view.

椎木俊介　　しいのき・しゅんすけ
ボタニカル・フォトグラファー

2002年、東信とともに、銀座にオートクチュールの花屋「JARDINS des FLEURS」を構える。東が植物による造形表現をはじめると時期を同じくして、カメラを手にし、刻々と朽ちゆき、姿かたちを変容させていってしまう生命のありようを写真に留める活動に傾倒していく。日々、植物に触れ、その生死に向き合ってきたからこそ導き出すことのできる、花や植物のみが生来的に有する自然界特有の色彩や生命力、神秘性を鋭く切り取っていく。

2011年には初の作品集となる東信との共著『2009–2011 Flowers』（青幻舎）を発表。常に独特の視点で東の作品を捉え、植物の美を写し続けている。

Shunsuke SHIINOKI
Botanical Photographer

Shiinoki opened the "haute couture" flower shop JARDINS des FLEURS at Ginza together with Makoto Azuma in 2002. Around the time Azuma first started creating his botanical sculptures, Shiinoki began to point his camera at the ever-changing forms of life, committing himself to capturing such processes of gradual decay. Having been working with plants and facing the cycle of life and death on a daily basis, he developed an ability to highlight the genuine color, vital energy and mystique of flowers and plants as specifically natural qualities. In 2011, Seigensha published *2009–2011 Flowers*, the first book showcasing the results of his collaboration with Azuma. Shiinoki continues to capture Azuma's works and the beauty of plants with his unique perspective.

Azuma Makoto Botanical Congress
Since 2012

東 信　　Makoto AZUMA
椎木 俊介　Shunsuke SHIINOKI

寺尾 まり　Mari TERAO
河合 美華　Mika KAWAI
成田 映里　Eri NARITA

上記メンバーにより、植物名リスト［Pages 368−439］
および索引［Pages 440−476］の監修に当たった。
The List of Flower Names (pp. 368−439) and
Index of Flower Names (pp. 440−476) were compiled
by the above members.

www.azumamakoto.com

ENCYCLOPEDIA OF FLOWERS III

植物図鑑

発行	2016 年 12 月 5 日　　　初版
著者	東 信──────────アートワーク 椎木俊介──────────写真
監修	AMKK（東信、花樹研究所）
ブックデザイン	原 研哉＋松野 薫＋大野 萌美 | 日本デザインセンター原デザイン研究所
発行者	安田英晃
発行所	株式会社 青幻舎 京都市中京区三条通烏丸東入ル 〒604-8136 Tel. 075-252-6766　Fax. 075-252-6770 http://www.seigensha.com
協力	和田京子
編集	中村水絵 | HeHe 鎌田恵理子 | 青幻舎
印刷・製本	株式会社サンエムカラー
プリンティング・ディレクター	谷口倍夫 | 株式会社サンエムカラー

ISBN 978-4-86152-571-1 C0072